RUSSIA'S ARMY

CAMPAIGNS & COMMANDERS

GREGORY J. W. URWIN, SERIES EDITOR

CAMPAIGNS AND COMMANDERS

Russia's Army

A History from the Napoleonic Wars to the War in Ukraine

Roger R. Reese

University of Oklahoma Press : Norman

PUBLICATION OF THIS BOOK IS MADE POSSIBLE THROUGH
THE GENEROSITY OF EDITH KINNEY GAYLORD.

Library of Congress Cataloging-in-Publication Data

Names: Reese, Roger R., author.
Title: Russia's army : a history from the Napoleonic wars to the war in Ukraine / Roger R. Reese.
Description: Norman : University of Oklahoma Press, [2023] | Series: Campaigns &
    commanders; vol. 76 | Includes bibliographical references and index. | Summary: "An
    overview of the history of the Russian Army in the nineteenth and twentieth centuries,
    arguably the most crucial time in Russia's history of warfare. Includes an analysis of twenty-
    first century events, including the Russian invasion of Ukraine"—Provided by publisher.
Identifiers: LCCN 2022059964 | ISBN 978-0-8061-9275-8 (hardcover)
Subjects: LCSH: Russia. Armiia͡. | Russia—History, Military—19th century. | Soviet Union.
    Sovetskaia͡ Armiia͡. | Russia (Federation). Vooruzhennye sily. | Russia—History, Military—
    20th century.
Classification: LCC UA772 .R4338 2023 | DDC 355.00947—dc23/eng/20221216
LC record available at https://lccn.loc.gov/2022059964

Russia's Army: A History from the Napoleonic Wars to the War in Ukraine is Volume 76 in the
Campaigns and Commanders series.

The paper in this book meets the guidelines for permanence and durability of the Committee on
Production Guidelines for Book Longevity of the Council on Library Resources, Inc. ∞

For Emily

Contents

Maps

PREFACE

This work is more than a survey history of the Russian army in the nineteenth and twentieth centuries; besides addressing the wars, as one would expect, it delves into the inner workings of the army from top to bottom, from the development of doctrine and strategy by general staffs to the lives of officers and soldiers in the regiments, and weaves the important dynamic connection between the army and society throughout. This book is a unique contribution to the study of the Russian military in that it spans three centuries and connects three eras of Russian history—the tsarist, Soviet, and post-Soviet—highlighting the many continuities and occasional discontinuities in war-making, strategic thought, and social relations within the army and with civil society. A synthetic study that draws on a wide range of scholarly monographs, memoirs, articles, journals, and published documents in English and Russian, this book incorporates the latest scholarship to show how Russia organized and prepared its army, and how that army fought to extend, defend, and maintain the empire and nation from enemies within and without over a period of more than 220 years. From the perspective of historians who focus on battles and campaigns, the Russian army is often characterized as a monstrous steamroller that, despite its flaws, habitually crushed its opponents, often at excessive cost to itself, but to be admired for getting the job done more often than not. From the perspective of social historians who study the internal workings of the army, it is often characterized as a monstrosity—brutal to the soldiers, led by incompetent and corrupt officers, and alienated from society. Both perspectives have their truths and merits—which are easily overstated—and are included here in moderated form.

The time frame 1801 to 2022 was chosen because the third partition of Poland more or less stabilized Russia's western border by 1800. The year 1801 saw the coronation of a new tsar, Alexander I, who would oversee the wars with Napoleon and initiate a number of military reforms. For more than one hundred years, the fixed western border with Austria and Prussia (later Germany) and Russia's desire to extend hegemony over the Balkans at the Ottomans' expense, caused Russia to consider the potential of war with those empires and plan accordingly. A firm western border in these years facilitated the expansion of the Russian Empire to the south in the Caucasus, to the southeast into Central Asia, and to the Pacific Ocean and the border of Manchuria in the Far East. Imperial conquest brought into the empire diverse populations that the government would have to keep in check and burdened the army with a lengthened border to defend. This study ends on 31 August 2022, six months into the Russian Federation's invasion of Ukraine.

The 1991 collapse of the communist government in a failed coup led to the disintegration of the USSR, the Eastern bloc, and the Soviet Army—and ended the Cold War. Subsequently, the new international environment called for a reappraisal of Russia's diplomacy and defense needs. The government and military of the new "democratic" Russia inherited the Soviet Union's defense and domestic challenges. The revolutionary destruction of Imperial Russia and the subsequent rise of the Soviet Union had entailed limited territorial and population changes, but the collapse of the Soviet empire resulted in substantial territorial and population losses in the west and northwest, and a great diminishing of Russian hegemony over Eastern Europe. Following the dissolution of the Soviet Union, the new Russian Federation found itself with no credible threat of invasion from the west and a more homogeneous population, thus requiring a reassessment of foreign and domestic security policies, and the role of the military therein. Thus, the start of the Napoleonic Wars and the apparent start of a new Cold War with the West enable the tracing of the major trends in Russian military history as they play out in the current war in Ukraine.

In the last one hundred years, the study of the Russian army has produced scores of excellent monographs covering specific wars, campaigns, and battles, or various narrow aspects of Russia's military development; however, few have written on Russian military history over the *longue durée*. So far, the longest time frame tackled by a scholar is David R. Stone's *A Military History of Russia: From Ivan the Terrible to the War in Chechnya* (2006). The next longest span goes to John L. H. Keep's *Soldiers of the Tsar: Army and Society in Russia, 1462–1874* (1985). William C. Fuller's *Strategy and Power in Russia, 1600–1914* (1992) is next in line. Frederick W. Kagan and Robin Higham cover the years 1453 to 1991 divided between two companion edited works, *The Military History of Tsarist Russia* (2002), which covers the years through the First World War, and *The Military History of the Soviet Union*. What the present work adds to the literature is a study focused on the army that spans Imperial Russia through the Soviet Union to the Russian Federation in one volume, with one voice. This book examines Russia's, the USSR's, and the Russian Federation's wars, campaigns, and battles as well as the social history of the army, personnel policy, and the institutional history of the army, drawing attention to the similarities and differences across the three major eras more deeply than Stone's work does and more broadly than Fuller's, which does not venture into the Soviet period. It includes the twentieth and twenty-first centuries, which Keep does not, and is a coherent narrative, unlike Kagan and Higham's edited volumes. Furthermore, it examines the army's strategy, tactics, and doctrine, placing them in the contexts of the diplomatic-international setting and of imperial expansion and decline. Finally, this study treats all the foregoing in relation to the interplay of the military and domestic challenges of empire and postimperial adaptation.

The notes and bibliography indicate the many sources I consulted to write this study, but it is worth highlighting the more significant works in English that informed my work. Janet Hartley's *Russia, 1762–1825: Military Power, the State, and the People* (2008) is the best source on the army under Alexander I. John S. Curtiss's *The Russian Army under Nicholas I, 1825–1855* (1965), more than fifty years on, is still of great value, and Frederick Kagan has enhanced the study of that period with *The Military Reforms of Nicholas I* (1999). Forrestt Miller's *Dmitrii Miliutin and the Reform Era in Russia* (1968) was indispensable. William Fuller's *Civil-Military Conflict in Imperial Russia, 1881–1914* (1985) has not lost its relevance. John Bushnell's *Mutiny amid Repression* (1985) stands unchallenged as the go-to book on the army during the Revolution of 1905. Nikolai Golovin's *The Russian Army in World War I* (1931, 1969) still has utility, but David R. Stone's *The Russian Army in the Great War* (2015) provides a current, more scholarly view of the war through a wider lens. Bruce Menning's *Bayonets before Bullets* (1992) has yet to be surpassed in elucidating Russian military thinking in the years 1861–1914. *The Russian Civil War 1918–1921* (2020), by A. S. Bubnov et al., translated by Richard W. Harrison, brings a valuable Soviet perspective of that war long denied the English-speaking reader. Sally Stoecker, with *Forging Stalin's Army* (1998), Richard Harrison, with *The Russian Way of War* (2001), and Mary Habeck, with *Storm of Steel* (2003), comprehensively cover the interwar development of Soviet military doctrine. Evan Mawdsley, in *Thunder in the East* (2011), and Alexander Hill, in *The Red Army and the Second World War* (2017), have used the latest scholarship to take us beyond where John Erickson's *The Road to Stalingrad* and *Road to Berlin* (1975, 1983) and David Glantz and Jonathan House's *When Titans Clashed* (1995) left off with their studies of the Great Patriotic War of the Soviet Union.

Like Kagan's, Higham's, and Stone's books, this is a study of military history for the nonspecialist. As a book for the general reader, jargon has been kept to a minimum, notes are limited, and little prior knowledge of Russian military history is assumed.

I thank my wife, Melora, for her support during the years it took me to write this book. I must include thanks to the editors at the University of Oklahoma Press: Adam Kane, who got the project rolling; Kent Calder, who took the handoff from Adam; and Katie Hall, for her enthusiasm and encouragement. I also gratefully acknowledge the excellent feedback I received from Jeremy Black and Mary Habeck, who both encouraged me to include the post-Soviet period and to comment on the invasion of Ukraine.

Introduction

The Imperial Russian Army and its successors, the Soviet Army and army of the Russian Federation, were instrumental in addressing the state's foreign policy challenges of projecting power and defending the empire, and the domestic challenge of containing internal unrest—unrest generated by nationalism, competing ethnic and religious identities, and political discontent. These twin challenges combined to drive foreign policy, defense policy, strategic war planning, manning policies, and the conduct of war. Because the needs of empire did not change even after the loss of most of Moscow's imperial possessions, continuities outnumber discontinuities across the imperial, Soviet, and post-Soviet eras. This book argues that the development of the army was driven by its striving to meet the challenges posed by the shifts in the European balance of power and the changes in global diplomacy, politics, economics, and society. Five interwoven themes make up the essential elements of Russian military history: the adoption of a strategy to maintain a defensive posture in the west; an offensive strategy in the Balkans; an expansionist policy to the east; maintenance of a large standing army; and a consistent unease about the loyalty of both the army and the non-Russian minorities to the state. These themes emerged at the beginning of the nineteenth century, matured during the late imperial period, and continued over into the Soviet era but ended abruptly with the collapse of empire and authoritarian rule; however, they were then resurrected by Vladimir Putin in the twenty-first century as he sought to restore authoritarian rule and hegemony over the former territories of the old empire. These themes are mostly considered within the context of the heads of state exercising their prerogatives as commanders in chief to force or allow the direction in which the army would develop in peacetime and to make operational as well as strategic decisions in wartime.

The Russian Army

Geographic, economic, diplomatic, and social realities led tsarist Russia to maintain a large military. There are five facets to an explanation of why Russia has historically maintained such large armies: the length of its frontiers; the potential size of the opposing forces; the need for troops to maintain domestic order; the intent to maintain great power status; and, until 1861, the institution of serfdom.

The size of Russia, with or without empire, shows why a large army could be justified. Between 1800 and 2022, Russia fought wars in Europe, European Russia, the Balkans, the Caucasus, Central Asia, and the Far East. The entire Russian armed forces could never be concentrated to fight in one area because defenses had to be maintained in the others. Some of the countries or empires on Russia's borders could field substantial armies, which reinforced the need for a large defense establishment; therefore, Russia had to be prepared to divide its army to fight on multiple fronts, such as in 1808 when Russia fought two wars simultaneously—against Sweden and the Ottoman Empire.

The need to maintain domestic order over an enserfed population that was prone to rebellion, and to keep the many conquered peoples cowed, also justified a large army. During the nineteenth century, the tsarist army fought two year-long campaigns to suppress Polish nationalism (in 1831 and 1863), which threatened the integrity of the empire. Tsar Nicholas II twice called on the Russian army during the twentieth century to quell domestic revolt while at war, earning for himself the nickname "Bloody Nicholas." During the Russo-Japanese War, in 1904–5, as the army fought in the Far East, it also defended the long German/Austro-Hungarian border and simultaneously ruthlessly suppressed nationalist revolts in the Baltic States, intimidated Polish nationalists, campaigned against rebellious peasants, and suppressed striking and rioting workers all across European Russia. During the First World War, the army fought simultaneously on its European border, in the Balkans, and in the Caucasus; it also suppressed a large-scale revolt against conscription in Central Asia.

The Red Army, in the course of the civil war (1918–21) and war with Poland (1920), was also called upon to suppress numerous large-scale peasant uprisings and Estonian, Latvian, Lithuanian, Finnish, Ukrainian, and Caucasian independence movements. It succeeded in suppressing the peasants and the Ukrainians, Georgians, Azeris, and Armenians, but not the others. The Soviet Army was employed in the 1920s 1930s (and later the 1980s) to suppress separatist, anti-Soviet movements in the Caucasus. For nearly a decade after the Second World War, the Soviet Army treated Ukraine and the reabsorbed Baltic States as occupied territories as they fought underground anti-Soviet, nationalist separatist movements. During the Cold War, the Soviet Army crushed

Hungary and Czechoslovakia (in 1956 and 1968, respectively), when their nationalism threatened the integrity of the Soviet bloc. The Soviets threatened to do the same to Poland in 1956 and 1980, all the while maintaining a large force against NATO and China.

The military of the Russian Federation at more than 1 million members is still large relative to its population of 144 million in 2022. There are no objective justifications for such a large army. Institutional interests, great power aspirations, the momentum of history, and politicians with feet of clay have kept it oversized and overfunded at the expense of the nation's economic well-being.

The institution of serfdom inadvertently led to a large standing army—sometimes larger than desired. Serfdom posed a problem for the army because conscription freed a man from serfdom placing him in the social category of soldier who no longer had a place in his former village. Releasing young soldiers into civilian life who had no social or geographic moorings, and who lacked skills useful in the economy, would, the authorities feared, make them ripe to become troublemakers. To avoid the release of large numbers of young free men into society, Peter I at first set the term of military service at life, though he later reduced it to twenty-five years. This meant that when the army expanded in anticipation of or during a war, the soldiers recruited for the war had to stay in uniform even after the need for them had passed. Keeping men in the army until their health was nearly broken prevented Russia from having a large trained reserve, which would have enabled a smaller standing army. Lacking a reserve, the standing army had to be oversized in peacetime if it were to be ready to fight immediately because it could expand only by conscripting raw recruits who would need time to be trained. Thus, at times the army was larger than either Alexander I or Nicholas I wanted, but their hands were tied by the social system. Thus, being frequently at war kept the army large because it was unable to demobilize to any significant degree at the conclusion of hostilities. Only after the emancipation of the serfs in the 1860s was the army able to create a reserve that it could call up in time of war and send home when peace was restored.

The army recruited officers on a voluntary basis. The Imperial Russian Army relied primarily on nobles to fill the officer corps, but the worthy enlisted soldier could also earn a commission. Until the 1860s, training and educating the officer corps was mostly by apprenticeship in a regiment; the few cadet corps produced only a small minority. Alexander II's reform era ended the apprenticeship system. Henceforth, entrance into the officer corps was through the military education system of cadet corps (for nobles only) and *junker* schools (open to all social classes). The Soviet period continued the practice of voluntary officer recruitment (except during the Second World War) with membership open to all classes except the former nobility. Despite its high social status, the officer corps was always undermanned during the imperial period. During the interwar years, the Red Army had trouble recruiting officers. Though one would think the officer corps would attract men who supported the state and the established order of things, the tsars, and then the Communist Party leadership, had good reason to fear dissent among the officers, especially in times of intellectual ferment. The officer corps' growing awareness of itself as a corporate body with an institutional identity and interest threatened the loyalty of officers to the state. Both Yeltsin and Putin ensured the loyalty of the army by enriching the high command by turning a blind eye to corruption. Putin, like Stalin, also intimidated the military with his close association to the security forces.

From 1801 to the 2020s, the heads of state insisted on exercising the prerogatives of commander in chief by intruding in military affairs including planning and overseeing operations. Monarchs taking to the field to command their armies in war had a long tradition in warfare, and Russia was no exception. The tsars clung to the idea of seeing war-making as the private preserve of the monarchy and insisted on having the last word on all important issues in peace and war and on many trivial matters as well. The tradition continued into the twentieth century until the February Revolution ended the Romanov dynasty.

Alexander I took to the field to command the Russian army in the coalitions against Napoleon. Nicholas I commanded the army during the Russo-Turkish War of 1828–29 but only dictated policy during the Crimean War. Rather than command the armies in the field himself during the Russo-Turkish War of 1877–78, Alexander II put his brothers in charge: Nikolai in the Balkans and Mikhail in the Caucasus. Hearing of Nikolai's incompetence, Alexander II paid a prolonged visit to the field headquarters in Bulgaria, where he participated in decision-making. Nicholas II refrained from traveling to Manchuria to command the army during the Russo-Japanese War but monitored the war from St. Petersburg and second-guessed the field commanders' personnel decisions. During the First World War, he, in 1915, claimed his prerogative to command the army, thinking his presence with the *Stavka* (the headquarters that ran the war at the front) would inspire the troops and the home front to greater efforts.

During the Soviet period and after, the heads of state also assumed the mantle of commander in chief of the armed forces more or less as forcefully as they deemed necessary. During the civil war, Vladimir Lenin sometimes overrode his military advisers and field commanders to insist on the allocation of manpower and the assignment of battlefield priorities. Stalin exercised his power to purge the officer corps three times: 1927–28, 1930, and 1937–38. Stalin's involvement in military affairs extended from the highest strategic level down to the operations of armies in the field. Nikita Khrushchev, Stalin's successor, personally dictated the scale of the reduction in the armed forces during the

1950s and pushed the adoption of missile technology and nuclear weapons at the expense of the ground forces. Following Khrushchev, Leonid Brezhnev tried in vain to rein in the military and reduce the economic burden imposed by the arms race. The last Soviet leader, Mikhail Gorbachev, mounted a purge of senior officers in 1987 and forced a reluctant high command to adopt his defensive doctrine of "reasonable sufficiency." Putin oversaw massive investment in high-tech weaponry designed to please the military and make the Russian army as modern as NATO. Without recourse to the State Duma, Putin sent the army to war to do his, rather than Russia's, bidding. In the imperial, Soviet, and post-Soviet eras, the heads of state played important roles in establishing military-diplomatic priorities and assigning human, economic, and financial resources as they oversaw national defense or imperial expansion. Commanders in chief participated in military decision-making as much to shape the conduct and preparation for war as to reinforce their political power.

Russia's Thoughts on War

Beginning with Alexander I, Russia's leadership accepted the western border to be fixed and adopted a defensive posture. When it came to war in the west, the Russian state worked to avoid being seen as the aggressor, but it always intended to attack and wage war on the enemy's soil if not immediately then as soon as feasible after a declaration of war. On the occasions when it was not prudent to attack early on, the leadership prepared to absorb the enemy's attack and then launch a counteroffensive. In contrast, up until the twentieth century, Russia's attitude to war on the rest of its periphery—from the Balkans, to the Caucasus, Central Asia, and the Far East—was overtly offensive. There, Russia usually planned to initiate conflict and strike first into enemy territory intending to maintain the initiative through to victory. In the twentieth century, Russia took a more cautious approach as it faced stronger adversaries first Imperial Japan and then Communist China.

After the Revolutions of 1917, how and where the Soviet Army intended to fight differed little from the calculations of the Imperial Russian Army. Lenin, leader of the Bolshevik Party, inherited the First World War, a war he had no illusions of winning. Lenin withdrew Soviet Russia from that war in March 1918 but immediately found himself embroiled in a civil war and a fight against foreign intervention. In 1920, Soviet Russia went to war with a resurrected Poland that sought to establish its eastern boundary at considerable expense to Russia. During the weeks when the Red Army had turned the tables on the Polish army, Lenin pushed for a military campaign westward in hopes of sparking communist revolutions. When this failed, the Soviet state adopted a defensive foreign policy while it rebuilt its shattered economy. In the 1930s,

Stalin undertook a foreign policy of territorial reacquisition. Using military intimidation and aggression, he worked to restore to the USSR the former territories of the tsarist empire lost during the civil war. Once the Baltic States, eastern Poland, and Bessarabia were reacquired (he failed to conquer Finland), the Soviet Union adopted a defensive posture on all its borders—except that of Romania. After the Second World War, the line to defend moved to the western borders of the Soviet satellite states of East Germany and Czechoslovakia. During the Cold War with the West, the Soviet government, like its imperial predecessor, did not intend to initiate war but planned to take the fight to the enemy once war began. In the post-Soviet era, Russia has been unabashedly the aggressor, acting almost without restraint in dealing with former Soviet republics, being held at bay in the Baltics only by the Baltic States' membership in NATO.

Reasons for War

The fundamental reasons Russia went to war—to defend its territory, impose its hegemony, or conquer new territory—remained constant over its history. In the cases when Russia went to war or used force against foreign adversaries in the nineteenth and twentieth centuries, it either initiated, deliberately provoked, or willingly sought all but four cases. Tsar Alexander I joined the Third and Fourth Coalitions to attack Napoleon and provoked Napoleon's invasion of 1812. He then formed the Sixth Coalition to continue the war. Alexander I sent the Russian army into the Balkans initiating the 1806–12 Russo-Turkish War. He also invaded Finland in 1808 to start the Russo-Swedish War. Nicholas I pursued the conquest of the Caucasus in the 1830s, a conflict that lasted some three decades. He took the offensive at the start of the Russo-Turkish War in 1828. Twenty-one years later, Nicholas also deployed his army to help the Habsburg Empire suppress Hungary's bid for independence. He did not shy away from war with the Ottoman Empire in 1853, which led to war with Britain and France. In 1866 and 1870, Alexander II supported the unification of Germany under Prussia by using his army to threaten Austria-Hungary at the behest of Prussian chancellor Otto von Bismarck. Following in his father's footsteps, he initiated war with the Ottoman Empire in 1877 to establish Russian hegemony in the Balkans. Alexander II oversaw the conquest of Central Asia beginning in the 1860s which his son Alexander III continued into the 1890s. Nicholas II was the unluckiest of the Romanovs when it came to war: he consented to the confrontation with Japan over Korea expecting it to result in a short victorious war; war did come in 1904, but Russia was not victorious. Ten years later, he allowed himself to be maneuvered into war with Germany by his generals and Foreign Ministry.

During the Soviet period, Lenin provoked a civil war with the other leftist parties by creating a one-party state. While fighting them, he simultaneously engaged in a war with counterrevolutionaries, which was likely inevitable. He also employed Red armed forces in failed attempts to prevent the secession of Finland and the Baltic States in 1917–19 but succeeded in reconquering Ukraine and the North Caucasus between 1918 and 1921. The war with Poland in 1920 was largely Poland's doing; however, in the weeks when the Red Army had the upper hand, Lenin considered extending the war to include an invasion of central and southeastern Europe to spread revolution across the continent. In 1939, Stalin launched two unprovoked wars: first in September against Poland in conjunction with Nazi Germany, and then against Finland in November. The following year, he conducted armed occupations of Estonia, Latvia, Lithuania, Bessarabia, and Bukovina, absorbing them all into the USSR. The German attack on the USSR in June 1941 was unprovoked though not entirely unexpected. At the time, Stalin was deep into preparations for war with Germany and Japan. The Soviet Army's last fight was the military intervention in Afghanistan in the years 1979–89, which was pushed for by a faction within the party's ruling body, the Politburo.

Under Yeltsin and Putin, the desire to restore Russian hegemony has been the driving force behind military aggression. This aggression has ranged from cyberattacks on Estonia to invasions of Chechnya, Georgia, and Ukraine.

Milestones in Military Development

How the Russian army prepared to fight and how it conducted operations evolved over time. The major reasons for change were social and technological. Social changes had profound effects on the scale on which Imperial Russia and the Soviet Union could wage war. Russia faced two major constraints in waging war: money and manpower. Political and social change led to economic development, which enabled Russia and the Soviet Union to wage modern war on a massive scale.

The first major milestone that changed how Russia would prepare for war was the emancipation of the serfs. This was linked to Russia's defeat in the Crimean War, which gave Tsar Alexander II the necessary leverage over the landowning nobility to make emancipation possible. The emancipation of the serfs radically altered how the army was manned, creating for the first time the ability to establish a large military reserve. Emancipation allowed the term of enlistment to be reduced to six years, after which soldiers could be recalled up to age forty. As a result, the size of the standing army was reduced, and war and mobilization plans were drawn up to handle a variety of mobilization contingencies.

In the 1860s, minister of war Gen. Dmitrii Miliutin initiated a series of military reforms. These reforms established a universal military service obligation and a reserve system, led to mobilization planning and the integration of railways into that planning, expanded the opportunity for nonnobles to enter the officer corps, and replaced the corps system with the military district system of administration. The military district system became the basis for administering, training, supplying, and mobilizing, and it was far more efficient than the previous decentralized method. Miliutin renewed the emphasis on the General Staff as a war-planning organ. Miliutin's organizational changes carried over into the Soviet period.

Another major milestone was the Bolshevik Revolution. In the heady days of the revolution and the civil war that ensued, Bolshevik ideologues and newcomers to the faith prophesied that "people's war" would be Soviet Russia's new way of waging war—hearkening back to the example of the French Revolution. The realities of world war and civil war eventually put an end to such thinking, and the new Red Army, in 1925, began to look much like the old tsarist army. What was significantly different, however, was the sober intent to do away with massed infantry assaults. Instead, the Bolsheviks wanted educated and motivated soldiers to defeat the enemy using fire and maneuver with the support of the latest artillery, armor, aircraft, and communications technology. The introduction of a new military doctrine that united the economic, political, and social elements of war to the military guided the development of war preparations and technological advancement. Due to financial and industrial inadequacies, however, the army only slowly acquired modern equipment and weaponry. The addition of a political administration to motivate the soldiery with Marxist ideology muddied the waters of command authority and leadership responsibility; it represented the Soviet Union's intent to infuse class consciousness into the soldiers' mentality. An important continuity between the tsarist and Soviet armies was that the Red Army adopted the tsarist army's methods to mobilize reserves to fill out partially manned active divisions, provide for replacements, and create new formations in time of war.

Stalin's drive to rapidly industrialize the USSR was the next major milestone in the Soviet era. His five-year plans included massive investment in defense industries, thereby enabling the Red Army to field extraordinarily large numbers of tanks, artillery, and aircraft during the Second World War. The results made it possible for the Red Army to engage in combined arms warfare—infantry supported by artillery, armor, and close air support—on a massive scale. Armed clashes with the Chinese in 1929 and the Japanese in 1939 seemed to validate the Red Army's new tactical approach of fire and maneuver. This was all undone, however, during the Second World War. First against the Finns, and then under the onslaught of Nazi Germany's Wehrmacht and its allies, the Red Army abandoned the fire-and-maneuver approach and instead relied on infantry attacks inexpertly supported by armor and artillery. Midway through the war, in 1943, combined arms warfare came to the fore and proved effective but still costly in lives.

The penultimate evolutionary milestone was the addition of nuclear weaponry in the 1950s to a fully motorized and mechanized force. The army planned to rely on huge numbers of tanks and self-propelled artillery accompanied by infantry transported in armored vehicles with close air support from airplanes and helicopters to first repel an attacker, and then launch a counteroffensive. The use of short- and medium-range nuclear weapons was always a consideration and seemed to be a foregone conclusion in the minds of some Soviet generals. Preparing to fight a combined arms war on a nuclear battlefield left the Soviet Army singularly unready to wage war in Afghanistan in the 1980s. Gorbachev forced the military to accept grudgingly a genuinely defensive outlook in 1989, marking the last change in how the military planned to wage war. With this change in posture came reductions both in the size of the armed forces and in their share of the national budget.

The post-Soviet era saw massive investment in high-tech research and development, especially in the areas of cyberwarfare, missile technology, smart weapons, drones, and manned aircraft. Tanks, self-propelled artillery, and armored personnel carriers have also been improved to give a qualitative edge to an army otherwise low in human quality, given its ongoing reliance, in large part, on unmotivated conscripts serving short terms of service.

The book is organized chronologically. The focus of the chapters varies because the Russian army was in a perpetual state of transition, sometimes slowly, sometimes rapidly; and the challenges to security, opportunities to project power, and the domestic security situation shifted over time. The first chapter has no mention of military doctrine, the second does mention that the army began to think in terms of doctrine, but not until the third chapter does military thought become institutionalized as the high command pondered how to defend the lengthy borders and maintain hegemony over eastern Europe. During the tsarist era, the focus on domestic unrest expanded from nationalist resentment of conquered minority populations to include economic discontent of the now free peasantry, and extremist political activity among the expanding intelligentsia that sought to stir peasants and workers to revolt. In the Soviet period, the focus of Chapters 4 and 5, when defense was seen through an existential lens, doctrine became all-important. All the while, domestic tranquility was never assured with nationalist resistance taking active form in the 1920s, 1930s, 1940s, 1950s, and 1980s. Chapters 1–3, on the imperial period, have more foundational discussions of the nuts-and-bolts workings of the army and detailed coverage of battles and wars, while the chapters covering Soviet Russia include more theoretical discussions on how Soviet leaders thought they should fight as technology provided more options. Chapter 6, covering the first thirty-odd years of the Russian Federation, reads more as a narrative of events rather than as historical analysis because the events are too close to the present and no truly historical materials are available to examine. Other factors that shape the narrative flow of this book are changes, such as the establishment of the Main/General Staff as a war-planning body in the mid-nineteenth century and the accompanying growth of professionalization and bureaucratization of military careers that characterized the evolution of the army over three centuries.

CHAPTER 1

THE REIGNS OF ALEXANDER I
AND NICHOLAS I, 1801–1855

In the years 1801–55, which spanned the reigns of Alexander I (r. 1801–25) and his brother Nicholas I (r. 1825–55), the elements that shaped Russia's military development were highly affected by the social structure of a serf society, the agrarian nature of the economy, the person of the tsar, and the experience of the Napoleonic and Crimean Wars. The Ministry of War, charged with overseeing the military, was bureaucratically still underdeveloped and concerned itself mostly with personnel, equipment acquisition, and budgeting.[1] The military and diplomatic corps focused on conducting limited campaigns revolving around decisive battles that would lead to negotiated settlements. No organization within the Ministry of War existed to think about establishing doctrine or warfighting strategy particular to Russia's needs and capabilities. Russian military thought and activity was largely in line with Antoine-Henri Jomini's ideas that war was primarily an art, and less so a science, and that putting superior combat power at the decisive point on the battlefield was the key to success. The Great Patriotic War of 1812 and the Crimean War were major milestones in this period. Fighting Napoleon necessitated a massive expansion of the army and focused attention on the threats to Russia as coming primarily from the west and less so from the north (the Swedes) or from the south (the Ottomans). Though victorious over the French, Alexander I recognized the pressing need to change the manning system to create a reserve force, which the army could draw on in time of war—a need he attempted to address with his military colony experiment. The shocking loss of the Crimean War proved to be a watershed in the development of the Russian army, in that it prompted Nicholas I's successor to enact major reforms in both Russian society and the military.

Russia being an autocracy, its military affairs naturally revolved around the person of the tsar. Under Tsar Alexander I, the army was commanded and administered variously by the War College, the Ministry of War, and the Main

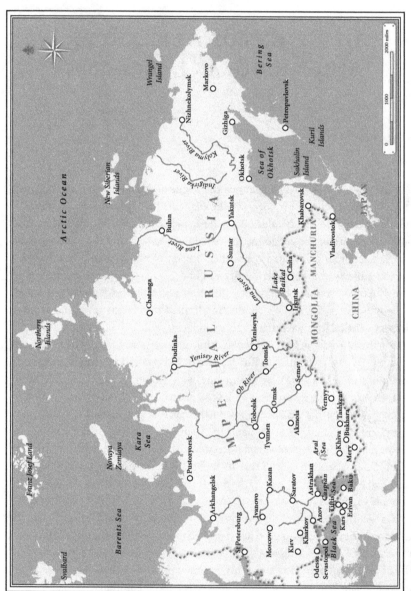

Imperial Russia, 1914

Staff.[2] Alexander I inherited the War College, a collection of senior generals who administered the army and advised the tsar on military matters, when he ascended the throne in 1801. The following year, he created the Ministry of War, which took over some of the functions of the War College eventually making the latter superfluous, thus leading to its abolition in 1811. As a result of the Napoleonic Wars, Alexander created the Main Staff to plan operations and oversee training, which answered to him, not the Ministry of War. Confusion in the chain of command resulted because the Ministry of War, which also was directly subordinate to the tsar, directed the major unit commanders on matters of administration and supply. This arrangement, by design, hindered the top military administrative organs from creating an institutional identity because they were designed to reflect and transmit the will of the tsar and not to encourage an independent military identity.

The Imperial Russian Army referenced the tsar as the source of all authority and as the object of its loyalty. Displays of loyalty were most pronounced in the socially elite Guards regiments, and less so among the poorer nobles and nonnobles in the line units. The tsars took an active role in the promotion and assignment of senior officers, colonels and higher. In judicial matters, the tsars reserved for themselves the right of pardon and clemency; they exercised it regularly, not just in the interest of justice, but to reinforce the idea that they were the final arbiter of officers' fates. The tsar had the ultimate authority to decide whether to initiate war or negotiate to preserve peace. As commander in chief, the tsar had the options to command the army in the field, lead through a council of war, or delegate the warfighting to his generals.

The Army under Alexander I and Nicholas I

During the reigns of Alexander I and Nicholas I, the Imperial Russian Army was almost exclusively a conscript army of serfs. Every other year in peacetime, the War College, then the Ministry of War, consulted with the tsar to determine the number of peasants and men from the unprivileged classes to be drafted. When Nicholas I ascended the throne in December 1825, soldiers still served for twenty-five years, but, in 1834, he reduced the time in active service to twenty years. After discharge, soldiers were liable to be recalled to duty for a period of five years, after which their military obligation ended. In practice, commanders routinely released well-behaved soldiers into civilian life as free men after fifteen years with only those convicted of civil misdemeanors or serious offenses having to serve longer. Between 1834 and 1850, the army furloughed roughly 17,000 men each year.[3] These men constituted Russia's trained reserves.

Peasant serfs, and men from the lower social orders of towns, dreaded the prospect of military service and often exerted considerable effort to avoid being selected because being drafted for life or even for twenty-five years meant one would likely never see his family again. Self-inflicted injuries and faking illness were common practices. A lottery system was used to select who would be sent to the army. Families desperate to save their sons would use their influence in the village to convince the elders or the landowner's representatives to keep their sons out of the drawing. Some who were wealthy enough hired substitutes. Losing a son to the army put the family at an economic disadvantage potentially even to the point of making families economically unviable in the labor-intensive agricultural economy. Villagers and landowners both agreed that it was in everyone's interest to send troublemakers to the army. Between 1801 and 1874, men became liable for conscription at age nineteen. They were supposed to be at least five feet two and a half inches tall and in good health. It was not unusual for age, height, and health criteria to be violated.[4]

Under Alexander I, there was no normal rate of conscription because the army was either at war, recovering from war, or preparing for the next war. The size of the army on Alexander I's death in 1825 was 729,000 (slightly down from its peak of 800,000 during the wars with Napoleon). Under Nicholas I, the average biannual intake of conscripts was 167,000 men. Between 1826 and 1850, the army conscripted 2,087,507 men. In 1850, the army's strength stood at 930,000 men. In any given year the army had about 30,000 officers.[5]

A soldier's life was brutal. At its essence, the social culture of the army reflected the national culture: officers saw the men as serfs in uniform and treated them as such. The words "teaching" and "beating" were used synonymously. Officers slapped, punched, and kicked soldiers and sergeants. Sergeants also beat the soldiers. To enforce discipline and punish crimes, the army employed running the gauntlet, exile to Siberia at hard labor, and execution. There is no evidence that the soldiers who experienced the same treatment on serf estates expected any different.

During the winter months and rainy seasons—up to seven months per year—soldiers outside of garrisoned cities would be quartered with peasants. Life was easier then because officers, billeted in towns, seldom checked on the men. When off duty, soldiers wore peasant garb. The prosperity of the village or rural district determined the soldiers' quality of life during winter quarters. Poor, unhealthy villages saw high levels of sickness and mortality among soldiers. Between 1825 and 1850, 900,000 men (roughly 36,000 per year) died of noncombat-related causes, making the official death rate among soldiers not engaged in combat 37.4 per 1,000. In other European armies in those years, the death rate was typically 20 per 1,000. The true figure may be higher due to intentional underreporting. Bad food, insufficient food, rough physical treatment, and unsanitary living conditions whether with peasants, in camp, or on campaign are to be blamed. Combat deaths during three campaigns over those same twenty-five years accounted for the deaths of just 30,000 soldiers.[6]

The training of the Russian soldier consisted of individual instruction in the regiments conducted during the winter months following his induction. Noncommissioned officers supervised training in which the soldier learned the basic ins and outs of soldiering: how to march, salute, and address his superiors, as well as marksmanship and bayonet drill; if in the cavalry or artillery, soldiers were instructed how to ride. In the summer, the soldiers assembled at training camps, lived in tents, and trained as units under the direction of their officers. Regiments conducted field exercises in which they practiced maneuvers, battle formations, and the bayonet or saber charge. Historians generally agree that unit training was not taken particularly seriously by the officers. Officers held the attitude that the key to battlefield victory was simply obedience on the part of the soldiers and courage on their part.

For the entirety of the existence of the Imperial Russian Army, from Peter I to Nicholas II, the state underfunded the army. Military spending under Nicholas I was the largest single line item in the imperial budget and accounted for 40 percent of annual expenditures, yet this did not cover the costs. In 1851, on the eve of the Crimean War, the Russian government was 400,667,799 rubles in debt, mainly due to military expenditures. This situation profoundly affected everyday life in the army; it caused the officers at the regimental level to devote a considerable amount of their time to economic activity to operate the unit, rather than prepare for war. Economics, rather than thoughts of war, dominated the life of the regiment. Instead of sending the regiments uniforms for the soldiers, the intendancy sent cloth, or money for cloth, and soldiers of the regiment tailored them. The same went for boots, saddles, and tack. A good number of men, therefore, were employed year-round, not in training, but in tailoring and leatherwork. To earn money for the regiment to buy what the army did not provide, commanders detailed soldiers to find paid employment in the civilian economy. Local landowners often hired men to work on their estates, especially during the planting and harvest. The money thus earned was shared between the soldiers and the regiment.[7]

The soldiers' diet consisted mainly of bread, porridge, and tea. Meat was not guaranteed until 1842, when it was decreed that soldiers should have meat at least once a week. Company commanders had responsibility for purchasing meat (usually on the hoof) for their companies. This regulation applied only to the summer months when the regiments were assembled for training. While quartered on the population, the soldiers ate with their peasant hosts, who determined the menu and were reimbursed by the regiment.[8]

The military intendancy, charged with providing the army with food and supplies, remained underdeveloped until nearly the turn of the twentieth century. Until after the Crimean War, commissariat and provisioning commissions that were subordinate to various departments within the Ministry of War were attached to the divisions. Regiments coordinated the filling of their needs for ammunition, saddles, tack, hats, cloth for uniforms, and leather for boots with these commissions. The ministry issued regiment commanders cash to buy locally what the intendancy could not provide, which facilitated widespread corruption. Sometimes a regiment might have to finance up to half of its need due to inadequate funding.[9]

According to a law passed in 1821, when units were on the march, villages along the route of march were required to house the men for free and feed them at rates set by the army. The weakness of the intendancy inhibited the Russian army's ability to project power and led it to rely on allies for logistical support on campaigns against Napoleon and during the suppression of the Hungarian War of Independence in 1849.

The Officers

Before the Miliutin reforms of the 1860s and 1870s, the Russian army acquired the vast majority of its officers through the volunteering of young nobles—very often in their early teenage years—directly to the regiments. As officer candidates they were known as junkers. To apply to a regiment to become a junker the only requirement was to be a noble. There were no educational requirements; it was not unusual for junkers to be illiterate and remain so throughout their careers. In general, junkers were commissioned with no formal instruction in the military arts and sciences. Instead, they served an apprenticeship in a regiment, the length of which depended on their age, personal qualities, rapport with their superiors, and the availability of officer slots. Promotions were entirely at the discretion of the regiment commanders. In regiments posted in undesirable locations, the time to commission could be as few as six months or up to two years, whereas in the more desirable regiments posted in or near the larger towns and cities where competition for slots was fierce, the wait could be five or six years.

A minority of officers came through the military school system comprised of the Corps of Pages, the Noble Regiment, the School of Guards Sub-Ensigns, the various cadet corps (there were only five in 1825, but this number grew to twenty-three by 1855 with fewer than four hundred cadets enrolled in each), and the Engineering School and the Artillery School. About half of these school-educated officers went to the socially elite Guards regiments.

To apply to a military school, besides being from the aristocracy one had to pass a test of basic education. The point of the instruction at the cadet corps was to instill in the students: "fear of God, piety, a feeling of duty, limitless loyalty to the Sovereign, submission to superiors, esteem for elders, thankfulness, and love of one's neighbors."[10] Only cadets who graduated at the top of their classes were given the option to serve in the Guards. The midlevel graduates went to regiments of the line. Those at the bottom of their class due to poor grades or conduct were not commissioned at all but were sent to line regiments as either subensigns or junkers to serve a few years in the ranks before being commissioned. At the end of Nicholas I's reign in 1855, 18.7 percent of officers had been commissioned from the cadet corps, 69.2 percent began as junkers, and 12.1 percent were serf conscripts promoted from the ranks. Half of all officers who served during the reign of Nicholas I came from the hereditary nobility, one-third were personal nobles, and the rest were nonnobles.[11]

Russian autocrats strengthened their personal power through their relationship to the officer corps. The tsar, or tsaritsa, showered honors on officers who proved their loyalty and satisfied the monarch's whims and expectations, thus inspiring others to serve loyally as well in hopes of receiving the same or greater rewards. Ceremony, social connections, and catering to the ego of the monarch trumped military proficiency as criteria for advancement, to the dismay of talented but unconnected officers who could not gain the attention of the tsar. This created an environment that stifled merit as the means to promotion and reward. The key to promotion lay not in an officer educating himself in the military arts but rather in getting assigned to St. Petersburg, where he could make an impression on the monarch or gain the patronage of a member of the royal family; yet this option was available only to the wealthy. Proximity to the throne was essential to secure top assignments in both the army and the civil service.

Wealth and social status affected careers more than military proficiency. Only the wealthy nobility could afford to send their sons to cadet corps or had the connections to get them into the socially elite Corps of Pages, the Noble Regiment, or the School of Guards Sub-Ensigns and thereafter afford the costs associated with service in the Guards. Consequently, wealthy nobles dominated the top ranks of the officer corps until its demise in 1917, regardless of their military qualifications. The social hierarchy also largely determined the distribution of officers throughout the army. Poor and less-educated nobles who began as junkers and nonnobles up from the ranks served mostly in the infantry. Wealthier nobles more often chose to serve in the cavalry, which had higher costs (officers had to provide their own horses) and expenses for social obligations. Sons of the wealthiest noble families who graduated from the more prestigious cadet corps sought to serve in the Guards, within which the cavalry had higher social status and costs than the infantry. Service in the artillery and engineers was reserved for the best-educated officers, conferring a status of its own and attracting officers of both moderate and great wealth. The egoism and arrogance of Guards officers who lorded their wealth and social status over line officers was irksome and the source of widespread resentment.

Before Alexander II's reforms following the Crimean War, service as an officer was far more avocation than vocation, especially for the wealthy who had no need of employment. Many young men were motivated to serve in the army less out of patriotism and more out of family tradition. Few stayed on for full careers; it required more than twenty years of service to secure a pension of one-third of one's annual salary, and thirty-five years to retire with a full salary. The pay was miserable and life in the hinterland could be mind-numbingly boring.[12] Therefore, young men of means usually left the service after only three or four years unless they had a strong affinity for the military life. Others stayed on because they needed the income, paltry as it was.

Life was fairly easy for officers because noncommissioned officers did most of the work. Officers could take months of unpaid leave or go on or off active duty on a whim. Officers were under little pressure to improve their military proficiency, and few opportunities existed to do so. The army had only a handful of infantry and artillery schools for advanced instruction, and they were reserved for the top graduates of the cadet corps. Officers learned their duties and responsibilities on the job and were required to memorize the detailed and extensive regulations governing training and maneuver. Seniority, social connections, vacancies in regiments, and one's standing with his regiment commander determined promotions. Without promotion by merit, there were no guarantees that senior officers would have a significantly better grasp of military strategy, tactics, and administration than the average junior officer.

Popular views of the military and military service depended on one's social class. The nobility saw it as an honorable pastime, yet few chose to serve and fewer still to make it a career. In the 1830s, only 10 percent of eligible males of the hereditary nobility served in the armed forces. During Nicholas I's reign, the cadet corps graduated 17,754 men, but nearly 20 percent of them declined commissions and instead chose to work in the civil service. Despite the apparent prestige of the officer corps, the army was consistently short of officers. Between 2,000 and 2,500 officer slots went unfilled every year. One attraction of military service was that it offered social mobility. Initially, under Peter I, a commission automatically conferred hereditary nobility. Eventually, the landed hereditary nobility grew jealous of their status and pressured Nicholas I, in 1845, into raising to major the rank at which hereditary nobility was awarded. Below that rank, officers had to settle for personal nobility, meaning their noble status was not passed down to their offspring.[13]

The Wars of Alexander I

Russia's success in the War of the Sixth Coalition (1814), following the 1812 French invasion of Russia, which led to the penultimate defeat of Napoleon, validated contemporary views on how to conduct war for the foreseeable future. When Alexander I became tsar in 1801, there was no military organization assigned to think about future war and how to prepare for it. The tsar and his generals planned for wars only as they loomed on the horizon, basing their plans on situational requirements not general principles.

Alexander I organized the Third Coalition against Napoleon in 1805 with the strategic goal of restoring the balance of power in Europe. He saw it as a war of choice, not a real necessity, and intended for Austria to do most of the "heavy lifting," as it were. The Russian army at the time was 300,000-men strong, but because of the need to guard the southern border pending war with the Ottoman Empire, Alexander I committed only 75,000 men under Gen. Mikhail Kutuzov to the war against France. To offset Russia's woeful inability to supply its army on the march, Alexander convinced Austria to provision the Russians while on their territory. Where the Austrians failed to deliver, the Russians lived off the land—to Austria's dismay.

Generals Kutuzov and Frederick Wilhelm Count Buxhöwden led the Russian forces in two columns marching west through Austria. The allied plan was to combine forces and attack together, but the Austrians attacked Napoleon at Ulm in October, before the Russians arrived, and were defeated. Kutuzov then marched to Austerlitz, where he joined Buxhöwden. Alexander I came to the army at this time, and, per Russian law, when the tsar was in the field, he became de facto commander in chief. Napoleon defeated the Russians and Austrians at Austerlitz in December, putting an end to the Third Coalition. Francis I of Austria came to terms with Napoleon in the Treaty of Pressburg on 26 December 1805; a humiliated Alexander I ordered the Russian army home.[14]

Russia and Prussia formed the Fourth Coalition in 1806. As in 1805, Russia's ally attacked Napoleon before the Russians arrived. Napoleon defeated the Prussians at Jena and Auerstedt in October 1806, knocking them out of the war. The Russian army under Gen. Levin August von Bennigsen then fought Napoleon in February 1807 at Preussich-Eylau, where it inflicted about the same number of casualties that it suffered—23,000. Without an ally and with no reinforcements at hand, Bennigsen retreated. Luckily for Bennigsen, Napoleon was in no shape to pursue and destroy the Russians. The next battle was in June 1807 at Friedland; there Napoleon again defeated Bennigsen, who lost 20,000 men. Abandoning hope of victory, Tsar Alexander I negotiated the Treaty of Tilsit in July 1807, whereby Russia agreed to comply with Napoleon's Continental System and become a nominal ally.[15]

Although it probably did not affect the outcome of the War of the Fourth Coalition, Alexander I's presence with the army did not help. During the campaign against the French in 1806–7, when Alexander I joined the forces at the front, according to Gen. Alexei Yermolov, "parades and foppishness took over." When the tsar demanded to review troops from each regiment, the commanders dressed their soldiers in the best uniforms and hid those men from whom uniforms had been taken. Commanders always presented their units in the best light, so Alexander I never knew the true material condition of the army.[16] Alexander I took great stock in a unit's appearance. Impressing the tsar on the parade ground, whether in peace or war, was every bit as important to an officer's career as battlefield success.

In response to the failures of the Third and Fourth Coalitions, Russia reorganized the army into divisions and corps following the French model. Each division comprised three brigades of two regiments of infantry each. Two brigades were infantry of the line, and one brigade was comprised of light infantry skirmishers. Two infantry divisions plus additional regiments of cavalry and artillery made up a corps. On campaign, corps headquarters had the responsibility for logistics, relieving the regiments and divisions of that burden. The adoption of the corps system after the Peace of Tilsit made it nearly impossible for Napoleon to rout the Russian army with single, decisive victories as he had in earlier campaigns.[17]

In combat, the regiment was the basic maneuver unit. An infantry regiment was authorized 2,033 officers and men, each battalion 646 soldiers, and each company 159. The Russians arrayed their regiments facing the enemy in lines three deep, with the front two lines firing in volleys. After firing, the soldiers passed their muskets back to the third line where they were reloaded and passed them back to the front.[18] If and when the regiment or higher commander decided the moment was right, he ordered a bayonet charge to drive the enemy from the field.

The Great Patriotic War of 1812

Napoleon's invasion of Russia in 1812, which became known in Russia as the Great Patriotic War (not to be confused with the Great Patriotic War of the Fatherland, 1914–17, or the Great Patriotic War of the Soviet Union, 1941–45), happened not solely by the emperor's choice. Alexander I needed to confront Napoleon to regain his prestige and reverse the steady decline of his reputation and power at home, which had begun after Tilsit. Defeating Napoleon and regaining Polish territory would, Alexander hoped, restore his international and domestic standing. Rather than initiating a war, Alexander I chose to provoke conflict by refusing to let Napoleon marry his sister, opting not to support Napoleon against Austria as he was obligated, and violating the Continental System by putting a prohibitive tariff on French goods and trading with Britain through neutral American shipping. The tsar and his generals began discussing war with Napoleon and how it should be fought as early as 1810. Some generals advocated a preemptive strike into Poland, others to wait and receive Napoleon's attack and adjust to it, and still others to retreat first and then counterattack once Napoleon's strategy was revealed and his forces weakened. All assumed that Napoleon would start with superior numbers. The tsar chose to cede the initiative to Napoleon.

On the eve of the war, the Russian army fielded 409,000 men and 1,344 cannons, though not all of them could be deployed on Russia's western border. War with the Ottomans in the Balkans (1806–12) tied down tens of thousands of troops. Against Napoleon, Alexander I divided the Russian forces into three contingents: two north of the Pripet Marshes, of which one was to guard the approaches to St. Petersburg, and the other to block a move straight east toward Moscow; the third contingent was placed south of the marshes to defend Ukraine. The total strength of the armies in the west was 213,759 soldiers. The forces north of the Pripet Marshes were divided into the 1st Army (120,210 men) and 2nd Army (49,423 men). South of the marshes was the 3rd Army (44,126 men).[19]

In this war, Alexander I consulted with his commanding generals on the overall strategy but at times arbitrarily gave direct orders to engage in battle. He and his entourage occasionally joined the army in the field, to which his generals politely objected; when he was away, he monitored events and sent orders and suggestions, first to Barclay de Tolly, then to his successor, Marshal Kutuzov. The tsar complicated matters by creating an unclear chain of command. At first, he placed Barclay de Tolly in charge, but he was not clearly superior to Gen. Petr Bagration, commander of the 2nd Army, because Bagration had the right to report directly to the tsar. Bagration (a Russian) detested Barclay de Tolly (a Livonian) and worked constantly to undermine him. Bagration hated the thought of giving up a single inch of Russian soil without a fight. It was not unusual for Alexander I's generals to second-guess him.[20]

In the weeks before the *Grande Armeé* attacked, when it was determined that Napoleon's force of more that 500,000 men was too large to be engaged by any of the dispersed Russian armies, Alexander dismissed any calls to attack. Instead, the tsar ordered, against the advice of some of his generals, that Russia cede the initiative to Napoleon and react to his movements. Napoleon attacked on 24 June 1812 against the forces commanded by Barclay de Tolly, minister of war and commander of the 1st Army, who immediately ordered a retreat to the vicinity of the Dvina and Dnieper Rivers. This decision was not well received by General Bagration, who had earlier argued for a preemptive attack.[21]

Because the Russian forces were divided, if Napoleon kept his forces concentrated neither of the Russian armies could stop him. Only if the Russians united their forces would they have a chance to win a battle. Bagration brought his forces northward to join with Barclay de Tolly, who deployed his forces at Vitebsk while his rearguard delayed Napoleon. All the while, Barclay de Tolly was under pressure by Alexander I not to let his army be decisively defeated and destroyed. When it became clear that Bagration would not arrive in Vitebsk in time, Barclay de Tolly destroyed his supply depot and withdrew to Smolensk. Bagration's refusal to subordinate himself to Barclay de Tolly complicated the situation. Barclay de Tolly arrived in Smolensk on 1 August and Bagration on 3 August. They held a meeting to decide on their course of action at which Grand Duke Konstantin Pavlovich, Alexander I's brother, insisted that they go on the offensive. Bagration and his staff agreed. Barclay de Tolly and Gen. Ludwig Wolzogen advocated continuing the retreat.[22]

After heated arguments, the generals decided to engage Napoleon with their combined armies at a time and place to their advantage. Barclay de Tolly left 15,000 men to defend Smolensk proper while the rest deployed several days' march away. They did not know if Napoleon was going straight for the city or if he would try to outflank it, so they tried to cover all approaches. When Napoleon went straight for the city, Bagration's 2nd Army was too far out of position to help, so Barclay de Tolly told him to head for Moscow. Barclay de Tolly sent his 1st Army (60,000 men) to Smolensk to engage Napoleon. It appears that Barclay de Tolly had no intention of holding Smolensk but planned a delaying action while his and Bagration's armies withdrew to the east. Fighting mostly in Smolensk proper on 14 August, Barclay de Tolly did not commit his army to a decisive battle, to Napoleon's dismay. On the first day of fighting, the French inflicted heavy casualties on the Russians and captured part of the town. When he was sure the city would fall, and having suffered at least 10,000 killed, Barclay de Tolly ordered the retreat to resume.[23]

The Russian command continued to be divided over strategy. Barclay de Tolly wanted to retreat along the lines of supply, but Generals Bagration and Aleksei Arakcheev wanted to turn and attack Napoleon's larger forces. Alexander I was caught between the two choices. The tsar sided with Barclay de Tolly, but under pressure from those at court to put a "real Russian" in charge, he gave overall command to the aging Marshal Kutuzov, who was popular with the other generals, though Alexander did not like him. Barclay de Tolly retained command over the 1st Army.[24] To Bagration's dismay, Kutuzov ordered the retreat to proceed. Several times Kutuzov's subordinates encouraged him to stand and fight, but to him the situation seemed too risky—until he got to Borodino.

Kutuzov's plan at Borodino, on the approaches to Moscow, was to fight a defensive battle anchored on field fortifications. The battle front extended for nearly six kilometers. The Russians had 120,000 men and 650 cannons divided into seven corps. Barclay de Tolly's army was on the right, with Bagration's army on the left. The battle proper commenced on 7 September and lasted just one day. Intense cannon fire inflicted horrendous casualties on the French and their allies (at least 6,550 French dead and 21,500 wounded), yet the Russian forces suffered more—50,000 casualties, both dead and wounded. Bagration died a week later of wounds received in the battle. With casualties so heavy, Kutuzov decided to fall back to Moscow.[25]

As the retreat began, Alexander I abandoned his original caution and sent orders for Kutuzov to fight another battle in front of Moscow, but Kutuzov had already held a council of war in which five of his generals voted to stand and fight and four to retreat. Kutuzov chose not to risk a decisive defeat of the army and sided with the four before the tsar's order arrived. When Kutuzov received Alexander's order, he did not change his mind and wrote back to the tsar that they were giving up Moscow to save the army. Alexander I reluctantly accepted Kutuzov's decision.

The Russian forces then retreated past Moscow and began to receive reinforcements. Earlier, in July, Alexander I had ordered the raising of the *opolchenie*, a volunteer force of free men who would serve only for the duration of the conflict. These men and a new levy of conscripts, though hastily trained, were sent to join the army at the front. Ensconced in Moscow in mid-September, Napoleon sought to negotiate an end to the war, but Alexander I cleverly dragged out the talks while his army gained strength and winter approached. Napoleon did not appreciate that Alexander I could not come to terms with him. To keep his throne, the tsar had to pay attention to the opinion of the nobility, who had not forgiven the humiliation of Tilsit and were angered by the retreat. Alexander I also feared that Napoleon was trying to destroy the Romanov dynasty and Russia as a great power, so there was every reason to keep fighting. He had to pursue the war to the bitter end.[26]

After a month passed with prospects for peace proving ephemeral, Napoleon began the retreat westward. There was no sense among the generals, or in the tsar's mind, that now was the time to engage in decisive battles to annihilate

Napoleon. Instead, Kutuzov followed a pattern of pressing Napoleon's rear-guard and keeping him on the Mozhaisk highway, where food would be hard to come by because the French had picked the countryside clean on their way to Moscow. At Maloiaroslavets, Kutuzov joined in battle to block Napoleon's retreat to the southwest. He was successful only because Napoleon, overestimating Russian strength, did not press the attack the next day. Napoleon backed off, and Kutuzov gave him space to retire, counting on the worsening winter weather and malnutrition to deplete the *Grande Armeé*. Napoleon then took his army on the Mozhaisk highway to Smolensk.

Kutuzov's next and last attempt at a decisive battle to possibly block Napoleon was at Krasnyi. Here Napoleon won, and the *Grand Armeé* continued its retreat, every day becoming weaker. According to General Yermolov, an eyewitness to events: "In his report to the tsar, Kutuzov portrayed the indecisive and sluggish action of our army at Krasnyi as a series of major battles fought over several days, whereas the engagements had been fought in isolation and none of these battles had been fought according to any general plan. Yet, our timid actions had to be presented in a positive light and what could have been better than describing them as battles? But, in reality, they were carried out randomly."[27] Still intimidated by Napoleon and desiring to maintain the strength of the Russian army, Kutuzov warned Yermolov to minimize his casualties and not risk becoming decisively engaged during the pursuit, and he forbade him to cross the Dnieper River.

Alexander I ordered Kutuzov (27,000 soldiers), Adm. Pavel Chichagov (24,000 soldiers), and Gen. Peter Wittgenstein (34,000 soldiers) to join forces and prevent Napoleon (110,000 men) from crossing the Berezina River at Borisov. None of these commanders were eager to tackle Napoleon head-on in a winner-take-all fight; ultimately, they did not have to because through lack of killer instinct and ineffective reconnaissance, they kept the bulk of their forces south of Borisov. French engineers built bridges across the Berezina, fighting a rearguard action on one bank and attacking on the far bank to prevent this route of retreat from being blocked. Kutuzov eventually succeeded in taking Borisov, but not before Napoleon got most of his army across, despite being heavily pressed. Admiral Chichagov received the blame for Napoleon's escape, and he eventually retired abroad in disgrace. The Grand Armeé's retreat ended on 13 December, four days after the army crossed the Niemen River. Kutuzov, recognizing that his forces had sustained considerable losses and that additional reinforcements would be weeks or months in coming, wanted to end the war now that Napoleon's forces had been expelled from Russia. The tsar, however, seeing that his throne was secure and encouraged by Prussia's betrayal of Napoleon in December (Frederick William III opened Prussia to transit by the Russian army), sought to reestablish Russia's position as a great power.

Allied with Prussia in January 1813, the two armies sought to engage Napoleon in Germany, much to Kutuzov's displeasure. There followed the Battles of Lützen, Bautzen, and Dresden, all of which the Russian and Prussian armies lost because they failed to coordinate their efforts. During a lull of a couple of months to regroup and absorb Russian reinforcements of 68,000 infantry and 13,000 cavalry, 66,000 of whom were volunteers for the opolchenie from the liberated western provinces, Prince Klemens von Metternich, on behalf of Emperor Francis I, sought to join Austria to the Russo-Prussian alliance against Napoleon. This union eventually created the Sixth Coalition, which soon added Sweden, Saxony, Württemberg, and Great Britain.

The allies adopted a strategy called the Trachtenberg Plan in which they agreed to engage Napoleon's forces in separate, small battles rather than when Napoleon had all his armies assembled. As a result, they were able to weaken the French while they built up their own forces to a size they thought even Napoleon could not overcome.[28] This strategy led to victory at the Battle of Leipzig during 16–19 October 1813, when an allied force of between 370,000 and 380,000 men went up against Napoleon's army of about 200,000 men. During the campaign, Alexander I held the title of supreme commander, but it was actually Prince Karl Philipp Schwarzenberg of Austria who commanded the forces in the field. The tsar relied on trusted generals to advise him, especially Bennigsen after Kutuzov died in March. Still, Alexander I provided useful insights into the planning of the great battle. After the great "Battle of the Nations," it took another five months for the coalition forces to push Napoleon all the way to Paris, which they reached in March 1814.

The Decembrist Revolt

Victory over Napoleon solidified Alexander I's hold on power, erasing the dissent caused by his earlier failures. The victory, however, led to the rise of a new opposition in the form of officers "infected" by European liberalism, which they had picked up from reading Western sources and by their experiences in central and western Europe during the war. These officers, some from the most prominent noble families in Russia, wanted to modernize Russia politically. The most significant of their goals were to end autocracy, adopt a constitution, establish individual rights, and emancipate the serfs. They were initially encouraged to work for change by Freemasonry, Alexander I's own early liberal tendencies, and his openly renewed interest in liberal reform expressed in 1815, as well as by recent liberal/nationalist revolutions in Spain, Italy, and Greece. These men were extremely well-read on liberal ideas and the constitutions of the United States, France, and Spain.[29]

Six army officers, all veterans of the Napoleonic Wars, formed the first conspiratorial group, the Union of Salvation, in 1816. Other liberal-reformist and Polish nationalist groups also formed, grew, and connected with the Union of Salvation (in 1817 the group changed its name to the Union of Welfare). As members of the socially elite Semenovskii Guards regiment, they practiced a humane style of leadership that was highlighted by literacy instruction and devoid of corporal punishment. In October 1820, this leniency inadvertently led to a mutiny by the men of the regiment against their new commander, Col. Fedor Shvarts, who insisted on restoring traditionally harsh discipline. The regiment was disbanded as a result, and the liberal officers were dispersed to various garrisons, where they continued to recruit idealistic young officers to the movement. The Union of Welfare grew slowly, and as a result of the Semenovskii revolt it divided in 1820 into two groups: renamed the Northern Society, led by three brothers—Lieutenant-Colonels Matvei, Ippolit, and Sergei Muraviev-Apostol—based in St. Petersburg; and the Southern Society, led by Col. Pavel Pestel, based in Ukraine.

Disappointed by Alexander's failure to follow through with liberal reform, the conspirators decided to act against him. Various schemes in 1823, 1824, and 1825 that considered kidnapping, assassination, and inciting mass mutiny all came to naught. Finally, Alexander I died of an illness in December 1825 while in Crimea, but in the weeks after his death, there was confusion as to which of his remaining brothers was the rightful heir (Alexander I had no sons): Constantine, the elder of the two, or Nicholas. The problem was that Constantine had renounced his right to the throne to contract a morganatic marriage with a Polish countess, thereby passing the throne to Nicholas, but this was known to only a few of the inner circle at court who were not sure he would honor his pledge. While the Russian Senate and the Romanov family sorted it out, members of the Northern Society saw their chance to seize power and create a liberal Russia.

The ill-conceived and poorly organized revolt was cobbled together in short order and put into action on 14 December. The conspirators lied to their soldiers telling them that Alexander I had wanted Constantine to take power and grant a constitution but that Nicholas was trying to prevent it from happening. This ploy succeeded in getting 3,000 soldiers to support the revolt. The coup was doomed, having been betrayed by a member of the Northern Society the night before, which enabled Nicholas to confront the mutineers with 9,000 troops, who, in a matter of hours, dispersed the soldiers and arrested the rebel leaders.

The Southern Society also rose in support with small numbers but, unable to recruit support from the rest of the army, was crushed in short order. All told, 579 men, mostly army officers, were arrested: 289 were subsequently cleared of all charges; 290 went to trial, and of them 121 were convicted of treason. For their crime, five were executed, thirty-one exiled to Siberia for life at hard labor, and eighty-five sentenced to shorter terms of Siberian exile. Nicholas's reaction to this revolt was to establish a secret police organization (the Third Section) that would henceforth keep an eye on society and the military in particular. The Third Section, which later in the century became the *Okhrana* (under the Ministry of Internal Affairs), had the right to investigate ordinary and political crimes in military units and had the authority to arrest officers without the permission of the military chain of command. Because of this, an adversarial relationship between the army and the Ministry of Internal Affairs reigned until the demise of autocracy.

The Military Colonies

After the Napoleonic Wars, the Russian army remained bloated, numbering at least 800,000 men. Maintaining this large force was financially burdensome (particularly so considering the debt the government had amassed during the war and the cost of rebuilding Smolensk and Moscow), yet Alexander deemed it unwise to release too many former serfs into society all at once. With the defeat of Napoleon and the attainment of satisfactory western boundaries at the Congress of Vienna in 1815, military-diplomatic policy became focused on protecting those borders. To defend those borders and still reduce the cost of maintaining such a large army, Alexander I returned to his idea of military colonies that he had begun to create in 1810 but had had to suspend to fight Napoleon. Military colonies were essentially both a utopian social engineering project designed to raise the cultural level of the peasantry and a military project designed to offset Russia's inability to create a system of military reserves.

Alexander I, and then Nicholas I, intended that the colonies be economically self-sufficient units of soldiers and state-owned peasant serfs. Between 1826 and 1831, military spending accounted for nearly 40 percent of the national budget, close to 160 million paper rubles annually. The colonies, then, were to cut costs by reducing the size of the standing army and to provide a reserve of soldiers. In peacetime, soldiers were to assist the peasants with their agricultural chores; in time of war, the soldiers would deploy to fight while the peasant farmers continued to farm and maintain their own and the soldiers' families. Soldiers and peasants lived together. Both soldiers and civilians did military training two or three days a week, and both worked the land the other days of the week. Male children born to soldiers and civilians in the colonies became state property destined to serve as soldiers in their adult years. By this method the tsars hoped, first, to no longer depend on drafts of civilian peasants to man the army and, second, to make the army self-financing through the production of its farmlands.[30]

The colonies were under the tsar's personal jurisdiction, outside the normal military chain of command and isolated from civilian government interference. Alexander assigned General Arakcheev to oversee them in 1816. By 1825, there were 138 infantry battalions and 240 cavalry squadrons dispersed throughout Novgorod, Kharkiv (Kharkov), Kherson, and Ekaterinoslav provinces. In 1826, of the Russian army's 800,000 men, about 80,000–84,000 served in the military colonies along with 200,000 civilians.[31]

Some historians think the project was doomed from the start. The aristocracy feared the tsar was creating a Praetorian Guard to use against them. Leadership and management suffered because the officers assigned to the colonies were often rejects from the regular army, did not care about the project, and enriched themselves by stealing funds and property from the colonies. The peasants detested it because they lacked freedom to run things in traditional ways. They did not understand the purpose behind most of the rules that governed their lives. Being treated like soldiers, being required to wear uniforms, and having to shave their beards antagonized them further. The women resented being forced to marry soldiers. Finally, they resented being subject to strict military discipline. The peasants suffered financially because Arakcheev heavily taxed and indiscriminately fined them to build up a working fund for the colonies.

On several occasions, discontent drove military colonists to revolt. Soldiers and civilians mainly targeted corrupt officers for revenge during riots. A major revolt occurred in Novgorod in 1831 as troops prepared to depart to quash the Polish uprising. During the uprising, the mutineers killed more than two hundred officers and officials.[32] As it turned out, the colonies did not cover the cost of their upkeep. Alexander II finally abolished them in the 1860s as part of his reforms.

The Wars of Nicholas I

In his foreign policy, Nicholas I explicitly rejected aggression against Europe; but he saw the North Caucasus as fair game. Russia conducted several small wars with the Ottoman Empire, Persia, and Caucasian tribes during his reign. According to William Fuller, Nicholas I's wars were more like punitive operations.[33] In all these wars, St. Petersburg chose to devote the least amount of manpower feasible for fear of being vulnerable to attack from Europe. Even during a major war against the Ottoman Empire in 1828–29, the Ministry of War did not commit more than 100,000 men. Because he devoted insufficient forces, the North Caucasus was not conquered until after the Crimean War when Alexander II authorized the army to use 300,000 men to finish the job, which they did by the forced mass migration of Circassians at great loss of civilian lives. Before that, the commanders in theater seldom had more than 60,000 men.

The Russo-Turkish War, 1828–1829

In 1828, Russia went to war with the Ottoman Empire largely because Sultan Mahmud II wanted a war (in order to maintain his power, he needed to show his people that he was not subservient to Russia), and after the naval Battle of Navarino, in which the combined fleets of Britain, France, and Russia destroyed the Ottomans' Mediterranean fleet, the Ottomans shut the Black Sea straits to Russian commerce thereby crippling the export of grain from southern Russia. Foreseeing the potential for conflict, the Ministry of War had begun to prepare for war as early as April 1826—two years before Russia attacked—with the strategic goal of extending Russian hegemony into the Ottoman Danubian principalities of Moldavia and Wallachia. Russia could pit approximately 115,000 of its 729,655 men and three hundred guns against the Ottoman army; Nicholas I wanted to keep large numbers of men to defend Russia's European borders. He usually kept more men back because poor intelligence regarding the intentions of Russia's neighbors, Prussia and Austria, nearly always led to overcautious calculations about the number of men needed to guard the borders. The tsars, their ministers, and the grand dukes who governed Poland tended to exaggerate the foreign threat, usually considering the worst-case scenario to be the most likely. Tens of thousands of men were required to secure restive Poland and Finland, and to police Russia's interior. During 1827, Nicholas I ordered the army to conduct a draft, the first since 1824, which brought in 59,906 men and barely offset the loss of 48,812 men to various causes that year. A critical shortage of horses and oxen proved to be a rather expensive problem to overcome.[34]

The Main Staff did not coordinate its plans for the war with the generals who were to lead major formations. The planners were prone to unrealistic expectations and wishful thinking and did not complete the plans before war broke out. As in 1812, command relations were unclear. The forces in the field were commanded by General Wittgenstein, but one month after the fighting began, Nicholas I (and his large retinue) took to the field and ensconced themselves at Wittgenstein's headquarters. Though Nicholas did not take charge formally, his presence hindered the initiative of the various commanding generals. The tsar had not articulated his war aims before the war began, and his indecision interfered with the generals' attempts to plan, leaving the army uncertain of its mission at the outset. Only after the failure of the 1828 campaign did Nicholas, while planning the next year's campaign, spell out his aims, which were limited to extending Russian hegemony over Moldavia and Wallachia and taking Armenia. Despite two years' lead time, neither the Main Staff nor the Ministry of War had gathered sufficient supplies for the number of men and draft animals they sent to war. Compounding the initial shortage, horses and oxen died by the hundreds for lack of water and forage, crippling the distribution of supplies. Besides personnel and animal deficiencies, Russia suffered financially. To cover the wartime increase in expenses, Russia secured foreign loans in 1828, 1829, and 1831. By 1 January 1832, the government had accrued a foreign debt equivalent to 823 million rubles.[35]

The Ottoman Empire declared war on Russia on 18 December 1827 but did not initiate hostilities. Nicholas I waited until 14 April 1828 to declare war in turn and ordered the army into Moldavia on 25 April. The advance guard crossed the Prut River on 7 May, and then the Danube on 8 June. After some indecision, Nicholas set the goal of marching on Constantinople by October to force the Ottomans to capitulate. Austria did move troops to the frontier to threaten Russia, but Prussia sided with Russia to keep Austria neutral. In the end, the conduct of the war did not match the aims; by not devoting sufficient forces to overwhelm the Ottoman defenders and by changing the focus of attack to unnecessarily reducing multiple fortresses, Nicholas I undermined the potential for a quick and decisive victory.

The Main Staff organized the Russian forces into three corps: III corps, with 38,000 men; VII corps, with 24,000; and VI corps, with 22,000. III Corps was to cross the lower Danube, march into Bulgaria, and take Varna. VII Corps was to besiege Brailov and cover the flank of III Corps; VI Corps was to occupy Moldavia and Wallachia, take Silistria, and guard the army's line of communication. VI and VII Corps crossed the Prut unopposed. To compensate for its unprepared and disorganized intendancy, Russian officers requisitioned food locally paying with promissory notes.

Besieging the fortress of Brailov in May was the first major action. Not until 3 June did the army make its first assault, which failed at a cost of 2,700 casualties. The fortress finally capitulated on 10 June, after Russia had suffered another 2,000 casualties, but the Ottoman force of 8,000 was allowed safe passage, whereupon they reinforced the other fortresses the Russians wanted to take.[36] In quick succession, the Russians captured the forts of Isakchi, Hirsova, Tultscha, and Kostendji (which was also a port the Russians would use to supply their forces). The Russian army had 45,000 men to besiege three remaining forts: Silistria, Varna, and Shumla. Nicholas I arrived at Karl von Dibich's field headquarters by 1 August. The tsar directed Dibich to maintain the siege of Shumla and personally accompanied the forces to attack Varna, which was put under siege on 6 August 1828. The Ottomans tried to break the siege from the outside but were driven back. The Russian navy blockaded Varna by sea. It fell to III Corps in October, but the corps did not have enough men to take the other two forts. The army did secure Wallachia by the end of October.

At the onset of winter, the army abandoned the siege of Shumla and retreated across the Danube, where Dibich used the time to plan a spring campaign and replace his losses. The number of men at his disposal had increased to 149,000 several months after the start of the war with the arrival of the Guards Corps and II Corps. By February 1829, Dibich had lost 40,000 men due to illness, combat, and the departure of the Guards Corps, which Nicholas had taken with him when he returned to Russia in December. To replace these losses, Nicholas I ordered three levies of new recruits (something he could have done in advance of the war), which brought in nearly 257,000 men, but the 1829 campaign began before they could be trained and sent to the Balkans.[37]

Helmuth von Moltke (the elder), a captain in the Prussian army at the time, observed the Russian army during the war. His assessment of the failed 1828 campaign highlighted the fact that by starting operations so late in the year, it was highly unlikely that the Russian army could get to Constantinople before winter. He noted that Nicholas I had not committed enough men. He also pointed out that they had not brought enough artillery to take on the fortresses they planned to attack and what they had they sent too late. It took more than three months to get the guns there. He suggested that the Prut and Danube should have been crossed simultaneously, which would have prevented the Turks from combining their forces to defend Shumla in strength. The Russians had unwisely dissipated their strength by occupying Moldavia and Wallachia, thus hindering their ability to overcome the unexpectedly strong resistance put up by Ottoman forces there. He thought the Russians should have gone straight for Varna with its port, rather than be distracted by taking Shumla. Russian deaths were higher than necessary, he thought, because they did not have safe or healthy places to take the sick and wounded for treatment. In von Moltke's words, "The preparations were insufficient, the campaign began too late, and the direction of the main army was not likely to ensure a successful result." Von Moltke gives credit to the "self-sacrificing obedience of their commanders, the steadiness of the common soldiers, their power of endurance, and unshaken bravery in time of danger" for avoiding disaster at Shumla.[38]

Nicholas I decided to return to St. Petersburg after the army had retreated beyond the Danube, but before he left, the tsar reorganized the command relations for the 1829 campaign, appointing Gen. Alexander Chernyshev to serve as both chief of the Main Staff and minister of war, and Dibich to command the 2nd Army. Only about 70,000 men were on hand to renew the campaign.

Waiting until May, Dibich sent his army across the Danube with the goal of finally taking Silistria. He besieged it on 1 May, and it surrendered on 1 July. Russian losses were about 2,700 officers and men. When the Turks moved from Shumla to attack VI and VII Corps, Dibich moved his forces to cut them off. A major pitched battle took place in May at Kulevcha, in which the Russians destroyed an attacking force of 40,000 Turks. After Silistria fell, those Russian troops moved to join Dibich, who then ordered an advance across the Balkan Mountains on 16 July. Simultaneously, the plague hit the Russian forces reducing them to about 35,000 men. A bold march on Adrianople in mid-August with only 10,000 men took the city without firing a shot. At this point, the Russians did not have enough men both to march on Constantinople and to secure their rear. Unaware of how weakened their enemy had become, the Ottomans called for negotiations, which ended the war. Through careful planning and bold leadership, Dibich—absent the interference of Nicholas I—managed to defeat the Ottomans with one siege, one battle, and a march of five hundred miles in a three-month span.

The Polish Revolt of 1830

Only one year after defeating the Ottoman army, the Russian army again found itself in major combat. This time it was to put down the revolt of its Polish subjects. Nicholas I ordered that the revolt be crushed mercilessly to dissuade other discontented national minorities from attempting to secede. Tsar Nicholas wanted the war wrapped up as quickly as possible to prevent other European nations from becoming involved given the widespread sympathy for the Poles in liberal circles. The "Polish Question" was a topic of discussion throughout Europe, with many people—particularly the French—urging their governments to intervene on the side of the Poles. The Poles started the war with the November Insurrection aiming to gain their independence. Nicholas I refused to negotiate with the Poles and sent in 120,000 men under General Dibich with the twin goals of annihilating the rebellion and subjugating Poland more thoroughly than ever. The tsar welcomed the opportunity to strip the Poles of the many liberal privileges previously granted by his brother, which Nicholas I felt had been ill-advised.

Dibich conducted the conflict like a campaign against a European army. The Poles had a regular army of 46,000 men and 146 guns, which had been authorized by Alexander I. Nicholas wanted a decisive victory and a quick end to the uprising so that he could then send his army, allied to Prussia, to suppress the Belgian revolt against the Dutch. Unlike the war with the Ottomans, this time he intended to allocate sufficient forces to achieve that end. He gave General Dibich 123,000 men and 348 guns. The Poles set up a defense east of

Warsaw and waited for the Russians to attack. Perhaps overconfident because of his numerical superiority, Dibich insisted on a frontal attack into the teeth of the Polish defenses at the first major engagement, the Battle of Grochow, in February 1831. The Poles were protected by the Vistula River on their right flank and swamps on their left. On 19 and 20 February, Dibich attacked head-on into the Polish defenses, failing to overcome them and taking heavy losses. Next, Dibich sent Prince Ivan Shakhovskoi's Grenadier Corps to get behind the Poles by coming down from the north, but they were held up by a Polish division. When Shakhovskoi finally joined him, Dibich attacked again. Nine Polish battalions battled twenty-five Russian battalions for hours before slowly withdrawing, causing the Russian forces to spread out and disregard their flanks. Soon, the leader of the Polish forces, Gen. Jozef Chlopicki, a veteran of the Napoleonic Wars on the side of France, sprung his trap: he sent two divisions into the Russians routing them and capturing some cannons in the process. Chlopicki ordered his forces to pursue the retreating Russians, but his subordinate commanders refused, wanting to be reinforced first. It was Dibich, however, who received reinforcements first, and the Poles wisely retreated into the Praga bridgehead defending the crossing into Warsaw, but not before first annihilating a Russian cavalry attack. The battle cost the Russians 9,400 casualties and the Poles around 7,000.[39]

The campaign to take Warsaw would last another seven months, foiling Dibich's expectations of a swift and easy triumph. He overestimated his abilities and underestimated the Poles. As Dibich regrouped and absorbed reinforcements, tens of thousands of Russian soldiers died of cholera, thereby depriving Dibich of the numerical superiority he had begun the war with. An early spring thaw turned the roads into a muddy quagmire that impeded the maneuver of men and the transport of supplies. Offensive action had to be delayed until May. On 26 May 1831, Dibich's forces, with superior numbers of infantry, cavalry, and artillery, routed the Poles in battle at Ostrolenka. Each side suffered around 6,000 casualties—the Russians a few hundred less and the Poles several hundred more. The Russians could replace their losses, but the Poles could not. After Dibich's death from cholera in June, Gen. Ivan Paskevich took command of the army and continued the march on Warsaw, the defenses of which he did not overcome until 8 September 1831. The capture of Warsaw spelled the end of the uprising.

Because the campaign had become drawn out, the army suffered many more casualties (mostly from disease) than anticipated. Manpower problems were made worse when the Lithuanians rose up in support of Poland in 1831. The tsar detached 26,000 men from the army in Poland to deal with them. Nicholas I suggested a draft of new recruits to form a reserve army to support the war without denuding the border with the Ottoman Empire or leaving St. Petersburg vulnerable after the Guards, Grenadiers, and II Corps had been deployed. A special committee of the Ministry of War to address the manpower issue, convened in May 1831, concluded that the Russian army had exhausted its manpower resources. The committee did not believe the peasants—who did not consider suppressing the Poles to be a foreign war—would tolerate another extraordinary peacetime draft. It recommended waiting for the fall to conduct a regular annual draft. After both the Polish and Lithuanian uprisings had been suppressed at the end of 1831, the army had a strength of 850,000 men. This represented 20 percent of all men liable for active duty and a significant burden to the state.[40]

Personnel Issues and Reforms, 1831–1849

The wars with the Ottoman Empire and Poland revealed a major problem with the army under Nicholas I: troop strength for warfare. Despite having a huge army, not all of it could be deployed to the battlefield. Besides the various defense needs that required the army to be spread out, the ill health of the army deprived it of manpower. Tens of thousands of soldiers died or suffered such severe sickness each year as to make them undeployable. Between 1825 and 1850, the military hospital system treated 16 million cases of illness. While on campaign, besides combat casualties, the army suffered huge losses from the elements, disease, and desertion. During the war with Poland, so many men died of cholera that operations had to be delayed. With woefully inadequate reserves, it was time-consuming to replace losses.

After 1831, at least four corps were kept in Poland to be on guard against Prussia or Austria, and to suppress nationalist unrest. In the 1840s and 1850s, about 500,000 men annually either were occupied as military laborers or were policing the interior and could not be committed to war. The army kept fifty local battalions spread throughout Russia, Ukraine, Belorussia, and the Baltics to handle domestic unrest. Nicholas believed that a revolutionary conspiracy existed that posed a major threat to international security—and more worrisome—Russian domestic security. He was obsessed by the fear of revolution, which was not completely unfounded as his reign had begun with the suppression of the Decembrist revolt of liberal-minded officers.[41] Twenty years into his reign, the arrest of the radical Petrashevskii Circle netted more than a dozen army officers, including Fyodor Dostoevsky. He and his fellow officers were treated to mock executions before being exiled to Siberia at hard labor.

Further hindering the army's ability to deploy men to fight Russia's wars was the fact that hundreds of battalions of soldiers were engaged in construction projects, primarily roads and fortifications. Finally, between 60,000 and

200,000 men were tied up attempting to maintain or expand Russian control over tribes in the Caucasus.[42]

Problems conducting the campaigns against both the Ottomans and the Poles led Nicholas I, always active in the internal workings of the army alongside his minister of war General Chernyshev and Gen. Ivan Paskevich, to consider reforms in the high command. After the Russo-Turkish War, Nicholas I briefly attempted to create a General Staff system in which the Main Staff planned the wars and the operations therein independently of the Ministry of War. The Ministry of War was responsible for supplying the material, animal, human, and nutritional needs of the army but had no say in planning wars. Nicholas dropped that system in 1832 in favor of putting the Ministry of War in charge of all military matters. He abolished the Main Staff and shared out its duties to various departments of the Ministry of War.[43] The reforms unified decision-making under one administration and provided for systematic, though not necessarily efficient, functioning of the entire military administration.

As part of his reforms, Nicholas I established the Academy of the General Staff in 1832 to produce the "brains" of the army, but after only a few years he ordered its curriculum shifted away from intellectual pursuits to an emphasis on tactics. Tactics, in the 1830s, meant tactical formations used in combat that were akin to those of the parade ground, as in the Napoleonic Wars. Nicholas I employed the renowned French general Jomini to advise the General Staff Academy, but the senior Russian officers ignored his advice on military education and training.[44]

The Hungarian War of Independence

Russia's next major military operation was to aid the Austrian Imperial Army in destroying Hungary's bid for independence from the Austrian Empire in 1849. With Europe still smoldering in the aftermath of the revolutions of 1848, Nicholas I was anxious that the liberal, nationalist, and socialist ferment might spread into his empire should the Hungarian effort succeed. Nicholas assigned General Paskevich, viceroy of Poland, to take charge of the operation. Paskevich had 240,000 men divided into three infantry corps (II, III, and IV) from Poland and western Russia to attack the rebel forces in Hungary. To keep his restive Polish subjects from taking advantage of the situation, Nicholas sent two corps along with some cavalry divisions into Poland. The Guards Corps was moved to Lithuania to maintain order after an abortive attempt by some Lithuanians to seize the arsenal in Vilnius.

Nicholas I took an active part in designating the units to be involved in the campaign and occupation duties. Initially, Nicholas I, oblivious to the stress his presence at headquarters would cause, relocated to Warsaw to keep an eye on the campaign and to participate in the planning alongside Emperor Franz Joseph I of Austria and his military commander, Prince Schwarzenberg. Gen. Count Alexander Chernyshev, Nicholas's minister of war, wisely avoided having his opinions second-guessed and authority undermined by staying in St. Petersburg.[45] The coalition against Hungary would have no overall commander and no joining of forces.

Paskevich assigned 140,000 soldiers to invade Hungary proper, 60,000 to occupy Galicia and cow potentially revolutionary Poles, and 40,000 to occupy restive Moldavia and Wallachia, whose own liberal nationalist revolution had been quashed just months earlier. He divided the forces that did the fighting against Hungary into three corps of ten infantry divisions and four cavalry divisions armed with 450 guns. Despite the strength of his forces, Paskevich was unenthusiastic and cautious, guided more by fear of failure than eagerness to win. Paskevich wanted one and a half to two times as many men as his opponent and so sought to engage the enemy only when his forces matched or exceeded that ratio.[46]

In a convention signed between Nicholas I and Emperor Franz Joseph, the latter consented to provision the Russian forces that crossed into Austrian territory. The Austrians agreed to help set up supply depots and military hospitals, and to replenish ammunition. Russian forces deployed to Galicia in June, but Paskevich did not seek battle with Hungarian forces until July, after he had amassed reserves of supplies and established a supply chain into Galicia.[47] The tsar accompanied Paskevich's staff from Warsaw to Galicia. Nicholas stayed in Galicia but sent his son (and future tsar) Grand Duke Alexander Nikolaevich with Paskevich. Alexander reported to his father regularly the state of the army. Within days of crossing into Galicia, the Russian forces began to suffer casualties from cholera. In some units, fifty men fell ill every day. By the time of the first engagement, Paskevich had lost 15,000 men to the illness, more than 7,000 of whom died.[48]

On 17 June 1849, II and IV Corps of Paskevich's army of 140,000 advanced into Hungary. They were divided into four columns advancing abreast under the commands of Generals Rediger, Paskevich, Liders, and Grotengel'. In a major battle on 21 July 1849, 62,000 Russians with 298 cannons took on 8,000 Hungarians with 41 cannons. The Hungarians crumbled as the Russian infantry advanced in close columns and then charged with fixed bayonets, drums beating and banners flying in parade ground fashion.[49] Recognizing that this was but a minor success, Nicholas I grew impatient with Paskevich for not closing with the forces under Hungarian general Artúr Görgey and inflicting a decisive defeat. Paskevich was indecisive, constantly changing his orders and shifting forces around as if to avoid a pitched battle. On 2 August, the

Russian forces, superior in numbers, defeated the Hungarians; yet the Hungarians again managed to withdraw from the field of battle intact. The tsar was displeased but Paskevich pled the need for caution. Recognizing the futility of further resistance against the combined armies of Austria and Russia, Görgey surrendered his forces on 17 August, fulfilling Nicholas I's war aims of suppressing revolt and preventing it from spreading into Russia. From the time that Paskevich crossed into Hungary until Görgey surrendered, the campaign had lasted a mere eight weeks. Of 190,000 Russian officers and men involved, 708 were killed in action, 278 died of their wounds, 2,447 were wounded; and 85,387 became ill, of whom 10,885 died. Of the Russian forces occupying Galicia, 23,000 became unfit for service due to illness. For its aid, Russia billed Austria 3.483 million rubles, which ended up being reduced to 3 million and was paid in installments over three years.[50]

The Crimean War

The complicated international politics behind the Crimean War are beyond the scope of this work; suffice it to say, Nicholas I accepted war as the logical solution to Russia's problems with the Ottoman Empire. Russia's strategic war aims were at a minimum to maintain, and at the maximum to increase, its dominant position against the Ottoman Empire in the Balkans and Black Sea. In contrast, the British and French wished to diminish Russian power in the eastern Mediterranean and so supported the Ottoman Empire to that end. Nicholas I and his generals limited their initial war plans to seizing Moldavia and Wallachia to draw the Ottomans into battle there.

Numerous problems beset the Russians from the outset. First, although the Russian army was as large as ever, in excess of 800,000 men in 1850 and growing, it predictably could not and would not deploy the majority of them into battle with the French, British, and Turkish invaders. Russia chose not move troops out of Poland because it was deemed to be the more critical theater of potential operations in the face of obvious Austrian hostility and Prussia's refusal to declare neutrality, meaning there was a real possibility that they could decide to intervene alongside Britain and France. There was also the fear of renewed Polish revolt. Indeed, many Poles and Lithuanians hoped that Russia would lose the war or that it would expand into to a wider European war that might lead to their emancipation from Russian rule. Caucasian tribesmen also hoped a Russian loss would lead to their freedom. More than 100,000 soldiers were kept back to defend the Baltics against amphibious invasion because the Russian navy was considered useless against the more modern British fleet. As always, the army had to garrison the country against potential disorder on the part of disgruntled serfs and the threat of upheaval encouraged by the growing antiautocratic left as the war dragged on. The garrisons of the military colonies were dedicated to defending the western frontiers and so could not be sent against the Ottoman Empire.[51] The reserves of early-furloughed soldiers were woefully insufficient to expand the army to the needs of the time. Nicholas, therefore, ordered the army to conduct an extraordinary conscription, which turned into five levies by the end of the war. To come up to wartime strength, the army drafted 865,762 men and recalled 215,197 men from indefinite leave. The army also used 647 officers recalled from indefinite leave. Late in the war, Nicholas I decreed the raising of the opolchenie, which brought in 364,421 volunteers. The Ministry of War also mobilized 3,640 Cossack officers and 168,691 Cossack soldiers.[52]

Assembling these men and training them took time. While the numbers look impressive, they mask the fact that the newly drafted men and the volunteers of the opolchenie were completely untrained, unarmed, and unequipped. Training and equipping them cost the army time and money, both of which were in short supply. Once trained, it took months for them to march to the war zones. Testament to the inefficiency of the recruitment and training system and lack of rail transport, few of the 1.3 million who joined the colors during the war made it to the battlefront. Conscription had taken hundreds of thousands of peasant farmers out of an agricultural economy to which they could not return, as they were no longer serfs.

Second, once the Ottoman, British, French, and Sardinian alliance formed but did not commit troops to the Balkans, the Ministry of War found itself in the position of waiting to react to the enemy's moves. This required keeping significant numbers of troops back from any commitment until the enemy's intentions could be discerned. The troops available to fight were divided between three theaters of operations: the Balkans and the Caucasus, where they engaged Ottoman armies; and Crimea, where they faced British, French, and Sardinian forces once the allies landed.

Third, Russia had fallen behind in military technology. At the outbreak of the Crimean War, the infantry had only 6,200 modern muzzle-loading rifles; the rest were smoothbore muskets. The opolchenie units were armed with obsolete smoothbore flintlocks left over from the Napoleonic Wars. The backwardness in small arms was compounded by a lack of musketry training. In peacetime, the officers had just not been interested in conducting and bearing the expense of such training. Their enemies, however, were armed with rifles that could accurately kill at 500 paces and farther, whereas the Russian muskets were only accurate to barely 100 paces. Finally, the production and distribution of artillery ammunition was pitiful compared to that of the British and French. During the war, the allies were able to fire 400,000 more shells at the Russians than the Russians could shoot at them.[53]

A fourth obstacle to success was logistics. The army's intendancy was ill-organized to support campaigns in both the Danubian principalities and Crimea. Collecting the necessary supplies for an army nearly three times as large as it had been before the start of hostilities proved to be nearly impossible. The army augmented the intendancy with civilian contractors paying them market prices, which drove up costs. Even more daunting was the task of delivering those supplies hundreds of miles by oxcart over unimproved roads. Along the way, grain spoiled and hungry soldiers slaughtered the draught animals for food. For the duration of the war, the soldiers at the front would live on the margins of hunger and with inadequate supplies of arms and ammunition.

The fifth disadvantage Russia faced was financial. The Russian government was operating at a deficit even before the war began, and it only worsened. Without a domestic small arms industry, Russia had to import rifles, but foreign credit became hard to get as the war dragged on, so ultimately it proved impossible to arm all the new conscripts.

The Danubian Campaign

Russia made the first move when Nicholas I, in May 1853, ordered the army into the Ottoman Danubian principalities of Moldavia and Wallachia with the goal to occupy the territory and hold it as a bargaining chip. He justified his incursion to the Russian people declaring that it was a holy war to protect the Orthodox and their rights in the Ottoman Empire. An army of 88,000 men under the command of Gen. Prince Mikhail Gorchakov began the occupation of the principalities in June unopposed. Gorchakov's superior and overall coordinator of the campaign was the aging Marshal Paskevich. Paskevich advised a defensive strategy, not wanting to risk a defeat as his career neared its end and because they already held Ottoman territory and the defensive line of the Danube. It was the Ottoman army, which numbered at least 50,000 men more than the Russians, therefore, that took the offensive after the Porte had repeatedly insisted that Russia withdraw. An Ottoman army crossed the Danube to attack the Russian army on 21 October, having declared war seventeen days prior. The first clash of arms at Oltenita was won by the Ottomans and led to the retreat of the forces under Gen. Petr Pavlov, which had suffered nearly one thousand casualties. At the Battle of Çatana in January 1854, the Turks again bested the Russians forcing them to withdraw.[54]

In the spring of 1854, Nicholas I, still not having laid out specific war aims or having enlisted the Ministry of War in planning operations, instructed Paskevich to cross the Danube and invest the Turkish fortress of Silistria. Paskevich suggested just the opposite: that the Russians should evacuate the Danubian principalities lest they be attacked by the Austrian army that had moved into Transylvania. Nicholas insisted, so Paskevich reluctantly proceeded to besiege Silistria in May. After several failed assaults, Paskevich, having suffered a concussion, handed command of the siege to Gorchakov and retired to Iasi to recover. Shortly thereafter, he ordered Gorchakov to abandon the siege and withdraw back across the Danube citing fears of Austria. Soon afterward, the Habsburg government demanded that Russian troops withdraw from the principalities entirely or else Austria would ally with Britain and France to force them out. Nicholas I agreed to stage a strategic withdrawal, and the humiliated Russian army moved back into Bessarabia.[55] Meanwhile, in the Caucasus, an outnumbered army poorly commanded by the elderly Gen. Prince Mikhail Vorontsov managed, over a period of two years, to defeat a wretchedly and corruptly officered Turkish army and eventually captured the city of Kars in November 1855.[56]

The Crimean Campaign

In September 1854, the British, commanded by Lord Raglan; the French, commanded by Gen. Armand-Jacques Leroy Saint-Arnaud; and Ottoman forces under Omar Pasha landed unopposed at Kalamita Bay, near Eupatoria, twenty-eight miles north of Sevastopol. The Russian commander of forces in the Crimea, Gen. Prince Alexander Menshikov, despite being warned that an allied seaborne expedition was being organized, failed to oppose the landing. The French unloaded expeditiously; however, it took five days for the British to complete their landing. All surprise was lost, yet Menshikov chose not to take advantage of the confusion in the landing areas to attack. He instead decided to fight on the defensive. The allies began their advance south to Sevastopol on 19 September with 60,000–65,000 British, French, and Turkish soldiers.

The first major battle of the war was the Battle of the Alma on 20 September 1854. Menshikov chose to defend a three-mile-long front at the top of the heights on the left bank of the Alma River, a natural barrier that dominated the road to Sevastopol, the obvious route on which the British and French would advance. Menshikov's forces numbered 35,000 men and 100 guns. He could have had more but kept several thousand in reserve to counter an anticipated allied landing at Kerch or Feodosia. The battle began when the British chaotically crossed the Alma on the Russian right flank by swimming and wading and charged up the hill to the Russian redoubts. Despite having the advantage of firing down from the high ground, the Russians briefly lost the redoubts. They counterattacked, regained their positions, and pushed the first attack back down the hill. Shortly thereafter, however, British reinforcements arrived and devastated the Russian defenders with long-range accurate rifle fire before mounting another charge up the hill. When he saw that the British had taken the redoubts on the right, Gen. V. I. Kiriakov, who was probably drunk at the time, ordered his men to retreat, but he did not direct them more specifically.

On the right, no one seemed to be in charge. Shortly after the British began to charge the heights, the French began to turn the Russian left flank by scaling cliffs that Menshikov, thinking them too steep to climb, had left defended by only a light force of infantry. The French were supported by naval gunfire from their fleet, which devastated the Russian infantry, who in turn retreated in panic. The battle cost the British approximately 2,000 casualties (362 dead), the French 1,600 (60 dead), and an unknown number of Turks. Menshikov's forces lost 5,000 men (1,800 killed).[57]

With the Russians retreating, the allied forces could have advanced directly on to Sevastopol and perhaps taken it, but Raglan and Saint-Arnaud dithered for two days afterward, clearing the battlefield of their dead and wounded. Menshikov gathered his retreating troops into Sevastopol. Once the British and French did begin to advance, instead of immediately attacking Sevastopol from the north, where its defenses were undermanned and weak, Saint-Arnaud and Raglan headed inland down to the harbor town of Balaklava, where they rendezvoused with the British navy. Meanwhile, the Russians reinforced the garrison with a further twelve battalions. Vice Adm. Vladimir Kornilov was charged with defending the city. He initially despaired at the unreadiness of the defenses and the troops but threw all his energy into creating fortifications that could withstand a siege.[58] The siege of Sevastopol began on 17 October and lasted 349 days. Shortly thereafter, in November, Kornilov was killed and replaced by Adm. Pavel Nakhimov.

The next major battle was the Battle of Balaklava. On 25 October, Menshikov sent a force of 25,000 men and seventy-eight guns under Gen. Pavel Liprandi with the mission to capture Balaklava, to deprive the British of their only port of supply and thereby greatly weaken the siege. Suffering heavy casualties (especially among the Light Brigade), the British prevented the Russians from taking Balaklava. The Russians considered it a victory, however, having cut one of the main roads from Balaklava to the British and French positions, yet this had no long-term effect on the war. In the aftermath, both sides reinforced their armies in Crimea.[59]

Menshikov initiated the next major battle, the Battle of Inkerman, on 5 November 1854. He had 60,000 men and 234 guns to commit to the battle, as well as support from the cannons of two Russian warships anchored in Sevastopol

Harbor. His plan was to attack simultaneously the British forces on Cossack Mountain and the French and British trenches facing Sevastopol. Menshikov's objective was to seize Cossack Mountain; the other two attacks were to tie down enemy forces so they could not reinforce the British holding the mountain. Under cover of fog and mist in an early morning attack, Gens. Fedor Soimonov's and Petr Pavlov's men ascended Cossack Mountain in piecemeal fashion. For eight hours the two sides engaged in fierce, sometimes hand-to-hand, fighting. The diversionary attacks failed, allowing the French to reinforce the outnumbered defenders, who eventually forced the Russians off the hill killing General Soimonov and then his two replacements in sequence, leaving those forces temporarily leaderless. Menshikov admitted defeat and recalled the regiments back into Sevastopol. His organization and management of the battle was a stunning display of incompetence. He failed to commit all his forces and gave few orders, which left his subordinates to act on their own initiative without coordination. Menshikov lost more than one-third of his force (12,000 of 35,000 men), compared to British losses of 2,600 and French losses of 1,800. The Russians did not sortie from Sevastopol again.[60]

During the course of 1855, 19,000 Sardinian soldiers arrived in the Crimea, helping to compensate for the British and French losses to combat and disease (cholera and typhus). Also, early in the year, a force of 35,000 Ottoman troops landed at Eupatoria, getting behind the Russians. An outnumbered Russian force could not dislodge them, to the frustration of Nicholas I. Shortly before he died in March 1855, Nicholas I dismissed Menshikov for his defeatist attitude (not his failed leadership) and replaced him with the equally defeatist and incompetent General Gorchakov, who, after the debacle in Wallachia, had no illusions that victory was to be won. To make up Russia's losses and perhaps to take the offensive again in the future without weakening the defense of its western borders, shortly before he died, Nicholas I ordered the calling up of the opolchenie, as Alexander I had in 1812. Eventually 365,000 volunteers stepped forward. Because of a dearth of officers and the time it took to arm, equip, and train the troops, few ever saw action—a repeat of Nicholas's tardy and therefore useless mobilization of 1828.[61]

Six months after the barely mourned death of Nicholas I, his son and heir, Alexander II, finally authorized the evacuation of Sevastopol. Alexander II accepted Austria's ultimatum that Russia either agree to negotiate with the allies, or it would join the war. It was a painful yet logical decision for Alexander II to make, considering that Russia had suffered 250,000 casualties, it was deep in debt, and no European government or banks would extend further loans. The Treaty of Paris, signed 30 March 1856, formally ended the war. Russia had not achieved any of its war aims (hegemony over Moldavia and Wallachia, and protector status in the Holy Land), and was left militarily, diplomatically, and economically weakened. A critical factor in Russia's loss of the war was that neither Nicholas I nor the Ministry of War offered any strategy for winning and focused their energies on supporting the besieged forces.

Ultimate success in the wars with Napoleon did not necessarily validate Russia's military system. It required taking hundreds of thousands of men out of the economy for decades, and it revealed the utter lack of a logistical infrastructure, which forced Russia to rely on its allies or its army to live off the land. While the Crimean War did not expose any fundamental flaws in how Russia performed on the battlefield other than poor leadership, it did show the weaknesses in Russia's tools for waging war: its serf army, which was unable to expand in a timely fashion; a lack of a body charged with war planning; a transportation infrastructure unable to provide adequate and timely logistical support; and the army's failure to modernize its weaponry. Despite having a Ministry of War and a Main Staff, neither of these institutions took it upon themselves to establish basic guidelines for planning and preparing for war, and neither Alexander nor Nicholas called on them to do so. In the era's conflicts, all had looked to the person of the tsar for direction, which often was not clear or forthcoming until war was imminent. Financial inadequacies and the reliance on serf conscripts seriously constrained Russia's war planning and war-making capacities. Much would change under the new tsar, who intended to make fundamental and sweeping reforms that would dramatically affect Russian society and the military.

CHAPTER 2

THE MILITARY UNDER
ALEXANDER II AND
ALEXANDER III, 1856–1894

After the Crimean War, Russian diplomats and military thinkers alike agreed that their country needed to be more purposeful in its preparation for war so as to win quickly, not only to reduce casualties and cost but also to preempt their enemies' ability to form coalitions against them. Alexander II and his generals concluded that the loss of the Crimean War resulted from Russia fighting without allies against a coalition. This thinking, as well as reactions to other material and human factors that contributed to Russia's defeat, guided the tsar and the Ministry of War in reforming the army. Some deficiencies for Russia to overcome were straightforward: it needed to replace the army's smoothbore muskets with rifles, its smoothbore cannons with rifled cannons; and the navy would need to complete the transition from sail to steam. The tsar and his military leaders understood that Russia would need to build more railroads to deploy and supply the army. During the Crimean War, all supplies and reinforcements for the forces in the Crimea had gone by foot, horseback, or oxcart over poorly maintained roads. Before the war, Russia had fewer than 600 miles of railroad—most of this being the line linking St. Petersburg to Moscow. Russia, at the time, was deep in debt as a result of the war and had no ready monies to immediately address any of these issues. The war showed that the few reserves on hand were inadequate to needs, and new recruits were often of poor quality and slow in coming. Serfdom was at the root of these problems. Alexander II understood that its abolition was necessary both to create a reserve system and to expand the economy as a precondition to revive Russia's military prowess and diplomatic standing in Europe.

In the decade after the war, the Ministry of War, under Gen. Dmitrii Miliutin, and the Main Staff, under Gen. Nikolai Obruchev, began to consider the threat from the west to be greater than ever as both Austria's and Prussia's economies grew and industrialized. Their strong economies enhanced their military development, and the building of many miles of railroad in Russia's direction improved their ability to project power eastward. Tsar Alexander II and his advisers unanimously agreed that Russia, because of its obvious military and financial incapacities, needed to adopt a defensive military posture for the foreseeable future and planned accordingly. They most feared an attack by a coalition of Austria, Sweden, and the Ottoman Empire, with Austria in the forefront. Fear of Britain, especially if it allied with a continental land power, lay in the back of Alexander's mind. Prussia also was seen as a potential member of a hostile coalition. Miliutin used the fear of Russia facing a formidable coalition to argue for universal military obligation based on conscription.[1]

Alexander II, no less involved in military affairs than his father, reestablished the Main Staff in 1865. He mandated that it deal with military operations and all matters immediately affecting them. The staff structure included the quartermaster general of the Main Staff, which dealt with imperial defense, military operations, military history, fortresses, and intelligence gathering. The Main Staff was further subdivided into sections for military communications, military topography, organization and training, personnel, and mobilization. The Military Education Section, also under the quartermaster general (after 1875 under General Obruchev), took over most of Russia's war planning. All told, the Main Staff employed more than 300 officers. The creation of the Main Staff institutionalized thinking on how Russia should prepare for and wage war and initiated a fundamental reorientation of the officer corps at the higher levels in the direction of professionalization.[2]

Thinking about Future War

In the nine years after the Crimean War until the reestablishment of the Main Staff, the Ministry of War mainly focused not on planning for war, but on cutting costs. It was the staff at the Nikolaev General Staff Academy that largely addressed the question of how to fight future wars. In the post-Crimean period, the academy's dominant thinkers were Gen. Genrikh Leer, who headed the study of Russian military history, and Gen. Mikhail Dragomirov, who held the chair of military tactics. The Main Staff and the Ministry of War relied on the General Staff Academy to guide their thinking on future war. Leer, obviously influenced by his reading of Clausewitz, concentrated on questions of strategy and doctrine and sought to identify universally applicable, scientifically based principles of war gleaned from the study of military history. Dragomirov focused more on the practical application of modern tactics based on the discretion of the commander and on identifying a particular Russian way of doing things.

Dragomirov's thinking reflected a widespread feeling that there was a unique Russian way of fighting that could be traced back to Peter I but was more recently illustrated by Alexander Suvorov in the late eighteenth century. That method was characterized by the willingness, or even eagerness, to engage the enemy at close quarters, as articulated by Suvorov in his famous quote, "The bullet is a fool, but the bayonet is a fine fellow." Those, who like Leer, believed in the primacy of firepower over fighting spirit dismissed the idea of Russian exceptionalism.[3] Both Leer and Dragomirov agreed that Russia had lost the Crimean War not only because it had fought alone, but also because the army had fought poorly and used the wrong tactics. A certain tension between the approaches of Leer and Dragomirov was felt throughout the army. Those who looked to Leer wanted guiding principles that would give some uniformity to the army's approach to war (a scientific approach), while those who looked to Dragomirov embraced the principle that the commander on the spot should be free to use his judgment to decide his course of action (a "war as art" approach), fearing that doctrine artificially circumscribed a commander's options.[4] Tension between the two outlooks lasted into the First World War.

In addition to conflicting ideas about general principles, debate flourished in the 1860s and 1870s about the merits of the bayonet assault and the need for attacking in open order rather than in formations of closed columns. There was strong feeling based on the experiences of recent wars in Europe and the United States that modern firepower made attack with massed formations unsustainable. Dragomirov, while not disregarding the lethality of modern firepower, was against deemphasizing the bayonet because he felt training for the bayonet attack was the foundation of soldierly courage. Others were worried that attacking in extended order would cause the leadership to lose control over dispersed formations. Nevertheless, regulations were rewritten to emphasize the need to attack in extended order, but compliance with the new regulations was spotty. There seems to have been no concerted effort to force new tactics on the army.[5]

The Miliutin Reforms, 1861-1874

Alexander II initially responded to Russia's defeat in the Crimean War and the ensuing budget crisis by ordering his new minister of war, Gen. Nikolai Sukhozanet, to reform the army based on the lessons of the Crimean War, specifically to address the issues of the incompetence of the officer corps and logistical failure. Furthermore, Alexander II ordered his minister of war to cut the army's budget. Sukhozanet, lacking imagination and with no specific guidance from the tsar, did nothing.[6] Alexander II, in 1856, took matters into his own hands to reduce the size of the army by ordering the immediate release of the opolchenie and those soldiers and officers who had been called up from indefinite leave. In addition, he ordered the discharge of the Cossacks called up for the war and the discharge of 69,000 of the longest-serving regulars. This amounted to sending about 490,000 men home. Alexander suspended recruitment between 1856 and 1858, and in 1859, he decreed a reduction in the term of active service to twelve years. It took until the end of 1864 to reduce the army's strength to fewer than 1 million men and until 1870 to reduce it to 683,000 soldiers, a level from which it would begin to expand later in the decade in preparation for war with the Ottoman Empire.[7]

In 1861, Alexander II replaced Sukhozanet with General Miliutin, a highly educated (he graduated from Moscow University and later taught at the General Staff Academy, where he wrote a book on Suvorov), competent, and farsighted officer from a well-connected noble family. He assigned him the same mandate he had given Sukhozanet—reform the army into a competent fighting machine and reduce the cost of maintaining it. Miliutin assembled a team of like-minded reformist officers with the overarching goal of recreating the army, almost from the ground up, to make it a modern fighting force not just materially, but also organizationally and socially. He addressed the critical problem of manpower policy, both officer and enlisted, which was the primary area where cost savings could be found, while simultaneously improving the army's capacity to fight. His solution was to create a viable reserve system to obviate the need for a large standing army. This was finally made possible by the emancipation of the serfs, announced in 1861 to take effect in 1863. Working in an entirely new social environment was a fraught enterprise in which the landed nobility, the socially dominant sector of the army and society at the time, stood to lose much, and so it was predictable that there would be resistance to change at the highest levels. The political battle over reforming conscription policy is masterfully detailed by Forrestt Miller and need not be delved into here other than to emphasize that there was tremendous resistance by social conservatives to any reform of the military.[8]

Despite the humiliating loss of the war and the diplomatic catastrophe that the Treaty of Paris represented, the conservative nobility resisted any change to the army's manning practices that would in any way prove detrimental to their social dominance. Opponents succeeded in blocking reform for eighteen years. The battle began before Miliutin became minister of war and lasted until the end of 1874 when the last stages of the reforms were finalized. Prussia's victory over France in 1870, which put a powerful, united Germany on Russia's doorstep and highlighted just how far Russia was behind the armies of its rivals, proved to be the tipping point in favor of reforming recruitment.[9]

In devising a conscription policy, Miliutin had to address not simply how many men would be conscripted and for how long, but also to answer the social question of who would be conscripted. Would it be mainly Slavs as before, or would Jews and Muslims also be conscripted? Would the nobility be exempt, or would all males of the empire be liable regardless of social origin? Because not all men of military age would be needed, should there be exemptions, and how would it be determined who would be exempt? What should be done with men who did not serve but who might be needed in an extended period of war? Would the Cossacks be liable for conscription or keep their special status? How would a reserve be formed? Would the reserves simply consist of rosters of discharged men held by the Ministry of War, or would it have a separate standing administration and organized units of men who had and had not done active service? How long would reserve service last? Miliutin's Ministry of War and the Main Staff tackled these questions together.

A vital social issue was that of how soldiers were to be treated now that they were no longer serfs. What rights would they have? Would corporal punishment as well as the normal brutal treatment at the hands of officers and noncommissioned officers be allowed in this new social environment? How would discipline be maintained if physical punishment were abolished? Miliutin favored changing the culture of the military to create vastly more humane officer-enlisted relations, thinking that would make for a more effective fighting force.

Miliutin was keenly aware of the reforms being undertaken in other European armies. In the 1860s, Prussia and Austria-Hungary adopted the manning policy of universal male obligation to serve. After its loss to Prussia in the Franco-Prussian War, France adopted the same policy in 1872. Britain maintained its army on an all-volunteer basis but endeavored to enhance recruiting by raising the quality of life for the soldiers. With these examples, Miliutin decided to retain a conscript army based on universal male service obligation. By universal he meant to include the privileged classes in the conscription pool. By obligation he meant not that all eligible males would serve, but that all were obliged to serve if called upon. In the end, Alexander II supported Miliutin largely because the German success in the Franco-Prussian War proved the value of the system of universal obligation. Alexander II finally signed universal male service obligation, announced to the public in 1874, into law on 1 January 1875.

In basic terms, the law established that all males in the empire between the ages of twenty-one to forty were liable for service, except for Finns and Central Asians. Service would last for six years of active duty followed by nine years in the first line reserve and then, until age forty, in the second line reserve, which he gave the name opolchenie. As a sop to the outraged nobility, Miliutin included exceptions to the length of service based on education. The higher the education level of a recruit, the shorter the time a man had to serve on active duty. Men with a university education were required to serve only six months on active duty followed by fourteen and a half years in the reserve.[10]

A critical aspect of conscription for the history of Russia was the issue of who or what the soldiers were to serve—the tsar or the nation. Alexander II and then Nicholas II assumed the former, but over time both officers and men began to consider it to be the latter. The idea that the universal obligation to serve now that they were free men gave them rights as citizens colored the men's attitude toward service, the tsar, and the state. In 1905 and 1917, that idea would contribute to soldiers' willingness to mutiny.

Between 1874 and 1883, in fulfilling its manpower needs, the army annually enlisted only 27 percent of the 2 million men liable for service, 85 percent of whom were from the peasantry. In those years, 52 percent of men eligible for the draft claimed exemptions for family reasons. About 15 percent were rejected on grounds of mental or physical health or disabilities. The army then held a lottery of those still eligible to serve, taking only the number it needed. The rest were deemed surplus to requirements and were excluded from the next year's draft.[11]

Despite the shortened term of service and the right to return to their place in the village, the prospect of military service still elicited feelings of dread in the peasantry. Peasants and workers adopted a host of subterfuges and practices to avoid service. These practices included having sons move away and change their names for a year or two when they were most likely to be called up, illegally hiring alternates to misrepresent themselves as those conscripted, and ingesting substances that would create symptoms of serious illnesses. A surprisingly large number of young men resorted to the extreme measure of self-mutilation to avoid service. Most often this entailed cutting off fingers or pulling an excessive number of teeth. The bribing of doctors on the conscription commission to grant an exemption occurred with regularity.[12]

Creating a Trained Reserve

Another achievement of Miliutin's was his successful creation of a trained reserve. Doing so finally enabled Russia to have a smaller peacetime army with the capacity to rapidly expand the forces to fight a major war on relatively short notice. Miliutin's new reserve consisted of two parts: the reserve of manpower created by discharging soldiers after six years and obligating them to recall for another nine, and the reserve known as the opolchenie. The former citizens' militia volunteer opolchenie was done away with by the reforms. The new opolchenie became a force administered by the Ministry of War, manned by those men who were eligible for service but had avoided active duty through the lottery. These men were now assigned to the opolchenie, but they were given no training and were considered the last manpower pool for mobilization.[13]

The reserves were organized to serve two functions. The first was to serve as a source of manpower to bring active units up to full strength before war broke out. As part of the reforms, Miliutin established three types of infantry divisions: those manned in peacetime at 75 percent; those manned at 55 percent; and those manned at 35 percent of wartime strength. How a division and its regiments were manned correlated to its proximity to the borders of the empire. The closer to the border, the higher the percentage of troops on active duty. In the event of war, the first reservists mobilized would be sent to the divisions to bring them to full strength. The second function was to create new units manned by reservists. To facilitate forming these new units, Miliutin created twenty-four reserve battalions that, in peacetime, conducted the few training sessions required of reservists and maintained the rosters of those who were to report in case of mobilization. In wartime, the battalions received mobilized reservists and organized them into infantry regiments.[14] This plan assumed that there would be sufficient warning to give the Ministry of War time to call up the appropriate number of troops and send them to the regiments in the numbers necessary with hopes that there would be time for refresher training and to build unit cohesion.

This reserve system preceded the 1874 law on universal military service. From the start, a problem with the reserves was the lack of equipment and uniforms kept on hand to fit out the men called up. In 1866, the Warsaw Military District estimated it would take four months to arm and equip the number of men it projected to receive in time of war.[15] This included everything from boots and uniforms to rifles and bayonets. For reasons of economy, weapons and gear for the reservists were not stockpiled in peacetime. This policy would have disastrous consequences in the First World War—the army never succeeded in arming all the soldiers. Furthermore, when a soldier passed into the reserves, he had to attend only two six-week training camps for the entire time he was in the reserves, meaning there would certainly be a drop-off in military proficiency.

The army held its first ten-day practice mobilization in the Kyiv (Kiev) Military District in September 1871. Of the men called up, 84 percent arrived within four days. Nearly all the rest eventually reported for duty by the end of the ten days.[16] Afterward, Alexander II ordered all military districts to have practice call-ups. These did take place, but not regularly, sometimes being decades apart, because of the costs and the disruption to the normal routine of the military districts. The Main Staff set itself the goal to reduce the time to mobilize the army from eight months to twenty-eight days. The results of the practice call-up were encouraging compared to 1859 when, reacting to a perceived threat from Austria, Russia had mobilized the army, calling back recently furloughed soldiers. It took five months for the designated units to be brought up to wartime strength. Then, the army had set itself the goal to complete the task in three months. Keeping up with the expanding reserves, the developing rail network, and the mobilization schedule became a major preoccupation of the Main Staff as mobilization planning became an essential aspect of war planning. The army wanted six to seven weeks to outfit mobilized reservists and give them refresher training before they would be ready to engage the enemy.[17]

Recruiting Officers

Because there was no reserve of officers and there had been no ready way to rapidly procure and train new officers, the army had fought the Crimean War with a deficit of leaders. Miliutin, then, had to address the issue of improving and expanding recruiting leaders for the army for the long haul. Besides active service, there was the issue of creating a reserve of officers. The obvious solution was to open the officer corps in a meaningful way to nonnobles. This proved socially contentious, however, as it would infringe on a fundamental aspect of noble identity. Regarding battlefield performance, it was widely agreed that, from top to bottom, officers had performed incompetently. Recognizing that the officer corps had performed so poorly during the war, Miliutin decided to pair reform of the education and training of the officer corps with that of recruitment.

Though Miliutin successfully created a reserve system of rank-and-file soldiers, he was unsuccessful in creating a reserve of trained officers. One thing Miliutin did to produce reserve officers was to copy the German army's program whereby educated individuals could join the army for one year with the express intent to be commissioned rather than take their chances of being drafted and serving as a private. These men, known as *vol'noopredeliaiushchiksia* (*vol'nopers* for short) could choose to be commissioned regular officers at the end of their one year and stay on active duty or to be commissioned as reserve officers and go home with the proviso that they return to the colors in time of war. Invariably volunteers came from either the nobility or the wealthy middle class—of whom there were relatively few in the first decades after emancipation. As it turned out, however, most educated men decided to take their chances with the lottery and the potential of serving as a private for six months to a year.[18] The odds were in their favor; in the first ten years of the draft, only 1.7 percent (35,000 men) called in the lottery were educated to the degree that they merited reduced time in the active army. Because Miliutin and his successors never devoted any energy to specifically building up a corps of reserve officers by direct recruitment, a meaningful number of reserve officers was never achieved.

Prior to the reforms, the rules were quite lax or lacking when it came to controlling an officer's time in service, and men could generally come and go as they pleased. They did so in large numbers, treating military service as a hobby or diversion rather than a vocation, much less a profession. Regulations stipulated that an officer could go on indefinite leave after ten years of service, but in fact officers routinely were allowed to "retire" from active service much earlier. In 1862, Miliutin promulgated a regulation to control the heretofore unpredictable coming and going of officers on and off active duty. It mandated an officer had to serve at least three years to become eligible to transfer to the reserve.[19] Then, in January 1865, Miliutin abolished the privilege of indefinite leave. Now an officer had to choose to stay on duty until retirement or to go into the reserve. The difference was that while on leave the officer remained a member of his regiment and his position had to be kept vacant pending his return, but officers in the reserve no longer belonged to their regiment. If they decided to come back to active duty, they would have to apply to join a regiment. These changes added a level of seriousness heretofore lacking in one's choosing a military career.

Officer Education and Training

Miliutin gave form and structure to officer education and training so sorely lacking from the earliest days of the Russian army. He drastically reformed officer recruitment by mandating that the military education system become the single gateway to the officer corps and that anyone who could qualify, regardless of social status, could enroll. Before Miliutin's reforms, there was no formal system or process for recruiting, educating, or training officers. With the abolition of mandatory state service by Catherine II in her 1785 Charter to the Nobility, the army took no steps to attract officers but passively stood by counting on nobles to serve in the military through family tradition, personal ambition, or financial need. Under Miliutin, the army continued to take a passive stance, but with the reforms, no longer would fathers be allowed to enroll their sons in a regiment to serve an apprenticeship in the ranks as a path to a commission.

In place of the apprenticeship system, Miliutin planned an ambitious and comprehensive reform of the military education system. To increase the size of the officer corps, he sought to open the military cadet corps to all classes. To get better officer candidates, he wanted to require a basic level of education before men could enter the commissioning process. Before the Crimean War, usually less than 15 percent of officer candidates had formal educations. Many had been tutored at home, and the rest were uneducated. Miliutin planned to change the curriculum of the cadet corps to deemphasize military drill and basic training, and instead focus on academic subjects, bringing them up to what might now be considered high school level. He envisioned that newly commissioned officers would receive advanced military training in two-year military schools after graduating from the cadet corps. The two-year schools already existed, but they were few in number and open only to the top graduates of the cadet corps. These proposals ran into resistance from the conservative noble elites who neither wanted commoners going to cadet corps nor wanted to be burdened with the expense of educating their sons themselves. After much debate, the tsar sided with the conservative elites on the issue of keeping the cadet corps socially exclusive, but he did agree to raise entrance standards and allow the change in curriculum.

Though he blocked them from cadet corps, Alexander II did accept the need to allow nonnobles to serve as officers in large numbers, and he recognized the need for them to be educated. Thus, Miliutin created a system of junker schools to educate and commission nonnobles as well as nobles who did not qualify for or could not afford to attend cadet corps. Like the cadet corps, junker schools had minimum prerequisites of at least six years of education and the passing of an entrance examination. The course of study in the junker schools lasted for two years. Instruction in the first year consisted of general educational subjects; the curriculum of the second year was more specifically military in nature. Eventually, the top graduates of the junker schools were allowed to attend military schools alongside graduates of cadet corps.

Because they were open to all males regardless of social classes, the junker schools eventually provided most of the officers for the Imperial Army and were the vehicle for diversifying the social makeup of the officer corps. By changing its social composition, Miliutin laid the foundation for a new military culture to grow in the officer corps, one in which promotion was based on merit and a military career was a vocation rather than an avocation. Men could apply to junker schools directly from civilian society, and the regiments were encouraged to nominate qualified conscripts to attend junker schools in their military districts. It was the first step in the bureaucratization of careers, taking the promotion and assignment processes out of the hands of regiment commanders and putting them under the authority of the Ministry of War where they were better regulated and made more predictable. By the turn of the century, the junker schools were producing most of the officers for the army, so by the outbreak of the First World War the majority of officers were commoners.

For most officers their formal military education ended at commissioning. Institutionalized military instruction was reserved for the select few who went on to military schools after graduating from cadet corps or junker schools. Those who did not attend military schools learned tactics in their battalions at the hands of their superiors. The problem with this was that battalion and regiment commanders routinely ignored instructions from the Main Staff on updating tactics to fit war experiences and changing weaponry. There were no higher schools or courses for officers as they rose through the ranks and assumed greater responsibilities where the army could force them to learn and adopt new methods. For example, after the Crimean War, the Main Staff issued numerous instructions on adopting new company- and battalion-level infantry tactics, but these were ignored by the vast majority of regiment commanders. Military district commanders usually failed to overcome the inertia and conservatism of the generals under their command; thus, the army would go into the Russo-Turkish War unprepared to use the lessons learned from the Crimean War.[20]

Other Changes under Miliutin

Miliutin created a military district system that significantly changed how the army was administered, and which vastly improved the army's ability to prepare for war. Miliutin divided the empire into military districts, of which there would eventually be fifteen. These districts had the tasks of recruiting, training, assigning personnel, and supplying the regiments. They also had a vital role in mobilization. After 1890, the Ministry of War decided that in wartime the district chiefs and their staffs would take on important command and staff functions. The commanders of the Kyiv, Warsaw, and Vilnius Military Districts, which shared borders with Germany and Austria-Hungary, would become the commanders of *fronts* (army groups) created from the units in their districts.[21] As with the positions of minister of war and chief of the Main Staff, assuming command of a military district was deemed so important as to require the approval of the tsar.

The professionalization of military service for officers and men was greatly enhanced with the onset of a barracks building program in the late 1870s. Over the next two decades, the majority of soldiers were no longer quartered on the peasants but were housed in regimental garrisons with barracks, mess halls, bathhouses, infirmaries, and chapels. The quality of life and the health of soldiers consequently improved. Officers benefited from the establishment of officers' clubs. These not only became centers of social activity that knit the regiments' leaders together but also served as forums for discussion of the latest ideas on doctrine, strategy, and tactics—thanks to their libraries that subscribed to the growing number of military periodicals.[22]

Miliutin's reforms barely changed daily life at the regimental level. Because of continued underfunding, officers still spent most of their time running the regimental economy rather than training for war. Soldiers continued to spend most of their time tailoring uniforms, making boots, gardening, and working in the civilian economy to earn money for the regiment. Through a concerted effort from the top down, brutal behavior by officers and NCOs against soldiers waned. Reform of the military legal code measurably reduced the arbitrary powers of regimental commanders. Soldiers now had the right to mount a legal defense against charges and to appeal verdicts. The use of the birch rod to flog men was curtailed; confinement to the guardhouse more often substituted for corporal punishment.[23]

Despite the tsar's emphasis on reforming and rejuvenating the army after the Crimean debacle, the position of the Ministry of War relative to the other ministries deteriorated. As Alexander II expanded his government's involvement in virtually every aspect of public life, the military, though it still held favored status with the tsar, lost primacy of funding. Whereas before the Crimean War defense could claim 40 percent of the national budget, between 1866 and 1885 it held steady at around 32 percent because other ministries' tasks were often seen as more important, especially if they stood to strengthen the economy. Finances became somewhat more challenging under Alexander III, who was less enamored of the military than his father and grandfather; he enabled the other ministries, especially the Ministry of Finance and the Ministry of the Interior, to gain the budgetary advantage over the Ministry of War. By 1902, the army's share of the budget had fallen to 18 percent. The actual amount of military spending grew by 27 percent, however, because urbanization and the greatly expanded industrial sector of the economy generated vastly increased tax revenue.[24]

The Polish Revolt of 1863

Just as Miliutin began his reforms, the army was called on to crush another Polish nationalist insurrection. Ever since the revolt in 1830, the Russian army had occupied Poland in force; in 1863 there were ten infantry and cavalry divisions with 150,000 soldiers dispersed among 180 garrisons in towns and cities, large and small, and especially in Warsaw, with the intent of deterring revolution and having forces on hand to deal with a revolt. Nationalist ferment had been percolating for several years and broke out in January 1863 in anticipation of an extraordinary draft of anti-Russian Polish youth.

Hostilities began the night of 22 January with surprise attacks against nineteen Russian garrisons in various parts of Poland. Most of these attacks failed to overcome the Russian units. In response, Gen. Anders Ramsay, commander of Russian forces in Poland, ordered the smaller garrisons to consolidate into forty larger garrisons, abandoning much of the countryside to the Polish insurgents. Though they had space to organize, the rebels, with no central command center or revolutionary government, could muster only small numbers. Only a few of the many rebel groups reached the size of 5,000 fighters. Most Polish units consisted of poorly armed civilians numbering between three hundred and five hundred men.[25]

The instigators of the insurrection had originally hoped to emulate the revolt of 1830 and fight a conventional war with the population rallied to the cause of nationalism. However, the war quickly devolved into a series of small-scale battles and guerrilla actions due to lack of popular support and Russian control of the large towns and cities. Polish tactics then evolved to massing units to attack garrisoned towns. The Russian response was to draw the insurgents into open battle with superior numbers.

Using one of the few railroads in the empire, the St. Petersburg–Warsaw line, Miliutin began to transfer reinforcements to Poland. Already by March 1863, Russian strength stood at 200,000 men, in April it increased to 270,000, and in July it reached 340,000. Russian tactics evolved to holding the towns and patrolling the countryside with large columns in hopes of drawing the Poles into battle. When a patrol was attacked, reinforcements converged to aid the stricken column and overwhelm the Poles. In the few conventional battles that occurred, the Russians maneuvered to keep Polish units from uniting and defeated them separately.[26]

Prussia sealed its border with Russian Poland to prevent its citizens from joining the revolt and to keep rebels from escaping the Russians. Austria, until November, turned a blind eye to Poles in Galicia organizing military units and launching forays into Russian Poland. Once they became aware of this, Russian commanders directed units to the border to prevent the use of Galicia as a haven. After that, and with international help not forthcoming, it was only a matter of time that the revolt was crushed. Alexander II ordered that rebel leaders be dealt with mercilessly; nearly all captured officers were executed for treason.

The conflict was officially declared over in April 1864. It had cost Russia 826 officers and men killed, and 2,571 wounded and missing.[27] Financially, crushing the revolt cost Russia 800 million rubles, which the Ministry of Finance used to justify cutting back on military-requested railroad construction. The revolt also delayed Miliutin's drawdown of the army for two years.

Fallout from the war included the execution of dozens of Polish officers who had defected from the Russian army to serve in the revolt. Henceforth, Poles were barred from attending the General Staff Academy and could not expect to be promoted above the rank of colonel. They were also discriminated against in admission to cadet corps. The army secretly set a quota on the number of Poles assigned to a unit to keep them to a minority. A handful of liberal-minded Russians had also joined the revolt, resulting in thirty executions and in 107 being exiled to Siberia. In protest of the harsh handling of the Poles and the seeming betrayal by Alexander of his liberalizing reforms, a few score Russian officers resigned from the army, which caused some unease in the Ministry of War and the Winter Palace.[28]

The tsar had good reason to question the loyalty of the officer corps. Although they constituted only an insignificant minority, a steady trickle of officers joined the revolutionary movement in the 1860s and 1870s. Some officers supplied munitions to the revolutionary group People's Will that were used to blow up a wing of the Winter Palace in an attempt to assassinate the tsar. The trend continued under Alexander III. Tight, yet ineffective, controls were placed over cadets in the cadet corps to keep radical literature away from them. The gendarmerie continued to keep an ever-watchful eye on the officer corps.

Planning for War

In response to the unification of Germany under Prussia, and in hopes of gaining support for universal military obligation, in 1873, Miliutin convened a secret strategic conference that the tsar attended. The result was the war plan of 1873, which was defensive in the west but allowed for an offensive start to a war with the Ottomans in the Caucasus or the Balkans. This war plan was the first to introduce the use of the railroads into the mobilization plans and stood as the basis of all war plans up to 1909. The defense in the west was based on mass of men, the use of railways, and fortresses. The participants debated whether to stand and fight or conduct a fighting withdrawal to trade space for time to complete mobilization. Obruchev argued against giving up Poland and advocated standing fast against any invasion. Grand Duke Nikolai Nikolaevich the Elder (Alexander II's brother) objected to the defensive nature of the plan, but was largely ignored. In line with Alexander's desire for both a smaller standing army and cost cutting, Obruchev argued for a smaller force that could be expanded by reserves and delivered to the front by rail. Both Miliutin and Obruchev lobbied for more strategic railways to enable rapid movement to the German and Austrian frontiers. Russia had 9,200 miles of railroads in 1873, which Obruchev sought to increase by 4,500 miles of track in the west by 1878.

In the event of war with Austria-Hungary and/or Germany, it was assumed that the Poles would revolt. If war broke out with the Ottomans, the Ministry of War expected the recently subdued tribes in the Caucasus to rebel. Either eventuality would require more troops to secure the rear. At the time of the conference, the Russian army did not have enough troops to wage an offensive war and defend the rear against rebellious Poles or Caucasian tribes. Therefore, a defensive option was seen as the most desirable.[29]

The results of the conference were that Alexander II accepted the defensive outlook of his top generals and agreed to commit additional funding to construct strategic railroads. By 1900, the amount of track in the Russian Empire had grown to more than 35,000 miles, but the amount devoted to strategic military purposes was less than the military wanted. Millions of rubles went into upgrading fortresses in Poland instead of laying track. Not directly related to the conference, but during the same time period, as part of Russia's looking to bolster its war-making power, the army convinced the government to invest in creating a domestic small arms industry.[30] Not until seven years after the conference did the Main Staff draw up a mobilization schedule to support the war plan.

The Russo-Turkish War, 1877–1878

The Russo-Turkish War of 1877–78 was the first major test of the reformed Russian army to project power. Historians generally agree that even though the Russian army forced its way to within fifteen miles of Constantinople and imposed a peace treaty on the Turks, it had not performed with distinction, and in some respects rather dismally. It paid a higher price than necessary in lives and treasure due to glaring deficiencies in both mid- and senior-level leadership.[31] Military and diplomatic planning for war began in 1876 with the strategic goal of establishing Russian hegemony over Bulgaria at the expense of the Ottoman Empire. In the spring, the Main Staff initiated talks with the government of Romania about the transit of the Russian army through the country and requested its cooperation. These talks were formalized in the Russo-Romanian Convention signed in April 1877. While the army talked with Romania, the Foreign Ministry succeeded in negotiating Austro-Hungarian neutrality through the Budapest Convention of January 1877.

A field staff (a subdivision of the Main Staff) to plan and prosecute the war was formed in November 1876 under the command of Grand Duke Nikolai Nikolaevich, whom Alexander II placed in command as a matter of royal prerogative, not because Nikolai merited it. Nikolai's personality worked against effective leadership in that he lacked a strong will but was stubborn; his mood swung from extremes of enthusiasm to discouragement in the blink of an eye. His work habits were haphazard and highly unsystematic. He lacked military credentials in the eyes of the generals, tolerated no criticism of his actions and tended to blame others rather than accept responsibility for mistakes. In practice, General Obruchev directed the planning of the campaign including the use of rail transport for troops and supplies. Scores of officers from the Main Staff did the reconnaissance work to prepare the attack across the Danube and simultaneously organized an intelligence-gathering network in Bulgaria. The

Main Staff created the mobilization schedule of men and horses. Neither staff, however, prepared maps of Bulgaria in a timely manner, which in the months to come hindered operations.[32]

Miliutin's new reserve system was put to the test when partial mobilization began on 1 November 1876. Of the army's forty-eight infantry divisions and eight separate infantry brigades and nineteen cavalry divisions, twenty infantry divisions, eight cavalry divisions, three separate rifle brigades, and two sapper brigades were allocated to fight the war. These units were divided between two armies: the Army of the Danube and the Army of the Caucasus. They were brought to full wartime strength with the call-up of reservists in November 1876, of whom 178,000 were transported to their units by rail. At first, the Main Staff anticipated calling up 225,000 men but eventually mobilized 372,000 with a second round of reservists called up in April 1877. They augmented the 722,000 men already on active duty; however, only one-third went to the Balkans. The Army of the Caucasus received 40,000 men, raising its strength to 100,000. A further 60,000 reservists went to units defending the Black Sea coast. The remaining 160,000 reservists either went to units on the western border or did not finish refresher training before the war ended. To bring the number of officers up to wartime strength, the Ministry of War canceled pending retirements, called up retired officers, commissioned qualified volunteers, and promoted promising noncommissioned officers without examinations. The senior classes of cadet corps and junker schools were allowed to graduate and receive commissions early.[33]

As part of preparing for war, the government also attempted to mobilize public opinion. The state promoted the campaign in the Balkans as a war to free fellow Orthodox Slavs from the yoke of Turkish Muslim oppression. The propaganda failed to generate mass volunteerism. Peasants, workers, and the privileged sectors of society were, however, inspired to donate tens of thousands of rubles to support medical treatment of the wounded. Three thousand women volunteered for Red Cross nursing courses and then served in army hospitals in the theater of operations. Fighting for the cause of freedom motivated hundreds of antiautocratic radicals to serve in the ranks and as medical personnel.[34] Thus, not all volunteerism in this war can be said to have been a patriotic show of support for the state. As for the soldiers and reservists, they responded out of obligation rather than any crusading motivation. Self-inflicted wounds began to mount as soon as the fighting began.[35]

General Obruchev's strategic plan, approved by Miliutin, was guided by the goal of obtaining a quick victory before Turkey could ally with any of Russia's other rivals. Obruchev planned to cross the Danube and build up a bridgehead, then bypass the Ottoman fortresses in the west while marching on Constantinople through the middle of Bulgaria. He planned to cross the Balkan Mountains at the Shipka Pass rather than along the coast roads, which were also guarded by fortresses. The western flank would be protected by forces taking Nikopol to block the transfer of Ottoman troops from Serbia. The east flank would be guarded by two corps at Ruse (Turk. *Ruschuk*) under the command of the tsar's son, the future Alexander III. Obruchev intended to maneuver away from the fortresses and other fortified areas to move quickly on the capital.[36] Once over the Balkans, he would risk leaving his flanks open and not secure his lines of communication, and rely instead on speed to keep the enemy off balance.

The plan did have its flaws. First, Obruchev naively assumed everything would work out just as planned, disregarding potential problems from the weather, enemy action, or the complete lack of an army logistical system. He had not prepared contingency plans if the main attack failed. Second, he expected the soldiers to hold up through five weeks of continuous campaigning without a break—a highly dubious proposition. He did not plan for reinforcements and replacements. Third, expecting victory to be secured in short order, he made no preparations to fight in inclement autumn or winter weather.

In April 1877, the Army of the Danube superbly executed the crossing of the Danube at Sistova—a significant challenge in the face of an armed enemy. The assaulting forces suffered losses of three hundred killed and just over five hundred wounded and missing. The crossing took the Turks by surprise, enabling the Russians to establish a bridgehead that served as the springboard for future operations.

Grand Duke Nikolai Nikolaevich took command of the campaign after the forced crossing of the Danube. The Grand Duke's lack of high level military experience immediately became apparent. Alexander Polovtsev, a member of the Russian Senate who was well-connected in the government, and no friend of Nikolai Nikolaevich, wrote in his diary at the time: "How difficult it is to have confidence in anyone so stupid."[37] Polovtsev had an equally low opinion of Gen. Artúr Nepokoichitskii, Nikolai Nikolaevich's handpicked chief of staff, who, for the previous twenty years, had held only administrative posts. He chose as his deputy General Levitskii, who also had no experience commanding large units in the field or making use of staff officers. A good number of generals had little to no confidence in the abilities of the trio in command and were disappointed that Obruchev had been denied the post of chief of staff.

Once across the river, things began to go awry. Grand Duke Nikolai Nikolaevich chose not to follow Obruchev's plan, instead modifying it to reduce the risks that Obruchev had accepted. He divided the army into three weakened groups instead of the planned two strong groups. Rather than making the main drive over the Balkans the focus of operations, he obsessed about the security of his flanks. He gave Gen. Josef Gurko 12,000 men to seize the Shipka Pass (the main pass over the Balkans) and told him not to proceed to Constantinople, but to act according to the situation. Gurko forced the pass and briefly marauded in the plains below; but without enough men to oppose converging Ottoman forces, he was forced to retreat to the top of the pass and wait for the advancing Russian army. That he was able to seize the vital mountain crossing and descend the far side with only light casualties is evidence that Obruchev's instincts for a rapid advance had been on the mark.

The weak main body, however, became embroiled in the Battle of Plevna and could not take advantage of Gurko's success. Not until winter would the army be ready to cross the Balkans. In the first attempt to storm Plevna in mid-July 1877, an outnumbered Russian division under the command of Gen. Iuri Schilder-Schuldner launched a poorly planned and ill-prepared attack. The effort failed and incurred losses of one-third of its officers and half its soldiers. Gen. Nikolai Kridener was then given a corps to take Plevna, but he worried more about avoiding defeat than securing victory and detached a considerable number of men to secure his line of retreat, leaving fewer men to find and exploit Turkish weaknesses. Kridener's assault on Plevna at the end of August failed owing to poor reconnaissance, inadequate communication, and lack of coordination as well as to a competent and determined Turkish defense. Although Russian artillery and small arms had improved over those of the Crimean War, the Turks' were even better. The Ottoman army was armed with the most recent models of Krupp steel cannons from Germany and American-made Peabody-Martini rifles. Russian tactics of attacking in close order against murderous rifle fire, in line with Dragomirov's thinking, also contributed to their high losses. The Russians suffered 7,000 casualties in the second failed storming, including one-quarter of the officers and an equal share of the enlisted men.[38] With the second defeat at Plevna, the Russians went on the defensive while Miliutin ordered 110,000 more troops to the Balkans.

At the beginning of September, a third assault on Plevna failed—this time costing 12,700 Russian and 3,000 Romanian soldiers killed, wounded, and missing—all before the eyes of the tsar, who had arrived with his retinue of some forty or so aides-de-camp to observe the siege. Alexander II knew by name many of the Guards officers killed in the failed assault and reportedly had tears in his eyes as the casualty list was read to him.[39] The tsar asked his brother and General Miliutin what they proposed as the next course of action. The Grand Duke suggested that they should retreat to the Danube, hold a bridgehead, and wait for reinforcements from Russia before resuming the offensive, just as in 1828. Miliutin disagreed, arguing that the army should remain in place while awaiting reinforcements. He did not believe that Osman Nuri Pasha, the commander of the Turkish forces in Plevna, had the strength to break through the Russian positions. Miliutin further argued that a withdrawal would damage the morale of the army. He did agree with Nikolai Nikolaevich that they should not resume the offensive until reinforcements arrived. The tsar, following his father's example from the Russo-Turkish War of 1828–29, had not taken command of the army yet used his royal prerogative to preside over all councils of war and to assert his influence over major decisions. He instructed his brother to follow the course of action proposed by Miliutin.[40]

By August, the Russian army had managed to trap itself within a semicircular pocket with a series of four Ottoman fortresses on the east, Plevna on the west, and the Balkans on the south. The Russians were in danger of being surrounded and overrun. Rather than reinforce their position at Plevna, the Turks put their main effort at the Shipka Pass. There 4,400 Russians heroically held their positions against attacks by 27,000 Ottoman soldiers in a three-day battle in August. Most Russian units suffered losses of between 30 and 40 percent. By the end of the battle, nearly all the junior officers had become casualties, their places taken by corporals and sergeants.[41]

Overriding his brother's objections, Alexander II brought in Gen. Eduard Todleben to take over the battle for Plevna. Todleben, with no concern for ending the war quickly, chose to put Plevna under siege and wait out the Turks. It took three months, but the siege succeeded in forcing Osman Nuri to attempt a desperate breakout at the end of November. This time the Turks suffered more casualties than the Russians and were destroyed.

The question of what to do next caused division in the ranks of the Russian high command. The ever-cautious Todleben wanted to reduce the risk to the Russian rear and flanks by taking the Turkish fortresses at Ruse and Silistria and put off going over the Balkans. Other generals promoted passivity and wanted to just sit tight and hope the Turks would conclude that they had been beaten. Grand Duke Nikolai Nikolaevich promoted an aggressive policy and argued for pushing across the Balkans immediately to force an end to the war. Nikolai got his way.

While the siege of Plevna was underway, the Russian army continued to hold the Shipka Pass. During those four months, the Russians lost more men to the elements than to combat action. The 24th Infantry Division, with 9,577 men, relieved the original defenders at the beginning of November; by the end of December, it had suffered 6,697 casualties, but only 134 at the hands of the Turks. The rest were victims of the bitter cold, or more accurately, the failure of the Main Staff to plan to fight in the mountains in the winter, even after it was decided to put Plevna under siege. The Ministry of War did not order winter clothing to be sent to the Balkans until the first snow had fallen in September, and it took until December for it to be delivered. Until then, the soldiers lived above the tree line in their summer uniforms. They accommodated themselves in shallow trenches and in mostly unheated shelters that barely protected them from the elements. The officers had not directed their men to construct shelters when the weather was favorable, and once it began to rain and snow the task became immeasurably more difficult in the frozen, rocky soil. Consequently, men suffered frostbite, trench foot, dysentery, and other ailments associated with exposure to the elements and unsanitary conditions. Because the approaches to the trenches from the rear were under enemy fire, food had to be hauled up by hand and was cold by the time it reached the men. The division commander, Gen. Konstantin Gershelman, made things worse when he refused to allow his men to wear the warm clothing because, in his eyes, it presented an unmilitary image. This foolish decision led to soldiers freezing to death on sentry duty. Not until casualties reached into the thousands did he relent, but by then the elements had destroyed his division.[42]

To cross the Balkans and march on to Constantinople, the Russians had to force three passes: the Araba Konak Pass, which was assigned to General Gurko; the Troyan Pass, assigned to Gen. Alexander Kartsov; and the Shipka Pass, given to Gen. Fedor Radetskii. In December 1877, the Russians had 528,000 men facing 183,000 Turks. Gurko went first, successfully forcing the pass and subsequently liberating Sofia. In doing so, his forces got behind the Troyan Pass, causing the Turks to abandon it thus enabling Kartsov's forces to push through. The attack through the passes was well executed, but it incurred high casualties, especially in the forces under Radetskii. His troops had to overcome most defenses without artillery because the narrowness of the road and the ice and snow, made it difficult to haul cannons up the mountain. Once in the plains, the Russians pushed the Turkish army back to Adrianople. Although many in the Russian camp aspired to conquer Constantinople, the tsar ordered that they not take it because of strong British objections. There they waited while peace negotiations ensued.[43]

Alexander II appointed another equally unqualified brother, Grand Duke Mikhail Nikolaevich, to oversee the campaign in the Caucasus, which proceeded simultaneously with the Balkan campaign. This campaign was designed to tie down Ottoman forces so they could not be sent to help in the Balkans. Although he had displayed competence as a young artillery officer, as commander of an army he showed himself to be notoriously indecisive. He chose as his chief of staff Gen. Dmitrii Sviatopolk-Mirskii, who had never commanded a unit larger than a regiment and for the past decade had been a provincial governor. So, though Grand Duke Mikhail Nikolaevich was formally in command, the real military expertise was provided by Generals Obruchev and Mikhail Loris-Melikov, whom he relied on heavily. Russian forces went on the offensive in July, but the advance in Armenia faltered quickly, in part because the Turks outnumbered the Russians. Miliutin sent 255,000 soldiers to reinforce the army there, bringing the number of Russian troops to just over 300,000. Once the reinforcements arrived, Grand Duke Mikhail Nikolaevich resumed the offensive. His forces succeeded in inflicting several serious defeats on the Turks, including the capture of Kars by Gen. Loris-Melikov in November.[44]

The Treaty of San Stefano formally ended the war in March 1878 (although the fighting had ended in early February). After ten months of fighting, Russian casualties stood at 34,742 killed in action or died from their wounds. An additional 82,879 officers and soldiers died from disease and the elements for a total death count of 117,621 Russians.[45] Several thousand Romanian soldiers and Bulgarian irregulars also perished.

In assessing the performance of the Russian army during the Russo-Turkish War, the Ministry of War recognized successes and failings. Mobilization of reserves before and during the war had proceeded smoothly and provided the necessary numbers to fight and win the war. The soldiers of the postemancipation army had fought just as well and loyally as those of the preemancipation army. Armaments, though they had been upgraded, were not as modern as the Turks', and the rearmament program in both rifles and artillery was still incomplete. Logistics were a mixed bag. In general, railroads did not live up to their logistic potential. More troops and supplies could be transported to the war zone in good order and in a timely fashion than ever before (254,000 men were transported to Romania in 1877); however, poor planning and coordination led to massive bottlenecks that delayed men and supplies for weeks. Because the army still relied mostly on the regimental economy for supply, it had not developed an intendancy that could support it when the army deployed outside the empire. Therefore, the supplying of the army was contracted out during the war to a civilian enterprise, which did a barely adequate job. Scandalously inadequate medical treatment led to the unnecessary deaths of thousands of soldiers. Poorly handled sanitation in the war zone caused many deaths; illness caused thousands to be combat ineffective for weeks or months.

Ultimately, Miliutin's reforms did not change the way the army fought in 1877–78 although they had made the army better prepared to fight. When the war lasted longer than anticipated, the army did not have to scramble to recruit new men and train them. Trained reserves satisfied the army's manpower needs. These same men were sent home in an expeditious manner with the conclusion of peace, which quickly reduced the army's payroll. One reason the army did not operate differently than before in the field was that the reforms had not been in effect for long, meaning the majority of large-unit command-ers had been inculcated into the military culture of the prereform era and had resisted change.

Granddukism and the War

"Granddukism"—the tsar's appointing of grand dukes and other assorted relatives to commands—prevailed during the war. By appointing a dozen relatives, Alexander II signaled his commitment to maintaining a personal hold over the army even though he had declined to take command of the army in the field. He assigned his son Alexis, a rear admiral, to command all naval operations on the Danube; the heir to the throne, Alexander, to command a corps; and son Vladimir to command a division—even though none had had such high levels of responsibility before the war. Alexander II also made two nephews (sons of his sister, Grand Duchess Maria Nikolaevna, and her husband, Maximilian de Beauharnais) brigade commanders. These young men were even less prepared to command than their cousins were. Prince Eugene Maximilianovich (5th Duke of Leuchtenberg) and Prince Nikolai Maximilianovich (4th Duke of Leuchtenberg) were in their early thirties and had negligible military experience; it is not clear that they even spoke Russian.[46] To compensate for their lack of preparation, the grand dukes and princes were assigned General Staff Academy–trained officers (*genshtabists*) to be their chiefs of staff.[47] There was no guarantee that the these aides would give sound advice or that it would be followed.

Granddukism was a slap in the face of Miliutin's attempt to raise the quality of leadership in the army through education and merit. Putting unqualified members of the royal family in responsible positions they did not deserve was an insult to officers who merited those positions. It reinforced the idea—held by many conservative officers—that only "character" (meaning noble lineage) was required to lead—not education, training, or experience. Putting Grand Duke Nikolai Nikolaevich in command instead of General Obruchev led to the most serious failure in that the grand duke altered the plan for the campaign to its detriment: under his command, the army failed three times to take Plevna, wasting thousands of lives in the process. Success at Plevna came only after Alexander II overrode the objections of his brother and sent for General Todleben, whose leadership and expertise made the difference. After the war, an investigation into wartime expenditures indicated that considerable mal-feasance had occurred under the grand duke's nose. In the face of this, he was "allowed to retire into private life."[48]

Another example of the failings of granddukism was Grand Duke Nikolai's and his relations' use of their status to support favorites and undermine those they did not like—all to the detriment of military operations and officer morale. Rumors circulated that in the third assault on Plevna, when Gen. Mikhail Skobelev's forces had taken an important redoubt, Skobelev sent word to the grand duke that he needed reinforcements to hold out against impending Turkish counterattacks. Nikolai Nikolaevich, it is claimed, deliberately withheld reinforcements out of jealousy of Skobelev's rising reputation. Without the reinforcements, Skobelev's men were forced out of the redoubt with heavy losses, and the siege ground on.[49]

Petty family disputes played out for the entire army to see. When Alexander II left Bulgaria to return to Russia, he assigned his son, Grand Duke Alexander Alexandrovich, to command the Guards units in Bulgaria. As soon as the tsar was gone, Grand Duke Nikolai countermanded the order and took command of the Guards himself. He was evidently perturbed by his nephew's suggestion that he replace the ineffective Nepokoichitskii with Obruchev. Grand Duke Alexander and many other officers appealed to Alexander II to dismiss Grand Duke Nikolai. Not surprisingly, this led to even more tension as the war reached its climax.[50] That granddukism turned out to be a factor in the war surprised no one because it had prevailed for over one hundred years—and would continue to do so until Nicholas II's abdication. Grand dukes could expect to be given important commands in the Guards or plum assignments in the military administration once—or even before—they had achieved the appropriate rank. The problems associated with granddukism should not divert attention from the faults of many other senior commanders who failed in their duties, thus contributing to a longer and more costly war. A bitter joke circulated among the soldiers and junior officers at Plevna that the "Turks had in consequence even been instructed by their superiors never to fire on a Russian general, lest he should unfortunately be replaced by a man of some military capacity."[51] Miliutin, despairing over the quality of the leadership, wrote in his diary: "The choice of these persons [by the tsar] shows to what extent we are poorly supplied with good, fighting generals; among these there are those who were not up to commanding a division."[52]

In addition to appointing relatives to high commands and awarding them medals they did not deserve, Alexander II's presence in the war zone signaled that he intended to exercise his royal prerogatives as commander in chief. According to statute: "The Commander-in-Chief of the armies in the field is directly responsible to the Emperor alone, from whom he receives general directions of the conduct of the operations."[53] In so doing, Alexander created a significant distraction for the field staff and raised the stress level of the generals, who naturally feared to fail in the presence of the tsar. This contributed to the excessive caution exercised at the highest levels of command. Witnesses had the impression that the tsar's field headquarters was more like a traveling carnival than a military organization. He was surrounded by aides-de-camp of the imperial suite, miscellaneous courtiers, and hangers-on who did nothing but seek promotions and rewards and get in the way of the business of war.[54] British military attaché Col. Frederick Wellesley believed that Alexander II had not intended to remain long in Romania, but the obvious ineptitude of Grand Duke Nikolai Nikolaevich compelled him to extend his stay to force his brother to follow the advice of the more competent generals like Obruchev and Todleben.[55] Why Alexander II did not take charge himself has never been explained.

Postwar Military Thinking

Russia's thinking about the next war was dramatically affected by the treaty-making after the Russo-Turkish War and would play a decisive role in leading Russia into war in 1914. The initial peace treaty between Russia and the Ottoman Empire, the Treaty of San Stefano, was hugely advantageous to Russia. Most importantly, it gave Russia hegemony over Romania and the newly created Bulgarian nation and potentially placed Russian forces within easy striking distance of Constantinople. It denied Austria-Hungary its promised gains in the Balkans while vastly increasing Russian prestige and influence. The resulting international uproar, led by Britain and Austria-Hungary, caused Russia to acquiesce to the demand for an international conference to rewrite the peace terms. This led to the Congress of Berlin hosted by German chancellor Otto von Bismarck. The outcome of the conference was the Treaty of Berlin, signed in 1879, which awarded Austria-Hungary the right to occupy Bosnia-Herzegovina, reduced the size of Bulgaria by half, and diminished the territorial gains of Russia's ally Serbia as well. Public outrage in Russia ensued. Military leaders, in particular, believed they had been cheated of the spoils of victory.

In the aftermath of the Russo-Turkish War, the tsars, the military establishment, and the diplomatic corps were of one mind—preserve peace and the status quo in the west, continue to exert influence in the Balkans and the Caucasus, and consolidate Russia's hold over Central Asia against potential British expansion. Beyond that, after the Congress of Berlin, both the military and the diplomats worried about losing the peace in future wars if it was left to be decided by international conferences. This led the Main Staff to desire enlisting allies and international support to bolster Russia's position at any future postwar peace talks. This new approach fed the desire for a Franco-Russian alliance, not just for war-making but also for peacemaking—by having a powerful partner at the peace talks. Thus, the eventual Franco-Russian alliance was not merely a defensive measure against Germany and Austria-Hungary; it was part of a larger appreciation of the benefits of international diplomacy.

The origin of the Franco-Russian alliance, which proved critical to the origins of the First World War, was twofold on the part of the Russians. First, Prussia's use of railroads to deploy its armies, and the speed and scale of Prussian mobilization of reserves during the wars of unification, greatly impressed all of Europe but truly shocked Russia, as it showed how inadequate the Russian rail network and reserves were in comparison. In response, General Obruchev drew up a plan for railroad construction to improve the speed of mobilization and westward deployment to counter the potential German threat. The Ministry of Finance rejected the Main Staff's plan for railroad development on grounds of financial inadequacy. Obruchev then sought out the French alliance which would offset Germany's ability to mobilize and deploy its armies far more swiftly than could Russia.

Russia's foreign minister Nikolai Giers initiated talks in 1891 that began as a military convention. Giers proposed that the two nations be allies that would "coordinate measures" if either was attacked. The French wanted an ironclad commitment to mobilization and military action on the part of both countries in the case of German aggression. Giers preferred that Russia have more freedom of action. Obruchev agreed with the French and supported the idea of a solid military commitment. Regardless of the terms of the alliance, it would mean Germany could not use all its forces against Russia. A German army divided between two fronts would compensate for Russian weakness in armaments and rail transport. Obruchev's thinking, and that of the minister of war Gen. Petr Vannovskii, considered Austria-Hungary to be the main threat to Russia. The French, however, wanted the Russians to focus their efforts against the Germans. Obruchev knew this, so he led the French to believe that he agreed, but for him fighting Germany was truly a secondary Russian interest. Still, Obruchev and subsequent Russian chiefs of staff and ministers of war believed war with Austria-Hungary would eventually end up involving German participation.[56]

Initially, Tsar Alexander III chose to back the military's thinking along the lines of solid commitment, but not as a treaty, just as a "project." Events moved talks between France and Russia forward. In 1892–93, Germany increased the size of its army by 72,000 men and reduced the terms of conscript service to two years. This led Obruchev and Vannovskii to revisit the French "project" in 1893 to convince the tsar to allow them to make it a binding treaty. Alexander III agreed. Soon thereafter, in 1894, the military convention was signed committing both France and Russia to mobilize if either Germany, Italy, or Austria-Hungary mobilized. If Germany attacked France with at least two-thirds of its forces, Russia was to attack Germany "with utmost dispatch" with at least 700,000 men. And if Germany attacked Russia with at least two-thirds of its army, France was to attack Germany with whatever forces it thought necessary.[57] With the terms of the treaty being strictly defensive, the Main Staff assumed that war would begin with Russia being attacked by either Germany or Austria-Hungary, or both. This does not mean that the Russian army thought of fighting and winning on the defensive. On the contrary, the main outlook of the military leadership was to fight and win on the offensive. Their plan was for Russia to receive the attack, blunt it, and then go on the offensive. What "utmost dispatch" meant was for the Russians to determine for themselves—until 1912.

At the time the treaty was signed, both Obruchev and Vannovskii knew that Russia could not mobilize sufficient forces to launch an immediate offensive against either Germany or Austria-Hungary. The standing army had approximately 940,000 men under arms and 2.7 million in the reserves, but the ability of the underdeveloped rail network to deliver those reserves and deploy mobilized units to the front in a timely fashion was doubtful. Furthermore, many men had to be kept back to guard the Caucasus and maintain domestic order throughout the empire. The French suspected as much but hoped for the best. What the Russians did think they could do to fulfill their treaty obligation was to launch large-scale cavalry raids to disrupt enemy deployments and mobilization on Russia's border to buy time for full mobilization, parry German and Austro-Hungarian attacks, and then launch an offensive. Thinking about and preparing for war with the Triple Alliance (Germany, Austria-Hungary, and Italy) would preoccupy Russian military planners until the outbreak of war in 1914. Ultimately, the Franco-Russian alliance and the growth of the Russian economy caused Germany to see Russia as a threat and led to the development of the Schlieffen Plan to conduct a two-front war.

The Army and Society

The Russian people and the other peoples of Russia have had an ambivalent relationship with their army. One can characterize the predominant emotion at the prospect of service as that of dread. According to Elise Wirtschafter, "Of all the obligations imposed on the poll-tax population, none was more terrible or feared than military service."[58] That fear was felt not just by the men being sent off to the army for years, but also by their families. For nearly 225 years, soldiers had little or no hope of ever coming home again. Only in the aftermath of the Crimean War, when the term of service was reduced to six years, could a soldier expect to return to his family. The government further reduced the term of service to just three years in the aftermath of the Revolution of 1905. With the accompanying reduction in the time of service, the prospect of being drafted was no longer terrifying, though still unpleasant.

The effect of conscription on the wives and families of soldiers was quite dramatic in the imperial period. During the era of serfdom, when a serf was conscripted, he permanently changed social status, becoming a soldier and no longer a serf; he thus forfeited his place in the village to which he was very unlikely to return. If he were married at the time of being taken by the army, his wife became a *soldatka* (pl. *soldatki*) and like her husband was no longer a serf; her place in a village on the estate of a landowner was no longer assured. If her husband's family would not take her (and any children) in or her family would not take her back, then she had no choice but to leave the village and make a life elsewhere. However, with no skills or capital to start a life, most soldatki fell into poverty, and many engaged in criminal or dissolute behavior to survive.[59]

There were limits to how many men the people would tolerate the government taking away. There was an unstated threshold of what the peasants thought they could bear economically in terms of the loss of men and also a point beyond which the taking of more men was considered unfair. Landowners shared the feeling that there was a threshold that the regime should not cross. The government was keenly aware of the potential for resistance if it took more men than the peasants and nobles deemed both justifiable and sustainable. This was one reason Alexander I in 1812, and Nicholas I in 1854, resorted to calling up the opolchenie. The government felt constrained in its recruitment during the Polish insurrection of 1863 for fear that the peasantry would not submit to extraordinary conscription for what they considered a domestic affair.

Throughout the imperial period, the reputation of the army as a brutal environment remained constant; however, there was always a trickle of volunteers in peacetime and modest surges in wartime. The opolchenie consistently attracted hundreds of thousands of volunteers in times of war. When the term of service was reduced to six years and the army needed soldiers to reenlist to serve as noncommissioned officers, it always fell short of its manning goals.

In contrast to the aversion to service as enlisted soldiers, men from the lower classes slowly began to take a positive view of serving as officers. When Miliutin's reform of officer procurement opened the officer corps to all classes based on educational requirements, peasants and men from the urban lower and middle classes began to enter the junker schools to pursue an officer's commission—a sure way to achieve social mobility. As education spread throughout the empire, more and more workers and peasants could meet the minimum requirements. In 1870, only 3.4 percent of recruits could read and write, but by the end of the decade over one-third possessed at least basic literacy and numeracy skills. In 1912, over half of all officers were nonnoble, mostly conscripts who had graduated from junker schools.

The military intruded into people's lives in ways other than conscription. For more than two centuries, the army quartered the bulk of its men on the population. Not until the 1880s did the army begin to build fixed garrisons with barracks and amenities for all the soldiers, which it only completed on the eve of the Russo-Japanese War. Peasants dreaded the prospect of soldiers being quartered on them. Soldiers filled peasant huts and their horses crowded the stables. Soldiers stole belongings, eggs, chickens, and pigs. They abused women, broke things, and disrupted family life. Soldiers fought peasants in the streets, and there were the occasional murders. Officers requisitioned food and fodder and then underpaid or failed to pay at all. Drunken soldiers caused many problems. Sometimes, the tsarist authorities quartered regiments on villages as punishment.[60] A regiment might stay in an area for months or even years before being sent elsewhere. Peasants could also be required to quarter soldiers on the march, which, while temporary, could be every bit as burdensome, and sometimes worse; because the soldiers knew they would be leaving shortly, they were more likely to steal and behave boorishly. Soldiers on the march also spread sickness and disease to the villages.[61]

Using the army to punish civilians or to repress disturbances added to popular alienation from the military. After the Miliutin reforms, when soldiers no longer shed their civilian identities and intended to return home, soldiers also became alienated from the army when they were made to use force to the point of killing civilians. One of the demands soldiers made during the Revolution of 1905 was to no longer be used against civilians. Between 1905 and 1908, many men deserted or evaded the draft because they did not want to be put in the position to harm civilians.

In contrast to peacetime, wartime generally brought society together in support of soldiers and the army. The wealthy and poor alike donated money to help ease the plight of sick and wounded soldiers. The nobility, the wealthy upper class, and businesses donated whole field hospitals and, in the late nineteenth century, hospital trains. To help the soldiers, thousands of women from all strata of society joined the Red Cross to work as nurses. From the mid-nineteenth century onward, during the last four wars of the tsarist era (the Crimean War, the Russo-Turkish War, the Russo-Japanese War, and the First World War), peasants and urbanites wrote letters of support to soldiers at the front and sent them gifts such as scarves, mittens, canned fruits, tea, tobacco, and the like at Christmas. At Easter, civic organizations would send the soldiers traditional Easter cakes. Many towns and cities adopted regiments and sent the soldiers gifts on all the significant holidays. During the Russo-Turkish War, peasants, workers, and the elites donated hundreds of thousands of rubles for the care of sick and wounded soldiers; during the Russo-Japanese War, such donations numbered in the millions of rubles; and during the First World War, in the tens of millions.

Alexander III initiated a Russification program in the 1880s aimed at homogenizing the people of the empire along the lines of Russian language, culture, and religion. This meant suppressing the native languages, religions, and cultures of millions of the tsar's subjects. The result was a raised awareness among the non-Russian minorities of their "otherness," which led to the emergence and coalescence of nationalist movements from Finland to Azerbaijan and to the strengthening of Polish nationalism. Non-Russian soldiers were made painfully aware that they were different in an inferior way—a way that would lead them to reject Russian domination. Later, during the First World War, the Latvians succeeded in forming several regiments solely of Latvians, asserting an identity within the army apart from the Russians. This inspired Ukrainian nationalists after the February Revolution to unite all Ukrainian soldiers into their own divisions under the command of Ukrainian officers—a prelude to their declaration of independence.

Under Alexander II and Alexander III, Russia's ability to wage war was enhanced. The emancipation of the serfs enabled Miliutin to create a system of trained reserves and consequently reduce the size of the standing army. Emancipation also initiated the expansion of Russia's industrial economy, which gave the army more resources to modernize its arms and equipment. Alexander II's reestablishment of the Main Staff further enhanced Russia's warmaking capacity by creating a military intellectual hub that pondered theory, strategy, and doctrine. Railroad building, which facilitated the mobilization of reserves and the concentrating of units at the borders, continued across the two reigns, though never on a scale extensive enough to satisfy the army. The Russo-Turkish War validated the usefulness and effectiveness of the new reserve system. The army was able to expand and then demobilize in a timely fashion and did not rely on new drafts of conscripts to fight the war. Finally, the Franco-Russian alliance gave Russia a powerful ally it hoped would deter German and Austro-Hungarian aggression.

CHAPTER 3

The Army during the Reign of Nicholas II, 1894–1917

Between the end of the Russo-Turkish War in 1878 and the outbreak of war with Japan in 1904 Russian diplomatic and military leaders oriented their thoughts toward the potential for and even desire for war. Within the military, Neo-Slavism and Pan-Slavism shaped the mindset of army officers regarding the army's role in foreign policy. To them, the plight of Slavs in central and eastern Europe merited Russian intervention. German economic growth was assumed to be a threat to Russia and led the Main Staff to consider the desirability of going to war before Russia was hopelessly outmatched. Many in the Ministry of Foreign Affairs and business circles promoted potential expansion eastward based on a "neo-Slavic" "East-Asian destiny." They were supported by a faction within the high command that believed it was in Russia's interest to expand the empire eastward at the expense of China and to head off Japanese expansion in Asia, especially along Russia's Far East border with Manchuria and Korea. The desire to control the Black Sea straits motivated some military, diplomatic, and economic leaders to seriously consider seizing Constantinople with an amphibious assault. Finally, many military and civilian officials desired revenge against Austria-Hungary for its double-dealing during the Crimean War. The Austro-Hungarian role at the Berlin Conference in 1879 that diminished Russia's gains from its victory over the Ottomans embittered both Russia's military and its diplomatic corps.

Furthermore, Austria-Hungary's embarrassing of Russia in 1908 over the annexation of Bosnia-Herzegovina, and then the successive Balkan crises in which Austria-Hungary predictably worked against Russian interests, embittered much of educated Russian society. Eventually, the fear of a too-powerful Germany and desire for revenge against Austria-Hungary led the Russians to use the alliance with France for offensive rather than defensive purposes. The

First World War and the consequent February Revolution resulted from the reorientation of the thinking about that alliance.

War Plans

Until Russia and France formed their alliance, Russia maintained a defensive military posture in the west, the idea being to begin any war against a Western power by fighting battles of attrition and then, when mobilization to a war footing was complete—the Main Staff estimated it would take forty-one days—transition to the offense to engage in battles of annihilation to force the enemy to the peace table. Although the alliance called for Russia to go on the offensive if Germany attacked France, there were those who argued that they should not honor this commitment if the Germans also attacked Russia in force. In that case, they thought Russia should fight on the defensive. It was not certain that either side would honor the alliance under all conditions, and until 1912, Russia claimed a degree of flexibility regarding its pledge. Initially, the expectations of the alliance were rather vague, but they became more specific over time. Through changes in chiefs of staff and ministers of war, what began as planning for potential war became preparation for an assumed war. The alliance became the major factor in how Russia envisioned and planned for the next war in Europe.

For eighteen years, Russian military leaders prepared for war in the west against the Triple Alliance assuming that, in the event of a German attack on France, they would attack Germany on France's behalf when they were ready, with as many men as they thought they needed. In the event of a German or Austro-Hungarian attack on Russia, Russia would defend itself and transition to offense when conditions made that possible. Every few years, as the size of Russia's military reserves grew, the Main Staff drew up new mobilization schedules. Minister of War Gen. Aleksei Kuropatkin wrote a memorandum to Tsar Nicholas II in 1900 outlining his vision of Russia's potential use of military power. He counseled against war with the Triple Alliance, saying there was nothing to be gained by victory. The idea to launch an amphibious assault to secure the Bosporus and Constantinople, an irresponsible idea advocated by a radical few, would lead to conflict with the Great Powers, Britain foremost among them, because by taking Constantinople, the Russian navy could threaten the eastern Mediterranean and the Suez Canal, a situation the British would not tolerate. Kuropatkin successfully quashed that idea. He also rejected provoking conflict in Central Asia to threaten British control of India—an improbable venture at best, yet one that some in the high command wanted. He did, reluctantly, endorse continued exploitation of Manchuria against his better judgment knowing that Nicholas II was enamored of that project, and he wanted to preserve his standing with the tsar. In 1902, Nicholas II directed the Main Staff to base its war planning on the assumption that the next war would be in the west and would begin with a full-scale German assault.[1]

At the turn of the century, Russia and France began to hold annual staff conferences to keep abreast of diplomatic changes and military affairs. Over the years, Russia's flexibility in responding to German or Austro-Hungarian attacks was greatly eroded by the French insistence that in the event of a German attack on France, Russia was to attack with at least 700,000 men by the fourteenth day after mobilization began (M+14). In the war plans of 1903 (Plan 18), Nicholas II proposed that in the event of a German attack, Russia should follow the example of Napoleon's invasion and stage a strategic withdrawal. General Kuropatkin and the Main Staff persuaded him instead to agree to abide by the agreement to attack by M+14 if it were determined that Germany was making its main effort against France. The Main Staff was not confident that France could hold out for more than sixty days without Russian assistance. For Russia's security, the staff considered it essential to keep France from being quickly knocked out of the war. The generals pointed out that Russia needed the Polish industrial and agricultural products they would lose by retreat and warned of the morale boost a Russian withdrawal would give the Austro-Hungarian army, and of the encouragement it might give other potential enemies (Britain, Turkey) to join a war against Russia. By 1903, the original defensive nature of the alliance had fallen away, and Russia's Main Staff began to think about waging offensive war against both Germany and Austria-Hungary.[2]

Plan 18's call to attack by M+14 led the army to position the bulk of its forces along the western border during peacetime because Russia lacked sufficient rail capacity to move large numbers of regular forces and mobilized reserves from the interior of Russia to the west in a timely fashion. At the time war broke out in August 1914, there were only eight main rail lines leading from Russia's interior to the borders with Germany and Austria-Hungary. Only five lines were double-tracked, enabling them to support significant two-way traffic; the other three lines required the use of sidings to allow trains to pass in opposite directions, which slowed rail transit during mobilization and the strategic deployment of the army at the outset of operations. At maximum capacity, barring accidents and bottlenecks, a double-track line could support a maximum of thirty-six trains per day. Because a single army corps of three divisions required about 130 trains to complete transport to the front, the movement of just one corps stood to occupy a double-track line for several days, and a single-track line for longer.[3] Time and again, the Ministry of War asked for more rail lines, but the Ministry of Finance prioritized railways that directly supported the growth of the economy over strategic military considerations. The Main

Staff's vision for the use of railroads ended at the Russian border. They did not devise a plan to use railroads to support the army if it advanced victoriously westward.

The Russo-Japanese War, 1904–1905

The Russo-Japanese War, which began in February 1904 and concluded in August 1905, was Russia's first war to rely heavily on railroad transportation, telegraphic communications, and vast numbers of reservists. It proved to be a failed test of Russia's ability to continue its imperial expansion. The war called into question the leadership, organization, and tactics of the army. Beforehand, the military establishment was divided on the merits of war: some, wanting good relations with Japan, thought it advisable that Russia limit its ambitions in Korea. The Foreign Ministry, those in the military who worried about the security of Siberia from Japanese encroachment, and certain business interests, who had the support of the tsar, sided with the prowar faction. The potential for war with Japan began to be considered with the Japanese victory in the Sino-Japanese War of 1895 and became a topic of general discussion in the Ministry of War and the Pri-Amur Military District in 1898. Mobilization planning within the Pri-Amur Military District began in 1900, and in 1902, the Main Staff began drawing up contingency plans for war.[4]

At the war's outbreak, Russia's strategic goal was to force Japan and the Great Powers to acknowledge Russia's hegemony in Manchuria and northern Korea. Because Russia had not massed forces in the Far East, the Ministry of War had no choice but to begin the war on the defensive and buy time to mobilize and send reinforcements to Manchuria. As a result, Japan held the initiative from the beginning. Nicholas II ordered General Kuropatkin to step down from his post of minister of war to command the armies in Manchuria.[5]

From the outset, Kuropatkin faced numerous obstacles. The most important was that neither the tsar nor the military establishment made the war in Manchuria a priority. The western border, thought to be threatened by Germany and Austria-Hungary, was deemed too important to weaken by transferring more than a handful of regular units to Manchuria. Kuropatkin agreed to fight the war largely with reservists and officers who volunteered to leave units garrisoned on Russia's western border. Another problem was that when Kuropatkin arrived in Manchuria on 15 March to establish his headquarters at Liaoyang, he did not have sole and uncontested command in the theater of operations. Adm. Evgenii Alekseev, viceroy of the Far East, refused to subordinate himself to Kuropatkin and used his position to influence operations and the use of military forces. Furthermore, the forces at Port Arthur under Gen. Anatolii M. Stessel' operated independently of both Kuropatkin and Alekseev.

In Manchuria, Kuropatkin, while building up his forces, allowed the Japanese to land men in Korea without interference. He did not anticipate going on the offensive until September, when he expected to have assembled a force large enough to make victory likely. He divided his forces into three groups: Eastern, Western, and Southern. He ordered the Eastern group, under Gen. Mikhail I. Zasulich, to fight a delaying action against the Japanese on the line of the Yalu River, using an active defense.

Complications arose immediately because Zasulich had received two sets of instructions: Kuropatkin's to delay, and Alekseev's not to give ground. He chose to obey Alekseev. Zasulich dug in on the banks of the Yalu to oppose a crossing and left the maneuvering up to the Japanese. On 12 April, the Japanese surprised Zasulich by crossing upstream of his positions and taking him in the flank while pounding his main positions with artillery fire from across the river. The Russians lost 5,000 men to 2,000 Japanese and retreated over the mountain passes into Manchuria.[6]

With the Russian Pacific Squadron bottled up in Port Arthur, the Japanese then landed an army on the Kwantung Peninsula to attack Port Arthur thereby cutting off rail communication. There followed the Battle of Nanshan, won by the Japanese despite an able and spirited defense by one Russian regiment that covered the withdrawal of the bulk of the forces into Port Arthur.[7] The Japanese put Port Arthur under siege for 241 days beginning on 23 April 1904. The senior commanders in Port Arthur seem to have done all they could to help the Japanese win the battle. Command in Port Arthur during the battle was divided between General Stessel', Lt.-Gen. Konstantin N. Smirnov (commander of the fortress), and Vice Adm. Vilgelm K. Vitgeft (commander of the naval squadron). Rather than working as a team or sublimating their pride and accepting one as superior, the generals and admiral ignored each other and often worked at cross-purposes.[8]

As the siege got underway, the Russians had 42,000 soldiers, plus several thousand sailors who could serve as infantry. The Japanese had 80,000 men. They employed heavy siege guns and massed infantry charges to storm the Russian defenses. The Japanese, despite taking heavy losses and failing three times (in August, September, and October), succeeded in their fourth attempt in capturing the hills above the port in November. With the loss of the heights, Stessel' needlessly and against the wishes of numerous of his subordinates and to the dismay of the men, surrendered on 20 December. As a result, 878 officers and 23,481 men went into captivity. The Russian garrison had lost nearly 30,000 killed and wounded; the Japanese attackers suffered nearly 60,000 casualties.[9]

In May–June 1904, while the siege of Port Arthur progressed, the Japanese sent three armies north along the railroad to Harbin. In several skirmishes, the Japanese forced the Russian army back through superior maneuvering and the Russians' lack of coordination and communication. The first major battle of the Japanese drive northward along the railroad connecting Port Arthur to Harbin was the Battle of Liaoyang, in July 1904. Kuropatkin's forces outnumbered the Japanese 158,000 to 125,000, but due to faulty and incomplete intelligence, he assumed that the Japanese were the superior force. The idea that he was outnumbered colored his planning, which was characterized by a defensive mindset and a fear of being outflanked. Russian forces succeeded in fighting the Japanese to a standstill, inflicting 23,000 casualties on the Japanese while suffering 16,000 themselves. Kuropatkin underestimated Japanese losses, though, and due to poor cavalry reconnaissance, he was ignorant that the Japanese had depleted their supplies, and so withdrew north to Mukden. He quite possibly could have won had he had an offensive mindset and taken advantage of several Japanese mistakes, or simply maintained his position on the battlefield. He did initiate one attack against the Japanese, but called it off when it ran into difficulty, unaware that it had achieved some success. Throughout not just this battle but during the entire war, Russian cavalry performed poorly at scouting.[10]

In September 1904, Kuropatkin for the first time believed he had numerical superiority in troops. He set out to engage the Japanese with a frontal attack, followed by a flanking attack, in what would become the Battle of the Sha-ho River. The terrain was not conducive to the planned flanking attack commanded by Gen. Georgii Shtakel'berg. Shtakel'berg had overwhelming superiority for the flanking attack but never brought it to bear. The Japanese reacted quickly to seize the high ground and dug in. Kuropatkin failed to coordinate the movement of his forces; he and his subordinate generals experienced several lapses in judgment and proved unable to either effectively construct adequate defenses against Japanese counterattacks or adapt them to the terrain.[11]

During the battle, Gen. Leonid Sobolev sent a regiment of infantry to attack across open ground in near parade-ground fashion, using the same tactics employed at Plevna twenty-seven years earlier and contrary to updated tactical regulations. In the span of a few minutes, Japanese rifle, machine-gun, and artillery fire annihilated the regiment, killing or wounding 2,000 men. Despite their costly tactics, the Russians managed to push the Japanese back several miles, but a Japanese counterattack led Kuropatkin to order a retreat to the Sha-ho River. The battle ended in stalemate with 41,351 Russian casualties against the loss of 11,000 Japanese.[12] When asked by a United States Army military attaché why he did not have his men take cover when advancing, a company commander replied, "My men have not been practiced in this method of advance. If I open out too much, and make them take cover, many will not move forward at command, so that as we advance the company is melting away and I cannot keep control."[13] Prewar training had clearly not followed the best practices identified by the Main Staff.

After replacing his losses with recently arrived reservists, Kuropatkin, in January 1905, ordered an attack on Sandepu. Due to poor maps and inadequate reconnaissance, his forces attacked in the wrong place twice and were repulsed with heavy losses of nearly 12,000 officers and men against Japanese losses of 8,900. After this battle, Kuropatkin openly criticized Gen. Oskar Grippenberg, who had been in command of the battle, whereupon Grippenberg claimed illness, resigned his command, packed his many bags, and returned to St. Petersburg.[14]

The final land battle in Manchuria came at Mukden in February 1905. Kuropatkin's forces outnumbered his opponent's 293,000 to 270,000, but he did not take advantage of several opportunities to maneuver against the Japanese or exploit their vulnerabilities. Even though his army inflicted catastrophic casualties on the Japanese (70,000 killed and wounded), the Japanese managed to outmaneuver Kuropatkin's forces, who fought primarily from well-prepared fixed defenses. Having suffered losses of 59,000 killed and wounded, he ordered his forces to retreat north toward Harbin. The withdrawal turned into a chaotic retreat in which the Japanese took nearly 30,000 men prisoner.[15]

Dissatisfied with Kuropatkin's repeated failures, the tsar relieved him of command in March. Gen. Nikolai Linevich replaced him. Linevich planned to take the offensive as soon as he replaced the losses from the Mukden disaster. Before sufficient reinforcements could arrive, however, the Russian Second Pacific Fleet was annihilated in the naval Battle of Tsushima in May. This disaster, as well as the overall financial burden of the war, led to the opening of peace talks, which culminated in the Treaty of Portsmouth in August 1905, ending the war and passing hegemony in Manchuria from Russia to Japan. The cost to Russia for this humiliation was more than 220,000 casualties, of whom as many as 58,000 officers and soldiers were killed or died of wounds on land and at sea, while a further 18,000 died of illness and disease. About 74,000 soldiers and sailors were captured during the war and repatriated afterward. The Japanese suffered 270,000 casualties, of whom 86,000 died.[16]

Some bright spots for Russia revealed by the war were the solid fighting qualities of the Russian infantry and the relatively smooth mobilization of reserves. Mobilization was smooth in the sense that orders were efficiently processed and delivered from the Ministry of War to the military districts, then down to the towns and villages, and most soldiers reported for duty in the time allotted. It became necessary to augment the regular forces and units already stationed in the Far East with ten distinct waves of mobilization because the

Ministry of War chose to transfer as few units from the western borders as possible and instead send units from the interior of Russia and form regiments and divisions of reservists. First, in February 1904, the army mobilized reservists residing in Siberia and the Far East. Military districts in European Russia did not begin to call up men until June. The last reservists were summoned in August 1905, while peace talks were underway. At the end of the war, more than half of all soldiers serving in Manchuria were reservists.

Reservists were called ups in February, June, July, August, September, October, and December 1904, and in April, June, and August 1905. Every military district experienced at least two rounds of mobilization; some had four. The army used reservists in three ways: to bring regular units up to full strength; to fill out and deploy reserve units; and to replace casualties.[17] By the end of the war, 1,754,146 men had been called up from the reserves. Of them, 1,669,454 reported for duty as required, a compliance rate of 95 percent. A noncompliance rate of 5 percent was not a great number, militarily speaking, though it was ten times the noncompliance rate of the Russo-Turkish War. The average reservist was often depressed, reluctant, and unmotivated. The war held no interest for them; separation from their families and livelihoods was painful. Their attitudes toward returning to the colors were also affected by the antiwar movement that emerged in the second half of 1904. Antiwar protesters picketed and agitated among the reservists at local military boards and mobilization centers.

Mobilizing officers proved to be a problem just as it had been during the Russo-Turkish War because of a lack of numbers to draw on. The army projected a need for 14,500 reserve officers but had only 5,000. To make up the shortfall, the army asked regular officers serving in active regiments that were not being sent to Manchuria to volunteer to fill out deploying units. The St. Petersburg Military District was able to call up 484 officers from the reserve and secure 369 volunteers. The army allowed senior students in cadet corps, junker schools, and military schools to graduate and commission early if they would serve in Manchuria.[18] It took months to secure the volunteers and to organize the called-up officers, which left the majority of infantry regiments short of junior officers at the start of hostilities. Most regiments fought the whole war without their full complement of officers. Combat losses compounded the shortage. As in the Russo-Turkish War, the competence of senior officers came into question as the fighting unfolded. A bit of black humor circulated among the officers and military attachés in which the Japanese emperor had offered to make peace with Russia and let them have Manchuria if the tsar could name: three competent Russian generals, three honest intendance officials, and three chaste unmarried Red Cross nurses.[19]

Another positive to come out of the war for the Russian army was the absence of "granddukism." Inexplicably, Tsar Nicholas II did not place any of his relatives in important command or supervisory positions as he later would in 1914. Conspicuous by his absence was the tsar's first cousin once removed General Staff Academy–trained Grand Duke Nikolai Nikolaevich, who considered himself a master of military affairs and who would lead the charge in reconstructing the army after the war. The tsar did send his first cousin, Grand Duke Boris Vladimirovich, a Guards officer, to represent him at Kuropatkin's headquarters, whence he was expected to send his observations of the goings-on directly to the tsar. Breaking tradition with his grandfather and great granduncle, he did not interfere with military operations, or decamp to the theater of operations; however, he did undermine Kuropatkin by allowing officers to send him letters complaining about Kuropatkin and seeking favors that Kuropatkin would not allow. Also, to the aggravation of many, Nicholas interfered with high-level personnel issues. In numerous instances, General Kuropatkin sought to relieve incompetent generals of command, but those with connections to the royal family succeeded in thwarting their removal.

The Revolution of 1905

While the army fought in the Far East, revolt, coupled with the antiwar movement, broke out at home. The Revolution of 1905 sorely tested the army's ability to maintain domestic order while conducting a war. Mutinies exposed the deep level of dissatisfaction of the soldiers at their quality of life and treatment by the officers. Unrest began with Bloody Sunday in January 1905 but did not manifest itself in the army until the summer. It then escalated rapidly with the tsar's promulgation of the October Manifesto. The manifesto promised constitutional rule and an elected legislature. While there was unrest in the army throughout 1905, mutinies were rare until October. Historian John Bushnell has conclusively established that the soldiers' mutinies grew out of the October Manifesto, which they viewed as the capitulation of autocracy to democracy. He convincingly argues that in the soldiers' minds the October Manifesto delegitimized the officers' authority over them. He concludes: "Soldiers acted as though the totality of the old rules and regulations had been annulled. Like peasants, they concluded from the obvious fracture of civil authority . . . that the fetters restraining them had also snapped, and that they could seize their own freedom."[20] The soldiers believed that autocracy was ended and that a new regime of, by, and for the people would therefore serve their interests at the expense of the officers. In the interim, many soldiers no longer believed they would be punished for insubordination and behaved accordingly. The insubordinate behavior was neither random nor mindless; soldiers aimed to achieve the goals of securing better living conditions and better treatment by their superiors. The mutinies finally ended in 1908, when it became clear that the new constitutional government upheld the authority of the tsar as commander in chief and that of the officer corps.

Considering how widespread the upheaval was in Russia in 1905, discipline in the army, other than the disaffection shown by reservists called up for the Russo-Japanese War, had held up well until mid-October. For most of 1905, the cities had been in turmoil, with large-scale strikes and rioting, and the murder of hundreds of government officials and policemen by revolutionaries. Radicals also targeted the royal family. The countryside had been equally aflame with peasant protest. Landowners and their bailiffs and stewards were frequently the object of violence at the hands of peasants. For ten months, the soldiers had remained obedient.

In the years leading up to 1905, the nation experienced persistent and pervasive discontent, and draftees certainly had the potential to bring some of that discontent into the army. The main sources of discontent likely to trigger protests in 1905–07 were the hard lives in the regiments and abuse by officers. From the middle of October 1905 to the beginning of January 1906, the army recorded 195 acts of collective protest by soldiers. Of these protests, 118 were peaceful, but 77 were violent. In 1906, there were 166 protests in the military, 32 occurring with the soldiers under arms. A total of 150,000 soldiers participated. This number includes soldiers' disturbances in the Far East that were organized by men impatient to go home. When one includes the disturbances that preceded the October general strike through to 1907, the total number of protests in the army and navy rises to 437.[21]

The nature of the mutinies was mostly peaceful, characterized by sullen refusals to obey orders; however, violence was prone to erupt when officers used loyal troops to disband protests and arrest ringleaders. As Beryl Williams observed about the peasantry, the soldiers' mutinies were driven more by "a concern for human rights, for liberty and equality within the system, rather than outright opposition to it."[22] It was about freedom, not socialism, and even though the demands were framed as economic concerns, they constituted a challenge to the political status quo. The soldiers' demands can be divided into five basic categories: desire that the material conditions and general quality of life in the army be improved; a wish that officers cease to use them to suppress demonstrations; that the length of service be reduced; that relations between officers and men in general and discipline and punishments in particular be more humane; and that civil and political rights be granted.

Quality of life issues made up about half of all soldiers' demands. They included demands for more and better food, and nearly always including requests for more tea and sugar. Soldiers demanded higher pay, just to meet their daily needs. After these issues, better treatment of enlisted men by officers and NCOs was the most common demand. Some soldiers called for the removal of abusive officers and NCOs. Others insisted on changes in the system of military justice and in the disciplinary powers of officers.

Officers tended to handle mutinies by first attempting to persuade the men to disband and cease their opposition. They either promised changes or threatened dire consequences. If that failed, officers used loyal troops to surround, disarm if necessary, and arrest if not all the mutinous soldiers then at least the ringleaders. Even if dialogue did succeed in defusing the situation, in the aftermath commanders usually sought to arrest ringleaders. An act of collective protest was considered mutiny when the soldiers threatened or declared their intent to disobey orders if their demands were not met. Officers whose units mutinied were routinely cashiered; therefore, to save their careers, officers did their best to cover up instances of mutiny. Many officers were thwarted in their cover-up attempts by the Okhrana, in whose institutional interest it was to expose mutinies and take credit for having incompetent officers dismissed. The antagonism between the Ministry of Defense and the Ministry of Internal Affairs was at its most intense between 1905 and 1908.

Especially worrisome to the tsar and the high command was officers' participation in mutinies and revolutionary activities in the years 1905–07. Despite the overall loyalty of the officer corps, in every military district small numbers of officers conspired to support reform or foment revolt. Radical junior officers (almost always of noble social background), some of whom were members of revolutionary parties, led a handful of mutinies. Others, more senior (also from the nobility), participated in creating manifestos to establish independent "republics" in Siberia. The occasional sympathetic liberal reform-minded officer refused to fire on mutinous soldiers. The consequences for these officers were uniformly severe, ranging from execution to exile or imprisonment.[23]

It is undeniable that there were positive long-term outcomes of the Revolution of 1905 for the soldiers. On 6 December 1905, the Ministry of War announced reforms meant to placate the men. These included the immediate increase of the daily meat ration from one-quarter to three-quarters pound, and the allocation of more tea and sugar. The ministry raised soldiers' and NCOs' pay by two and a half to three times, depending on rank. The army promised to begin issuing additional underwear and boots in January 1906 and to issue, for the first time, blankets, sheets, field shirts, towels, and handkerchiefs. The Ministry of War abolished the practice of having soldiers work in the civilian economy to raise funds for their regiments. Also, the terms of service were reduced to three years in the infantry; four years in the cavalry, artillery, and engineers; and five years in the navy.

The war, mutinies, and the use of the army (often under the direction of Okhrana officers) to suppress revolts among the civilian population disrupted training in the army, not just in 1904–07 but for the rest of the decade. Between 1904 and 1907 virtually no unit training was conducted. The annual large-scale summer maneuvers were cancelled. As the revolution wound down and mutinies ended in 1908, 13.8 percent of infantry and 15.9 percent of cavalry units still were unable to fulfill the designated training regimen because they were employed in pacification duties. On the eve of the First World War, things were even worse. Due to a massive increase in the number and scale of workers' strikes and demonstrations in 1914, more than one-third of infantry and nearly half of cavalry regiments failed to conduct the required training because they were being used to put down disturbances.[24] Needless to say, the loss of the Russo-Japanese War, the extensive mutinies, and the lack of training dismayed Russia's ally France. The reports of the French military attaché to Paris led the French military and government to not expect much of the Russians in the event of war.[25]

Losing the war against Japan and the upheaval of revolution made Russia both look and feel weak and vulnerable. In the Far East, Russia ceased its aggressive and imperialist diplomacy and adopted a more moderate and realistic foreign policy. Russia joined the Anglo-French Entente in 1907 at the urging of France, which stabilized Russian relations with Britain over the issues of Afghanistan and Persia, and gave Russia another ally at any future peace conference. Russia then signed a treaty with Japan to normalize relations in Manchuria, Korea, and Mongolia. Together these agreements gave Russia security in Central Asia and the Far East, enabling it to concentrate its attention on Germany and Austria-Hungary.[26]

New War Plans

Russia's preparation for what became the First World War was overseen by an establishment that had not made up its mind on how to fight a war with Germany and/or Austria-Hungary though it expected such a war to involve millions of men and probably to be drawn out. Indecision over whether to begin by attacking or defending stemmed from the uncertainty of which Germany would strike first: Russia or France. Gen. Nikolai Mikhnevich, commandant of the General Staff Academy and author of *Strategy* (1906) and *Principles of Strategy* (1913), advocated for dispositions away from the western border that would enable Russia to defend, while Col. Alexander Neznamov, author of *Contemporary War* (1911), *Modern Warfare: The Action of the Field Army* (1912), and *War Plan* (1913), advocated forward positioning to enable Russia to attack first. The planners' thinking was affected by the fact that most Russian divisions, including those in the border districts, were manned at partial strength and would not be ready to fight until mobilization had brought divisions up to wartime strength. The thinking behind partial manning was that it would be more efficient to have the desired total number of divisions that would then be brought to full strength by trainloads of reservists than to have a lesser number of full-strength divisions that would be supplemented with divisions created from scratch.

In the years after the Russo-Japanese War, disagreement arose in the General Staff (the Main Staff was renamed Main Directorate of the General Staff in 1905) and Ministry of War over whether to direct Russia's military power to the east or west. "Easterners" pushed their fears of war in the Far East even after diplomacy had achieved stability. They believed that the Japanese were not satisfied with what they had gotten from the Treaty of Portsmouth and would be back for more. As a precaution, the chief of the General Staff, Gen. Feodor Palitsyn, an "Easterner," wanted to send 138 battalions from western Russia to Siberia, the Caucasus, and eastern Russia but was denied. His successor, Gen. Vladimir Sukhomlinov, on the advice of the General Staff, was able, in 1908, to shift some 128 battalions from the west to central Russia so they could mobilize and concentrate there, in position to deploy either to the west or to the east. Sukhomlinov was convinced that war was more likely in the east than in the west. There was a latent fear among some senior officers that Russia could face the worst-case scenario of a two-front war. Sukhomlinov, in 1909, openly advocated conducting a fighting withdrawal from Poland in the event of war with Germany; his repositioning of troops away from the border supported this line of action. In the end, Mobilization Plan 19, written by Sukhomlinov and quartermaster general (head of planning and operations) Gen. Iurii Danilov in 1909, and approved by the tsar in 1910, envisioned Russia potentially giving up as many as ten provinces in Poland to an attack by Germany and Austria-Hungary and then, after mobilizing, counterattacking.[27] The French, already doubtful about Russia's ability to hold out for long against such a combined attack, fretted about the ramifications of Mobilization Plan 19. To them, it indicated a lack of intent to attack by M+14.

Mobilization Plan 19, however, did not stand unaltered for long. When the French assured Danilov and chief of the General Staff Gen. Iakov Zhilinskii in 1912 that the British would commit their navy and send an expeditionary force to France in the event of war, Zhilinskii called for another planning conference. Factions of the General Staff, the Ministry of War, and the military district chiefs presented competing scenarios to the tsar and minister of war. One faction, led by Danilov, thought Germany posed the greater threat, so it wanted to plan for an offensive against the Germans while holding against Austria-Hungary. Generals Danilov and Zhilinskii assumed it would take Germany two months to finish off France, thus giving Russia a sixty-day window to attack and turn the tables on the Germans. The other faction, led by Gen. Mikhail Alekseev, thought Austria-Hungary was the greater threat and should be attacked first. Rather than side with one over the other, Sukhomlinov fatally changed the mobilization schedule to support simultaneous attacks on Germany and Austria-Hungary.

Sukhomlinov's Mobilization Schedule 19 (A) became the dominant way of seeing war in the west among the military leadership from 1913 on. It allocated two armies to attack East Prussia or defend on that border as the situation dictated and three armies to attack Austria-Hungary if Germany attacked France first. If Russia were attacked first, then three armies would go against Germany and two against Austria-Hungary. Nicholas II accepted this final version of the plan. If Germany began war by attacking France first, Danilov was determined to see the Russian army attack on M+14, ready or not. Zhilinskii then promised the French that Russia would attack with 800,000 men no later than M+15.[28] In advance of the outbreak of hostilities, neither the army, the Foreign Ministry, nor the tsar articulated a clear strategic goal for a war with Germany and/or Austria-Hungary. There was a general but vague sense that victory would enable Russia to impose a harsh peace treaty that would somehow lead to long-term security on the western border.

The General Staff also wrote up Mobilization Schedule 19 (G) in case there was a war only against Germany. Unbeknownst to the tsar, however, the General Staff did not create a mobilization plan to conduct war only against Austria-Hungary. By relying on Schedule 19 (A) in 1914, Russia faced a crisis in July because it could not meet Germany's demand to stop mobilizing on its border and still have the war the tsar really wanted—a war with Austria-Hungary.[29] What happened between 1891 and 1913 was the army transitioned from first seeking a way to deter Germany, to committing to an alliance in which the Russians would begin a war on the defensive, and then to committing to respond to the threat of war by attacking both Germany and Austria-Hungary only fifteen days after the onset of mobilization.

Besides making the mistake of promising to attack on M+15 knowing they would likely not be fully mobilized, the Russian planners erred by not allocating decisive mass to either axis of attack. Because they were not mutually supporting, and because neither could be adequately supported logistically, this was the worst possible outcome for a war on the western frontier. All the while, it was assumed that once Russia took the offensive, it would remain on the offensive until victory.

Failure to Reform

Losing the Russo-Japanese War made it clear that the Russian army needed to make changes. In February 1908, Nicholas II charged his Council of Ministers to come up with a plan to reform the army. Prime Minister Petr Stolypin subsequently instructed the General Staff to develop a plan of national defense within which to frame military reform. Minister of war Gen. Alexander Rediger told Palitsyn that the goal was to increase "Russian military power, provide security and maintain its political position in the world."[30] Despite the tsar's mandate and the obvious need for change, there were highly placed, well-connected, hidebound generals who feared and resisted progress. Others reluctantly accepted the need but dragged their feet. Lack of agreement on if or when there would be another war, or whom it would likely be against (the Triple Alliance, the Ottomans, or Japan) led to the pitting of reformers against each other. By the outbreak of the First World War, the army had failed—despite considerable effort—to fully reform. Bruce Menning aptly sums up the reforms between 1905–14 as "incremental, superficial, and often disjointed change."[31]

A major impediment to reform was competition between the army and navy for funding. The navy insisted on quickly rebuilding the Baltic Fleet. It had lost sixty-nine ships, including fifteen battleships, to the Japanese. The admiralty was given several billion rubles, all of which were wasted—not a single ship was completed before the outbreak of the First World War. Both the army and navy had to wait years to begin to rearm and reequip according to a dedicated plan because it was not until 1910 that they received a firm financial commitment from the State Duma. The delay was not because of antimilitarism in the Duma, but simply because the empire's financial state was in shambles due to the recent war and revolution. In 1910, the Duma ratified a ten-year program to modernize the army with a budget of 53.8 million rubles in 1911 and 70 million in 1912. The army had asked for 2.1 billion rubles for 1908, to be followed by an additional 145 million each year. In 1913, the modernization program was boosted by the "Big Program to strengthen the army." The Duma voted a onetime allotment of 430 million rubles to the Ministry of War to be paid out over three years.[32]

Grand Duke Nikolai Nikolaevich, with Nicholas II's permission, in 1905 formed a State Defense Council to plan and oversee the recovery and reform of the armed forces. The State Defense Council was independent of the Ministry of War and answered directly to the tsar. The newly created Main Directorate of the General Staff (GUGSh) was subordinated to the council. Rather than centralizing the reform effort, this change resulted in the eruption of a bureaucratic turf war. The Ministry of War opposed the interference of the grand duke and the diminution of its power. Other ministries refused to subordinate themselves to the needs of the military.

The struggle distracted both the General Staff and the Ministry of War and impeded reform. The General Staff was in charge of training and doctrine; the ministry oversaw administration and personnel. Both submitted competing reform programs to the State Defense Council and the tsar. The tsar did not strongly support either side, which slowed progress toward reform. Because of infighting, resistance to his ideas by various generals, and opposition from the Duma, Grand Duke Nikolai Nikolaevich, his feelings bruised by Sukhomlinov's criticism that the council was merely "a haven for out of work grand dukes," resigned in 1908. Shortly thereafter, the tsar disbanded the State Defense Council, making himself once again the apex of military decision-making. In 1910, the Ministry of War (under Sukhomlinov since 1909) reabsorbed the General Staff and deliberately minimized its influence. A cohort of up-and-coming colonels and generals, self-styled "Young Turks," many of whom served on the GUGSh, advocated stridently for radical reforms and made such a nuisance of themselves that in 1912, with the blessing of the tsar, Sukhomlinov dispersed them to garrisons around the empire.[33]

A contentious atmosphere surrounded the implementation of reforms, much of it caused by differing conceptions of how to fight the next war—either exclusively on the offensive or beginning on the defensive. Those such as Sukhomlinov who thought the initial phase of a war with Germany and/or Austria-Hungary would depend on defensive maneuvering wanted to decommission most of the fortresses in Poland and transfer their men and armaments to the field forces. His proposal caused a huge controversy as the traditionalists who feared that starting on the defensive risked yielding territory. The contest ended with Sukhomlinov on the losing side. Not only did the old forts stay, but worse—Nicholas II, supported by archconservatives in the State Duma and his imperial suite, forced the Ministry of War to divert funding to upgrade them at the expense of the field forces' acquiring more artillery and ammunition. Eventually, the numbers of light artillery were made good, but not heavy artillery, with unfortunate consequences during the world war.

On the positive side, before its demise, the State Defense Council established a Supreme Attestation Commission, which had the task of weeding out incompetent and superannuated officers. In what was called "the slaughter of the innocents," the commission forcibly dismissed or retired 7,000 officers, scores of whom were over seventy years old. The minister of war, General Rediger, replaced nearly every regiment, brigade, division, and corps commander. Incompetence was measured by failures in Manchuria and in maintaining order during the Revolution of 1905. In their place, younger and generally more proficient officers were promoted.[34] Although many ultraconservative officers remained, the move did give a boost to the rising generation of professionally minded officers, making its voice more prominent in the debates about military reform.

Doctrine Revisited

In the aftermath of the Russo-Japanese War, Russian military intellectuals debated how Russia should reorient its thinking about preparing for and waging future war. Building on ideas that had circulated since the 1890s, many argued that modern wars were not destined to be like the relatively short wars of recent years (the German wars of unification, the suppression of the Polish revolt, the Russo-Turkish War, the Boer War, or the Russo-Japanese War) but could easily—due to the growth of industrialization, economic potential, and the size of populations—turn into protracted struggles that called on the total material, human, and moral resources of a nation to achieve victory.

General Mikhnevich challenged the assumption that the next war would end quickly in victory. Instead, planning needed to anticipate the potential for protracted operations that required a firm link between domestic and foreign policies. According to Mikhnevich's *Strategy*, Russia had the advantages of a strong monarchy (presumably better for fighting wars than weak monarchies or democracies) and the Russian people's supposed "combative spirit," and Russia's economic backwardness meant that it would be less disrupted by prolonged war. He was against taking the offensive too early in a war, before Russia was ready, and therefore advocated starting on the defensive and, if necessary, trading space for time. He did not, however, advocate intentionally giving up territory.[35]

Colonel Neznamov argued that the scale and fluidity of modern wars, such as the Russo-Turkish War, the German wars of unification, and the Russo-Japanese War, indicated that armies needed a unity of outlook on how to prepare for and conduct battles and operations rather than Russia's current practice of leaving everything up to the discretion of unit commanders. This led Neznamov to propose a "Unified Military Doctrine" just as Russia was preparing its new (1912) field regulations. In 1911, in *Contemporary War*, Neznamov advocated that for success in twentieth-century warfare, in general terms, the state and nation needed to coordinate all military, economic, and diplomatic resources to maximize their potential in the interests of conducting successful operations and sustaining a protracted conflict.[36]

Reaction was swift and immediate in the military press. While developing Mobilization Schedule 19, Col. Alexander Svechin—a Young Turk of the General Staff—took Mikhnevich's and Neznamov's thinking in a slightly different direction: he argued that the army should think of going on the offensive at first but needed to be prepared to revert to defense if the offensive did not return decisive results. The time on defense would then be used to prepare to resume the offensive. All other Russian thinkers on the subject thought in terms of being perpetually on the offensive and retaining the initiative. Svechin's idea did not gain wide attention or acceptance.

Russian nationalists branded Mikhnevich, Neznamov, and the "Young Turks" who looked to the West for inspiration with the pejorative "Western-izers." These nationalists, who included such prominent figures as Generals Ku-ropatkin and Sukhomlinov, wanted to look to Russian history for inspiration and not have "alien" Western ideas forced on them. They believed in Russian military exceptionalism and carried forward Dragomirov's earlier objections to the idea of any doctrine as though it would quash the power and right of the commander in the field to make judgments according to the tactical situation. They imagined that doctrine would bind commanders to respond to all battle-field situations according to some formula. In their minds, doctrine equated to dogma. A debate raged in the military periodical press in 1911–12 until Nicho-las II intervened, forbidding further discussion of a Unified Military Doctrine. He proclaimed, "Military doctrine consists of doing everything which I order."[37]

Besides the tsar's objections, perhaps the greatest obstacles to creating a unified doctrine were the rivalry between ministries and the resistance of the government to working with the State Duma, which prevented the nec-essary unity to coordinate the empire's resources in the interest of national defense. There was a perception among the tsar's ministers that the legislature was antimilitary. Distrusting the patriotism and loyalty of the majority of the State Duma as well as the competence of civilians to judge military affairs, the Ministry of War and Ministry of the Navy kept secret from the State Duma their legislative programs and proposals. The Duma, in reaction, created the Commission for National Defense with the right of interpellation to inquire about important matters. This alarmed military leaders because they thought leftist legislators would use information gained thereby to obstruct their rear-mament programs. To assuage their fears while trying to make progress, some conscientious generals in the Ministry of War formed an unofficial committee to work behind the scenes sharing information with Duma moderates on the commission. This unofficial committee kept itself secret from the tsar and his other ministers.[38]

The tsar's behavior created disunity in the army, which served to keep him the focal point of decision-making. While the State Defense Council existed, members of the General Staff, the inspectors general, and even military district commanders could go to the tsar through it and avoid the Ministry of War. At other times, high-ranking and well-connected generals used personal relations with the tsar or members of the royal family to plead their cases when rebuffed by the minister of war. When minister of war, General Rediger critically observed that "in the military department there is no place for dual power."[39]

New field regulations published in 1912 reflected the army's divided vision of war. On the one hand, they laid out new procedures and methods for commanders to adapt their tactics to reflect the changes in the lethality and effectiveness of modern weaponry, which the Russian army had experienced firsthand in Manchuria. Tactical doctrine emphasized fire and movement, use of cover and concealment, field fortification, and the action of all arms (infantry, artillery, and cavalry) in concerted offensive action. The regulations also raised awareness of the effects of machine-gun fire and rapid artillery fire. On the other hand, those procedures were grafted onto the outmoded battle formations of the nineteenth century. Offensive action and maintaining the initiative against the enemy were emphasized, along with the need for spirit and skill of commanders to keep the enemy off balance. The field regulations reaffirmed the long-held thinking that victory came through direct, head-on assaults against the enemy.[40]

The Desire for Professionalization

From the turn of the century to the demise of the Imperial Russian Army in 1917, the officer corps gradually increased its level of professionalism, the hallmark of which was promotion based on talent and merit. The transition was pushed forward by numerous factors. The advance of technology placed ever more emphasis on technical knowledge and expertise at the expense of natural leadership qualities. The bureaucratization of careers put officers' advancement in the hands of the Ministry of War at the expense of regiment commanders. Social change associated with economic development and the expansion of public education created opportunities for more commoners to serve as officers who then expected to advance by merit, not by virtue of social background or wealth. Finally, the failure of the army in Manchuria laid bare the deficiencies of the autocratic system that primarily promoted men based on social connections and standing. Society at large, as revealed by the Revolution of 1905, expected fundamental changes in Russia's social and political structure, which the army needed to mirror. The creation of the State Duma under the Fundamental Laws promulgated in 1906 transformed Russia into a constitutional monarchy in which many officers saw themselves serving the nation first and the tsar second bolstered the basic underpinnings of a professional army.

Before the Russo-Japanese War, some officers, bravely challenging the status quo, called for an end to the favored position of the Guards in promotion and command assignments, reiterating the long-held desire of line officers for promotions based on merit. Nicholas II harshly rejected such appeals. The desire for a merit-based promotion system only increased after the loss of that war, which revealed the pervasive incompetence regnant among senior officers. Those who favored advancement by merit supported the bureaucratization of careers under the Ministry of War to remove preferential treatment for the royal family's favorites. With the adoption of the 1906 constitution, the officer corps became more politicized, seeing themselves as an interest group that could use legislative politics to their advantage, to Nicholas II's anger and dismay. Military intellectuals generally accepted the Duma and the constitution as positive developments and accepted the army's subordination to the legally constituted authorities at the expense of the personal control of the tsar. Nicholas II jealously guarded his prerogatives over the army from the State Duma and State Defense Council, and quashed talk critical of the Guards. He had no intention of relinquishing control over officer personnel matters, into which the State Duma tried to insert itself, and he was suspicious of Ministry of War–Duma contacts.

In January 1906, a group of young officers—Lt.-Col. V. A. Apukhtin, Cols. V. F. Novitskii and A. V. Shvarts, and Capt. N. K. Shneur—founded the newspaper *Voice of the Military*. In its pages they raised the issue of military reform and suggested concrete actions, a veritable call to change the military culture of the Imperial Army. In an article that conservatives found provocative, Gen. D. Parskii wrote that the spirit of the army had been destroyed by the Russo-Japanese War and needed to be reborn. He noted that both officers and soldiers needed to be better educated, and he advocated that education standards be raised for officer candidates; they had not changed since Miliutin established them in the 1860s despite the expansion of public education over the past forty years. Parskii pointed out that discipline in the army was based on fear and called for officers to create disciplinary procedures based on a sense of duty and patriotism. He again voiced the feeling of many officers that special treatment for the Guards and General Staff–trained officers should be done away with so there would be a uniform and predictable system of career advancement open to all officers. He wanted the Ministry of War to devise a better way of assessing the merits of men nominated for promotion to general—a veiled criticism of the unchecked favoritism all knew existed. Promoting the idea that soldiers were also citizens, he advanced the idea that the military legal system ought to ensure the protection of individual and collective rights of soldiers, treating them as individuals under the law. This, he argued, would improve discipline, and motivate soldiers to fight harder. These and similar progressive ideas for internal reform raised the ire of powerful, conservative elements of the army who conspired to have the newspaper shut down after only nine months in print.[41]

Minister of War General Rediger proposed in 1906, in response to criticisms of the dysfunctional culture of officer promotions, to create promotion commissions to take charge of promotions at the regimental and divisional levels. One aspect of the problem was, according to Gen. Aleksei Brusilov, that "with characteristic Russian good-nature and spinelessness, they [corps and division commanders] gave undeserving candidates favorable reports in the hope that they might get rid of them to some other appointment without their having any cause for resentment or complaints of harsh treatment."[42] The General Staff was notorious for sending incompetent genshtabists to command regiments just to get them off the staff with no intention of letting them return. A similar problem was that of incompetent Guards officers being sent to command line regiments to get them out of the Guards. The powerful military district commanders, however, opposed creating promotion committees because that would diminish their own influence. When the State Defense Council took up the matter, Grand Duke Nikolai Nikolaevich spoke strongly against the commissions. He thought regiment and division commanders should merely do a better job vetting their subordinates. As a result, the army created advisory commissions at division, corps, and district levels—which changed nothing.

Rediger, intending to raise the level of officer competence, founded infantry and cavalry courses of instruction for officers slated to take command of companies or squadrons. He instructed every military district to create them. For the infantry, instruction emphasized tactics and the use of the machine gun. For cavalry, the focus was reconnaissance and fording rivers. Indicative of the resistance to reform was the inspector general of infantry forces, Gen. Nikolai Zarubaev, who claimed there was no need for such precommand schools and argued against their creation. The inspector general of cavalry, Gen. Mikhail Ostrogradskii, also considered them unnecessary. Ignoring their objections, the Kyiv and Moscow Military Districts founded precommand schools in 1907. Four more districts added courses in 1908. After Rediger left the Ministry of War in 1909, the remaining districts failed to establish precommand courses. His successor, General Sukhomlinov, considered them superfluous.[43]

The Outbreak of War, 1914

As anticipated, Germany and Austria-Hungary declared war (on 1 August and 6 August, respectively), thereby triggering Russia to take the offensive at the outset as the General Staff had promised the French. On the eve of the war, the Russian army was the largest in Europe with 1.4 million men, and plans to add another 480,000 over the next twelve months. The Russian army rapidly expanded by successfully calling up more than 3 million reservists. For the duration of the war, the army maintained a strength of around 6 million men by conscription and calling up the opolchenie.

During the July Crisis, the Ministry of War, expecting the imminent outbreak of hostilities and wanting to gain all the time it could, secretly began to mobilize on 24 July, with General Sukhomlinov issuing a "premobilization" order, setting the wheels in motion even before the Serbs replied to the Austro-Hungarian ultimatum. Nicholas's impulse was to order a *partial* mobilization against Austria-Hungary on 29 July, which the army had no way to implement without Schedule 19 (A) being fatally undermined. Sukhomlinov set about convincing Nicholas II to declare a general mobilization, which the tsar did the next day, at which time the army began mobilizing in earnest according to Schedule 19 (A), intending to attack both Germany and Austria-Hungary on M+15. The order for reservists to report for duty went out to the military districts, where preliminary steps had already been taken, and from there to cities, towns, and villages throughout the empire. Millions of reservists said their goodbyes and headed to their designated military commissions to report. Reacting to German protests, Tsar Nicholas II directed the army to cease general mobilization, but to instead selectively mobilize against Austria-Hungary. After some hours of confusion and indecision, Sukhomlinov convinced the tsar that any change would throw the whole process—especially the carefully planned railroad time schedules—into chaos. Nicholas II relented and informed his cousin, Kaiser Wilhelm II, that Russia would not cease to concentrate troops on the East Prussian border, though saying he had no intention of attacking Germany (despite the fact his military did!). On 31 July, Wilhelm II issued his infamous ultimatum that if Russia did not cease to mobilize against Germany, it would mean war. Thus, both the German and the Russian generals got the war they wanted, whereas Nicholas II had wanted to wage war just against Austria-Hungary.

The initial mobilization in 1914, which lasted to the end of August, gathered in more than 3.4 million men and 1.1 million horses, bringing the strength of the army up to 4.9 million men. The war plans called for conducting operations to victory with 5.3 million men organized into 28 cavalry divisions and 114 infantry divisions (78 of which existed before hostilities commenced and 36 of which were created at the time of mobilization). The other 400,000 men would come from drafts of new recruits and the second line of reservists, the opolchenie. Despite many disturbances, protests, and drunken riots, the mobilization succeeded in delivering the requisite number of soldiers, thus enabling the Russian army to attack on time and in great strength.

As in every previous war, procuring sufficient officers to man an expanded army required emergency measures. As in the past, the Ministry of War allowed cadets in cadet corps and junker schools to graduate and commission early and called up reserve officers. These measures did not come close to meeting the leadership needs of an army that had tripled in size overnight. To make up the shortfall, the army reduced the time of instruction in the junker schools and of all the military schools from two or more years to just three to four months for the infantry and six to eight months for the artillery, engineers, and cavalry, to get officers to the units faster. With this accelerated training, the cadet corps and junker schools produced 78,581 military school–trained junior officers.[44]

In an unprecedent move, the army appointed 172,000 temporary wartime officers at the rank of ensign, which did not carry the status of a regular commission. The variation in social backgrounds led to a diverse mix of men. They came from all classes: nearly 25 percent from the peasantry; large numbers of teachers, middle-class urbanites, tradesmen, shopkeepers—virtually all walks of life. Fewer came from the nobility, and the working class contributed the fewest. Educational requirements were lowered to just four years of primary schooling. Many ensigns came with good educations and positive motivations. The army also promoted many enlisted men who were tactically proficient and related well with the men.

To prepare them for their duties, the army created dozens of schools for ensigns with courses of instruction lasting up to six months. These schools produced 108,970 junior officers. Another 30,000 ensigns were added by direct promotion, of whom about 10,500 were vol'nopers and NCOs who passed the officer examination administered by military district and were then sent to three months of officer training. An additional 11,500 soldiers and NCOs were promoted for bravery or outstanding service in combat. Regimental commanders used their authority to promote about 8,000 men with satisfactory educational backgrounds to ensign. Nearly 20,000 men, many of them non-commissioned officers, were awarded battlefield promotions but were not sent to get additional training.[45]

Snobbery on the part of aristocratic regular officers created tension between these new lower-class, hastily trained, and often undereducated officers and the prewar regular officers. The Russian officer corps had a saying that a chicken was not a bird, an ensign was not an officer, and his wife was not a lady, and in this spirit regular officers sometimes maltreated ensigns in front of the men, diminishing respect for both officers and ensigns. Nobles were often condescending and, worst of all, rarely took ensigns seriously as officers; therefore, they did not invest in their professional development, to the detriment of overall military effectiveness. Noble regular officers generally treated noble ensigns well, viewed middle-class ensigns with suspicion, and had no regard at all for peasant or working-class ensigns. Nonnoble regular officers generally got on well with their ensigns. Nonetheless, on the whole, the ensigns carried out their frontline leadership duties with courage and to the best of their abilities.

The Course of the Great Patriotic War of the Fatherland

The plan against Germany was to attack and crush the small number of forces in East Prussia using two Russian armies that outnumbered the Germans nearly four to one, and then to march on Berlin. The three Russian armies assembled against Austria-Hungary were to advance through Polish Galicia, cross the Carpathian Mountains, and advance on to Budapest and thence to Vienna. Even before operations commenced, however, Stavka altered the mobilization and war plans. As mobilization proceeded, Stavka began preparing a supplemental operation at the request of the French. The First Army of the Northwest *Front* lost a corps (I Corps) that, along with the Guards Corps taken from the Southwest *Front*, would form the basis of a new Ninth Army. The Ninth Army was to conduct an offensive aimed directly at Berlin, while both the Northwest and Southwest *Fronts* were still fighting their opening engagements with the Central Powers.[46]

Tsar Nicholas II chose poorly when he appointed Grand Duke Nikolai Nikolaevich to serve as head of the field army; that is, commander of Stavka. The grand duke had no strategic vision and "led" by consensus. Rather than propose a course of action and ask for feedback, he posed a problem and left his subordinates to suggest plans of action, chose from among them, and then worked to achieve consensus through compromise. The tsar, perhaps cognizant of Nikolai Nikolaevich's shortcomings, did not let him pick his own staff. Instead, Nicholas assigned the chief of the General Staff, Gen. Nikolai Ianushkevich, to be the grand duke's chief of staff and General Danilov to be Ianushkevich's chief of operations. These men had a "Germany first" bias and therefore focused their energies mainly in that direction, rather than toward Austria-Hungary. They felt driven by the need to defeat Germany in the first sixty days, before Germany could defeat France and redirect its forces to the eastern front.

Due to poor Russian generalship and competent German leadership, the attack on East Prussia in August 1914 turned into a major defeat for Russia and led to the destruction of two Russian armies, the First Army under Gen. Pavel von Rennenkampf, as well as the Second Army under Gen. Alexander Samsonov. Together, the armies suffered 250,000 casualties at the twin Battles of Tannenberg and Masurian Lakes in August and September 1914. Some of the same defects that led to defeat in Manchuria in 1904 were evident in East Prussia, especially poor reconnaissance by cavalry. Samsonov's career had not prepared him to command an army-sized unit of six corps—it was his good standing with the tsar and peacetime position of military district commander that got him the assignment, which he had not sought. Amateurish use of radio communications, namely talking in the clear, enabled the Germans to intercept Russian orders and react accordingly. A lack of communication with and co-ordination of the two Russian armies by Zhilinskii doomed Samsonov's army to be surrounded while the overly cautious Rennenkampf's army stood idle.[47]

The attack into Galicia against the Austro-Hungarians fared much better. After fierce fighting, the Russian armies occupied Galicia and advanced to the Carpathians, where they stalled after sustaining considerable casualties. Nevertheless, the initial successes against the Austrians failed to be decisive for several reasons: first, the Austro-Hungarians were able to retreat rapidly enough to avoid being encircled or overrun; second, Germany sent reinforcements to shore up the Austro-Hungarian army; third, inadequate logistics, especially overtaxed railroads, could not support further advance; and finally, Russia was unable to deliver reinforcements to replace losses and rotate out exhausted units.

In East Prussia, the Russian army went over to the defensive, whereas against the Austro-Hungarians they continued to fight through the winter in grueling attritional warfare, with neither side making appreciable gains. In central Po-land, it was the Germans who took the initiative in October, launching a major offensive against Warsaw. The Russian forces, directed by General Nikolai Ivanov, not only successfully defended the approaches to Warsaw but turned the tables on the Germans, forcing them back.[48] For the rest of 1914, there was near-continuous campaigning in Poland with neither side able to achieve break-throughs, encirclements, or inflict serious defeats. Historians agree that had Russia attacked either Germany or Austria-Hungary and defended against the other, it would have had a decent chance of success, but events show that Russia did not have the resources to mount and sustain successful offensive operations against both Central Powers simultaneously.

1915

Rather than concentrate their forces against one foe, Stavka and Grand Duke Nikolai Nikolaevich planned to undertake twin offensives in 1915: one against the Germans in East Prussia, and the other against the Austro-Hungarians. They hoped to win a battle of annihilation against the Habsburg army, break through to the plains of Hungary, and force Austria-Hungary to the peace table. These plans came to naught when a combined German and Austro-Hungarian offensive thrusting out of Galicia in the vicinity of Tarnow-Gorlice in mid-May caught the Russians by surprise, overwhelmed them, and threatened to get behind the forces in the Carpathians. To avoid encirclement, the Russian army beat a hasty retreat. Then the Germans attacked in central and northern Poland and, in a period of five months, forced the Russians out of Poland and back nearly to Riga, while in the south the Russian armies gave up all their gains and were forced back into Belorussia and Ukraine. Losses in the 1915 summer campaign were an astronomical 1,410,000 men killed, wounded, or missing, and 976,000 taken prisoner. For the entire year, the Russian army suffered 2 million killed and wounded soldiers and lost 1.3 million men lost as prisoners, which precipitated crises in morale and manpower.[49] The Ministry of War handled the personnel issue by lowering the draft age from twenty-one to nineteen. Another problem that challenged the army's ability to wage war and was never fully overcome was a shortage of weaponry and ordnance: from heavy artillery to rifles to ammunition.

Frustrated by Grand Duke Nikolai Nikolaevich's failure in command, Nicholas II decided to make himself the commander in chief in the field, which he thought would restore the military's morale and raise public confidence in the army. This decision was not welcomed by Stavka and most senior officers, who had little regard for Nicholas either as a person or as a ruler, and certainly not as a military commander. Nicholas II did not really intend to command the army or direct the war; he wanted to play the role of inspirational figurehead. He appointed Gen. Mikhail Alekseev to be his chief of staff and de facto head of the army in the field. Nicholas's presence at Stavka proved to be every bit the distraction his grandfather's had been in the Russo-Turkish War. Court politics and intrigue inevitably made their way to Mogilev, the location of Stavka. In the tsar's absence from the capital, renamed Petrograd at the start of the war, salacious rumors about the Orthodox monk Rasputin and the empress began to circulate, further undermining confidence in the government, the war effort, and Nicholas himself. Nicholas and Alexeev did no better than Nikolai Nikolaevich and Ianushkevich; they too failed to devise a grand strategy to win the war. The tsar and Stavka generally accepted the idea that Russia would not be able to force a decision on the eastern front and that the war would be decided in France.

1916

In 1916, the army made no progress against the Germans in the short-lived and disastrous Lake Naroch offensive in March meant to aid the French at Verdun and to bring Romania into the war on the side of the Entente. The pompous and indecisive Gen. Aleksei Evert, commander of the Northwest *Front*, divided its armies to attack on the north and south of Lake Naroch, with the goal of cutting off the right flank of the German positions in the direction of Kovel. The *front* also launched diversionary attacks to hold German reserves in place. The Germans, however, perceived the intent of the Russian maneuvers and prepared accordingly. Although the Northwest *Front* unleashed an intense artillery barrage on 15 March, the attack was doomed because the spring thaw had come, and combined with rain, warmer temperatures turned the flat and wide-open no-man's-land into a muddy morass ideal for German machine gunners to mow down the slowly advancing Russian soldiers. After only a few days, the offensive was called off. The Russians, who began the offensive with 360,000 soldiers against 50,000 German defenders, suffered 100,000 casualties; German losses were negligible.[50] Russian morale suffered accordingly.

In June, the Russian army enjoyed a major success against the Austro-Hungarians in the Brusilov Offensive launched out of Ukraine, which pushed the Austro-Hungarian army back along a two-hundred-mile front. Stavka's strategic goal for the offensive was to inflict serious enough losses on the Austro-Hungarians to convince them to withdraw from the war. The immediate goal was to push the Austrians back, in hopes of restoring Russian morale and forcing the Germans to fall back to protect their open flank. Stavka hoped that success would make up for the failure at Lake Naroch, take pressure off the French at Verdun, and bring Romania into the war. The offensive was driven by the immediate needs of the alliance, rather than a larger strategic vision.

The plan was to launch a coordinated two-pronged offensive: one thrust led by General Brusilov, commander of the Southwest *Front*, against the Habsburg forces, and the other led by the incompetent and ill-fated General Evert, recently transferred to command the Western *Front*, against the neighboring German forces. It was hoped that the Southwest *Front*'s attack would draw the Germans off General Evert's Western *Front* preparatory to his attack. Brusilov's forces attacked according to plan, and the Germans did send troops to bolster the Austro-Hungarian forces. Evert, however, without warning Brusilov, delayed his attack by two weeks, claiming his forces were not ready. He thus missed the opportunity to advance against a weakened German force. While Evert dithered, the Germans used the time to transfer troops from France, thereby enabling them to defeat his tardy strike.[51]

Still, the offensive did manage to eviscerate the Austro-Hungarian army, and morale among the Russians slightly improved, predictably relations between Brusilov and Evert suffered. Russia's casualties for the year were 2,060,000 killed and wounded (most of whom were lost in the Lake Naroch and Brusilov offensives) and 344,000 men lost as prisoners of war. Despite the victory, the extent of Russian losses prevented a significant rise in morale. The people of Russia and the soldiers began to think that the high command was incompetent and that the losses were unnecessary. People were skeptical that the recent offensive had brought Russia any closer to winning.[52] There is no evidence to suggest that the offensive caused General Alekseev to change his pessimistic outlook on the war. In March, he had told Stavka, "You see, I know that we will lose the war, that we cannot possibly win it."[53] A few still hoped that Russia could hold on until the war was decided in the west.

Some of Alekseev's pessimism may have stemmed from manpower issues. In the spring of 1915, the tsar had ordered the calling up of the second tier of the opolchenie, the men who had escaped the lottery and never served. These men thought they were exempt from ever serving and protested their call-up with petitions and demonstrations. Most did report for duty but with very poor attitudes. In 1916, to further augment the army, the Ministry of War decided to conscript Central Asians (who had never before been subject to conscription) for army labor detachments. This led to open revolt by Kazakhs, Kirghiz, and Turkmen that required the diversion of several divisions of Russian troops to suppress the uprising.[54]

After Brusilov's success, Romania did enter the war alongside Russia on the eastern front in August 1916, but this proved to be a burden rather than a blessing. In short order, the Germans overran most of the country, causing Russia to divert manpower from the other *fronts* to save what was left of it.

In addition to fighting Germany and Austria-Hungary, Russia had to deploy forces to take on the Ottoman Empire, which had come into the war in November 1914. The Russian army did well in fighting in the Caucasus, taking the key city and fortress of Erzurum in 1916, after which both sides limited their investment of men and munitions, preferring to focus their efforts on other military fronts.

1917

Morale among Russian soldiers was never high during the war, and civil society failed to fully invest in the conflict. Though the tsarist government tried, it was unable to convince the majority of its citizens of the justice of its cause and of the need for the level of sacrifice that resulted. Draft evasion and desertion plagued the army from the beginning. By October 1917, the army had suffered close to 1 million cases of desertion. Thousands, perhaps tens of thousands, crossed enemy lines to surrender. A great many soldiers did not believe in the war and distrusted their officers. Others were skeptical of the efficacy of the autocracy and lost faith in the tsar. Still others were alienated by the failure of the constitutional system to improve the lot of the peasantry. These feelings were reinforced by the rather small urban-based antiwar movement of mostly leftist students whose main activity was to denounce the war to workers and disrupt the draft of university students. The soldiers' doubts and feelings manifested themselves in a hesitancy to press home attacks because, though they believed

Russia was worth defending, they did not consider it worth dying for on the offensive. Still, individual acts of valor, daring, and courage abounded.

Discipline began to unravel in mid-1916 with refusals to attack, to return to the trenches on rotation, and to carry out work details. Officers considered collective refusals of this nature to be mutiny and dealt with them harshly, which further alienated the men. From November 1916 to February 1917, executions of ringleaders of mutinies became commonplace. Obedient troops were used to force recalcitrant soldiers forward to the trenches at the point of bayonets. The huge number of casualties motivated many of the mutinies. By mid-1916, men routinely referred to themselves in letters home as cattle being led to slaughter.

The February Revolution

The disloyalty of the common soldiers, the high command, and the Petrograd garrison were instrumental in the revolution that brought down the autocracy. On the fourth day of rioting in the capital brought on by hunger and economic hardship, the soldiers of the garrison joined the workers in calling for an end to the autocracy. They marched on the Tauride Palace and called on the Duma to create a new government. The Duma contacted Stavka and sent a delegation to negotiate a transfer of power with the intention of keeping the tsar as a figurehead while creating a responsible parliamentary government headed by a prime minister. The generals at Stavka, headed by Alekseev, having weeks earlier entertained the idea of supporting Grand Duke Nikolai Nikolaevich in a coup to replace the tsar, whom they blamed for Russia's problems, opted (with the endorsement of every *front*, army, and corps commander) to force Nicholas II to abdicate. Nicholas did abdicate to his son Alexei on 2 March but then reconsidered and abdicated again naming his brother Grand Duke Mikhail Alexandrovich tsar. Mikhail, taken by surprise and facing death threats from the revolutionary parties in Petrograd, refused the throne, which left Russia to become a republic—something neither the Duma nor the generals had sought.

With the tsar's abdication and the creation of two competing centers of power—the Provisional Government of State Duma members, and the Petrograd Soviet of Workers' and Soldiers' Deputies—command and control in the army began to unravel. Order No. 1 of the Petrograd Soviet, issued even before the tsar had abdicated, called on the soldiers of the Petrograd garrison to form committees to defend their interests against the officers. Soldiers at the front and in other garrisons, when they heard about Order No. 1, also formed committees. From that point on, officers could no longer expect their orders to be obeyed without the soldiers first holding meetings and voting on whether they would comply. Discipline, fraught since the previous summer, worsened.

Soldiers demanded that unpopular officers be removed from command and, in many cases, elected officers to replace them. It seemed improbable that the army would ever be able to launch another offensive. The French had insisted that Russia launch an offensive early in the spring, but Stavka wisely refused.[55]

Unlikely as it first seemed, the Russian army was able to go on the attack late in June 1917. Minister of War Alexander Kerensky managed to convince the majority of soldiers in the Southwest *Front* to agree to launch an offensive (called both the "June offensive" and "Kerensky offensive") against the Austro-Hungarians. When it came time to attack, the soldiers of several divisions changed their minds and refused to engage. Nonetheless, the attack went ahead and sent the enemy reeling, but only temporarily. The Austro-Hungarians regrouped and, with German support, counterattacked, forcing the Russians to retreat beyond their initial positions. After almost three weeks of fighting, when the Austro-Hungarians and Germans were exhausted, the Russians had lost hundreds of square miles of territory and suffered about 60,000 casualties. From that point on, discipline became tenuous, and the army would stay on the defensive until the Bolsheviks signed the Treaty of Brest-Litovsk in March 1918 quitting the war.

The Franco-Russian alliance determined the course of Russian military history between 1894 and 1917. In the span of a few years, it morphed from a defensive idea to an offensive plan. Military planning revolved around preparing for war with the Central Powers. The Russo-Japanese War, though militarily a fiasco, showed again the efficacy of the reserve system created by Miliutin. The loss led to a major rearmament program to update the weaponry and equipment of the Russian army and a purge of superannuated and incompetent senior officers.

Contrary to a century's worth of opinion, the tsarist army did not lose the First World War. At the time of the tsar's abdication, the army was still in the field and ready to fight, reluctantly, to be sure. At the time of the Bolshevik seizure of power in October 1917, despite the chaos in command and control, and deterioration of discipline, the bulk of the army was still in the field determined to defend the nation, and Germany had not dared to weaken its forces on the eastern front. Germany did not begin to transfer soldiers to the west until after the Bolsheviks had concluded an armistice in November and abolished the officer corps in December. Despite its inability and unwillingness to go on the attack, Russia's army did not become militarily ineffective until February 1918, when the breakdown of peace talks led to mass desertions from the front. At this point, under Bolshevik command, the war was lost.

CHAPTER 4

THE FORMATIVE YEARS OF THE RED ARMY, 1917–1945

O ver the span of the thirty years from 1917 to 1946, the Russian military was in continual transformation: first attempting to move away from the practices and mindset of the tsarist army to a revolutionary army based on Marxist ideals, followed by gradual mutation along the lines of traditional Western models of national armies but with a substantial continuity with modes and methods of the old army. The October Revolution began a deliberate radical transformation, the lessons of the Russian Civil War tempered the radicalism, then the Second World War served as the catalyst for conservative change. In 1939, the army of the Soviet Union began the Second World War as the Workers' and Peasants' Red Army (RKKA), but within a year of the war's conclusion, it was renamed the Soviet Army. Behind the change of name were the effects of two decades of political maturation of the Soviet state, serious study of contemporary military developments through the lens of tsarist military thought, and the cataclysm of world war. After the civil war and war with Poland, the new government reduced the size of the army dramatically, against the wishes of the military, but a decade later it would begin to grow again. In the 1920s, the Soviet state initially adopted a policy of defense, which, in the late 1930s gave way to a foreign policy of territorial reacquisition under Stalin. Using military intimidation and aggression, Stalin intended to restore to the USSR the former territories the tsarist empire lost during the civil war. Once those territories were regained, the Soviet Union again adopted a defensive posture. Like the tsars, Bolshevik Party leaders exercised their prerogative as commanders in chief to make operational and strategic decisions.

Bolshevik Conceptions of the Military

The years 1917–23 saw the abolition of the Imperial Russian Army and the creation of the Red Army. These years included the First World War, the

Russian Civil War, the Polish-Soviet war, wars with secessionist national minorities, and fighting with anarchic peasants and the forces of foreign armies intervening in the civil war. The Red Army that eventually emerged from this period of strife was the result of compromises between the real and the ideal. It was founded by revolutionary socialists who feared armies and did not really want an army because they viewed armies as repressive organs of the bourgeois state.

Before they seized power in October 1917, the leaders of the Bolshevik Party—Vladimir Lenin and Leon Trotsky in particular—having chosen to mount a coup rather than mobilize a popular revolution, reluctantly admitted that they needed some sort of an armed force to maintain their party in power, and then to defend the country until the imminent world revolution obviated the need for armies. In the months before the October Revolution, they discussed creating what they termed an "army of a new type." Rather than remake the Imperial Army along socialist lines, they, following Marx's urging in his *Communist Manifesto*, decided to abolish the old army altogether. The soldiers were exhausted by the war, and the officers were thought to be all reactionary defenders of the old regime. To replace it they planned to create an entirely new military based on a popular militia—an all-volunteer force filled with class-conscious workers who understood their social obligation to serve the interests of the revolution and a free people. In their idealism, the Bolsheviks imagined that the leaders and led would be comrades rather than superior and subordinate, united by a desire to serve the revolution. Rather than being a tool of imperial aggression or internal oppression, the primary purpose of this army would be, first, to defend the revolution against aggression by capitalist states and, second, to carry Marxist revolutionary ideals and freedoms by the force of arms to the workers of the world. Above all, it was to be the antithesis of the Imperial Russian Army, which treated its soldiers brutally and was used to suppress Russia's peoples.

The Bolsheviks struggled to reconcile their ideology and revolutionary goals with the idea of having an army. Ignorant of the immensity of what he proposed, Lenin and his fellow revolutionaries failed to appreciate that Russian society was unprepared to create his army of a new type. Thus, during 1918–23, the Bolsheviks' army was an improvisation beset by contradictions, which translated into ad hoc organizational decisions being made mostly by people who did not consider or care how those decisions would affect the army in the long run and by others who, contrary to Bolshevik ideology, were working to create a more traditional military institution.

In the months before the October seizure of power, Lenin began to recruit armed workers' detachments (Red Guards) to the Bolshevik cause and send agitators to destabilize the old army. The Bolsheviks greatly benefited from Order No. 1, which undermined the authority of the officers. By the time the Bolsheviks succeeded in overthrowing the Provisional Government, the power of the generals over the army had been broken. Soon after the Bolshevik seizure of power, Lenin's government sought to negotiate an end to the war with the Central Powers. By this time, soldiers had forced out unpopular tsarist officers, and reactionary officers began to desert their posts.

Lenin, determined to pull Russia out of the war, succeeded in arranging a truce in December 1917. In the meantime, the Bolsheviks, while maintaining defenses at the front, began to demobilize the old army and build a new military force based on volunteers and Red Guard detachments. Lenin created a People's Commissariat of War in December 1917, appointing fellow revolutionary Nikolai I. Podvoiskii—at the time serving in the army as a mere ensign—to lead it. The transitioning of Red Guard detachments into army units lasted longer than expected because of deliberate foot-dragging by independent-minded soviets, factory committees, or the Red Guards themselves, who were reluctant to subordinate themselves to Bolshevik control.[1] When they put out the first call for volunteers in February 1918, the Bolsheviks hoped to attract some 750,000 volunteers over the course of a few months; they fell short of their goal, garnering just 450,000.[2]

After the truce expired in February without a peace treaty, the Germans attacked intending to force the Bolsheviks into accepting Berlin's peace terms. The Bolsheviks' ill-trained, ill-equipped, and lightly armed forces were easily swept aside by the German army advancing into Estonia. Subsequently, the German and Austro-Hungarian armies launched an offensive that advanced deep into Ukraine. What was left of the old army melted away in front of them. At that point, Lenin was able to convince the party leadership to accept the humiliating Treaty of Brest-Litovsk.

Founding the Red Army and the Russian Civil War

Immediately after the signing of the peace treaty in March 1918, the Bolsheviks found themselves embroiled in civil conflicts with other leftist parties that they refused to share power with: counterrevolutionary Whites, who were inconsistently supported by foreign powers; anarchist peasants; and subject nationalities seeking independence from the Russian Empire. The fledgling Bolshevik regime, ignorant of the niceties of bureaucracy, cobbled together an inefficient and confused structure of military organizations. There were few clear lines of authority and responsibility between the civilian government, the Bolshevik Party, and the emergent military bureaucracy, which added to the difficulties of running the army and fighting the Bolsheviks' growing list of enemies. Ultimately, the party decided all questions of military policy that had even the remotest of ideological implications.[3]

Lenin responded to the Brest-Litovsk disaster by appointing Trotsky to be commissar of war and instructed him to organize a new standing army, which marked a profound break with the party's previous stand on armies. On 4 March 1918, the Bolsheviks created the Supreme Military Council to co-ordinate all the necessary aspects of raising an army. A former tsarist officer, Gen. Mikhail Bonch-Bruevich, and two Bolshevik commissars headed its staff composed primarily of former tsarist General Staff officers. Trotsky wisely suspended any Marxist utopian strictures that interfered with the practical aspects of forming a regular army based on hierarchy, regulations, and formal discipline. The regime accepted that, at least in the short term, it could not rely on volunteers for manpower and introduced conscription of workers and poor peasants in May 1918. By the end of the year, slightly more than 1 million men had been drafted. The party leadership quickly became infatuated with the potential of the army to teach obedience to hierarchy—both of which the party woefully lacked—and seeing military service as a way to test the loyalty of party members, it vigorously recruited communists.

To administer, train, and even command some units of the Red Army, Trotsky chose to employ (most by compulsion) former tsarist officers—referred to as military specialists. Initially, between July and the end of December 1918, the Red Army mobilized nearly 37,000 former tsarist officers and civilian em-ployees of the army. More than 128,000 former noncommissioned officers were also ordered to report for duty with the Red Army. Within a few months, many of the NCOs were promoted to junior officer rank. By the end of the civil war, some 48,000 former officers, 214,000 former NCOs, and 10,000 former civilian employees had served in the Red Army. Red Army military schools trained more than 53,000 men to be the first cohort of "Red Commanders." Tens of thousands of party members and politically reliable men were simply elected or appointed to be officers with no formal training.[4]

Trotsky's controversial decision to use former officers led to the creation of military councils consisting of the commander, his chief of staff, and a com-missar to command major units. Employed by the Political Administration of the Red Army (PUR), commissars answered to the Bolshevik Party Central Committee, not the Commissariat of War.[5] They were not members of the military, which at times led to rivalries and confusion over who was superior to whom. Trotsky wanted commissars to be responsible for overseeing the loyalty of the military specialists in a relationship in which commissars acted virtu-ally as cocommanders. Many commissars, because of their political reliability, considered themselves superior to the commander.[6]

Besides watching over unit commanders, the Political Administration of the RKKA was to be the party's main mechanism to guide and shape the ideological development of the army. PUR expanded from its initial role of recruiting commissars to organizing communists in the army into primary party organizations (cells), recruiting soldiers into the party, conducting political education of soldiers, and providing literacy instruction. With the help of PUR, the Bolsheviks intended to use the Red Army as a "school of socialism."[7] In the short-term crisis of civil war, the Bolsheviks hoped that political education would bolster the loyalty of the conscripts to the party's cause. In the long term, the Bolsheviks hoped that instruction in Marxism, as well as basic literacy, would create a new class-conscious military.

In the years 1918–23, civilian Bolshevik revolutionaries wielded paramount political power and influence in the army. Tight control by the party shaped the development of the Red Army. Political and class considerations dominated recruitment, retention, and promotion. When it came to selecting leaders from postrevolutionary society, the party looked first to class and political reliability. The party eschewed military professionalism, fearing it would sway the new generation of officers to attach their loyalty to the army rather than to the party.[8] Stalin favored his cronies, and they tended to favor other Bolshevik veterans of the civil war for promotion and important posts. Thousands of military specialists subsequently joined the party to advance their careers.

Military specialists provided vital expertise to the Bolshevik military establishment, particularly its administration. Col. Sergei Kamenev became Trotsky's right-hand man in the Commissariat of War, and Col. Ioakim Vatsetis became the first supreme commander of forces in the field. Without the help of the former tsarist officers, the Red Army would have struggled far longer than it did to achieve what limited organization and capacity it did during the the civil war.

Despite their differences, distrust, and occasional treason by former officers, the Bolsheviks and military specialists managed to work together well enough to win the civil war—but not the war with Poland. All told, throughout the civil war period, the Red Army relied on a few thousand qualified, talented, and energetic individuals to hold together the fractious masses of poorly trained, undependable, mediocre, and unenthusiastic leaders and men. Trotsky often shifted the able from front to front, and from crisis to crisis, because the army's pool of talent and reliability was so shallow. The qualities that the more successful revolutionaries-cum-officers from the peasantry or working class such as Kliment Voroshilov, Semen Budenny, Vasilii Chapaev, Semen Timoshenko, and Josef Apanasenko brought with them to the battlefield were determination, enthusiasm, and the ability to connect with their men. Trotsky labeled future Commissar of War Voroshilov, a worker turned cavalry leader, "a first-rate rabble-rouser," neither in praise nor criticism, but in recognition that his methods worked with the motley assortment of workers, peasants, and Cossacks he led.[9] Lacking technical and tactical expertise, these men led by personal example, showing courage in the face of the enemy. Despite their ignorance of military matters, with the help of mostly unenthusiastic former tsarist officers, the Bolsheviks won the civil war against an ill-supplied, disunited opposition that had scant popular support.

During the civil war, Lenin acted in much the same way as the tsars. As head of state, he acted like a commander in chief inserting himself into strategic and operational matters. Lenin's strategic goals for the war were first and foremost to impose Bolshevik power on the empire, secondly to retain the boundaries of the empire, and thirdly to export revolution. Lenin mostly followed Trotsky's and Vatsetis's advice on which to prioritize but at times intervened to side with one over the other. In November 1918, Lenin overrode Vatsetis, who wanted to concentrate all available forces for a decisive campaign in southern Russia. The eastern front commander begged for more troops to fend off a strong White advance. Vatsetis refused to give up any units, but Lenin intervened and ordered Trotsky to take a brigade from Vatsetis's southern campaign and send it to the eastern front. In June 1919, Lenin and the party's Central Committee again sided with the eastern front at the expense of the southern front. Vatsetis resigned in protest and was replaced by Kamenev. Trotsky also submitted his resignation, but Lenin refused it. Lenin also gave instructions directly to commanders in the field assigning them their priorities.[10] He was not above giving special treatment for military assignments to friends and family.

Like the Imperial Army, the Bolsheviks sought to create a huge army for reasons similar to the tsars': to fight on more than one front and to maintain internal security. Recruitment—voluntary and compulsory—had returned large (nearly 1 million men) but still insufficient numbers of troops by the end of 1918. Facing a better organized foe in 1919, Lenin insisted on further expanding the army to 3 million. On the way to this goal, the high command set a target of recruiting 700,000–800,000 infantry and cavalry by mid-May. Between 100,000 and 120,000 of these men were assigned to suppress internal revolts. Until these numbers could be recruited, the existing soldiers were used to the point of physical and psychological exhaustion because they could not be withdrawn for rest.[11]

Achieving and then maintaining Lenin's 3-million-man army proved to be a difficult task because of widespread aversion to serve the Bolshevik cause. From 1918 to the middle of 1919, more than 1.5 million men refused to report for duty, failed to pass the physical exam for legitimate health reasons and by duplicity, or deserted after reporting for duty. By mid-1919, the army's strength stood at 1.6 million men. By the end of 1920, the Red Army, which had grown to 5.4 million men—on paper—had suffered 3.4 million cases of draft avoidance and desertion—more than 500,000 in the first six months of 1920. Some men deserted multiple times. To combat draft evasion and desertion, Trotsky instituted draconian measures including exemplary executions. He also ordered major units to form blocking detachments and special cavalry battalions to comb the rear areas for deserters. During large-scale sweeps of the rear areas in 1919, the army rounded up 837,000 deserters and draft evaders, of whom 612 "hardcore" deserters were executed and nearly 6,000 imprisoned.[12] Losses through illness and death also depleted the army. In 1919 and 1920, there were more than 1 million cases of illness that kept men from duty. The total death toll of Red Army soldiers from all causes by mid-1921 was 939,755— the majority from disease.[13]

Logistics were a nightmare. The Russian economy, dealt a heavy blow by the Treaty of Brest-Litovsk, steadily contracted during the civil war. Production of all but the most essential military goods virtually ceased by the end of 1919. Even those goods were often in short supply. There was a persistent shortage of boots. The army used its power of requisition extensively, sometimes taking what it needed from civilians at bayonet point. By 1920, roughly half of Soviet Russia's production of sugar, fish, meat, tobacco, soap, textiles, and footwear was taken by the Red Army.

The Bolsheviks' operational strategy for fighting the civil war was essentially defensive at first. Their immediate goal was to hold the major industrial areas, Petrograd and Moscow, and leave the initiative to the enemy while they created their army. In 1918 and 1919, the Red Army attempted a few limited counteroffensives to push back White advances. The summer of 1919 was one of crisis for the Red Army. White offensives out of Siberia, Latvia, and southern Russia threatened to capture Petrograd and Moscow. A massive recruitment drive of workers and Bolsheviks ensued. Trotsky issued an amnesty to all deserters who would return to the colors—hundreds of thousands, mostly peasants, did. Once it achieved superior numbers, the Red Army was able to turn back all three White offensives. After these successes, most of the returned deserters again abandoned the army.

During the autumn of 1919, in the aftermath of the failed White offensives to capture Moscow, the Red Army saw success in the Urals and southern Russia. Trotsky launched campaigns to push the Whites out of southern Russia and into the Crimea, and, aided by a ruthless partisan movement, to push east through the Urals and Siberia to destroy the White forces there. In 1920, when the White cause was waning and the Western allies began to withdraw their support, Lenin was able concentrate on consolidating Bolshevik control over Ukraine, in part through the destruction of Ukraine's former anarchist allies, and to consider a counteroffensive against Polish advances into western Ukraine. Because the Bolsheviks fought on multiple fronts simultaneously in northern and southern Russia, Ukraine, the North Caucasus, the Urals, and Siberia, and had to divert hundreds of thousands of soldiers to requisition grain and suppress peasant anarchist movements, the forces committed to each battle or campaign were never very large, seldom reaching 100,000.[14] The Reds succeeded in conquering Crimea in November 1920 when the White forces under Pyotr Wrangel were evacuated by the British and French navies. Although the leader of the White forces in Siberia, Adm. Alexander Kolchak, was captured and executed in 1920, it took the Reds until 1922 to secure the entirety of that region.

War with Poland

Toward the end of the civil war, the nascent Bolshevik state found itself in a war against Poland, which was trying to establish its eastern border well into Ukraine. The Red Army formed two *fronts*: the Western *Front* commanded by Mikhail Tukhachevskii, and the Southwestern *Front* under the command of former tsarist colonel Alexander Egorov. Lenin's initial strategic goal in this war was to preserve Russia's territorial integrity but exporting revolution westward into Europe became a secondary goal as the war developed. At first, the war went badly for Russia. In the late spring of 1920, the RKKA had a roster of approximately 3.5 million men, including troops of the internal security forces; however, only 640,000 were available to fight on the various fronts. The others had deserted or were being trained, fighting peasant revolts, being treated for wounds or illness, requisitioning food, guarding the railroads, or serving as labor. A bloated rear-area administration also tied up thousands of troops. Against the Poles, the Western *Front* fielded 52,763 men and the Southwestern *Front* 122,786.[15]

Poland attacked in April 1920 driving the outnumbered Soviet forces all the way to Kyiv, capturing it in just two weeks. While the Red Army regrouped preparatory, tens of thousands of men needed against Poland had to be diverted to put down a large-scale peasant revolt in Tambov province—provoked not by ideology but by the Reds' excessive requisitioning and burdensome conscription—and to deal with a White foray out of Crimea. To deal with the manpower crisis brought on by having to fight on three fronts while also suppressing peasant uprisings, the army launched another recruitment campaign. Nearly 1,500 former officers who had to that point evaded serving the Bolsheviks volunteered to fight the Poles.[16]

Having reinforced the Western *Front* with new recruits and by transferring several divisions from other fronts, the Red Army was able to launch a counteroffensive in July. Under Tukhachevskii's able leadership, the Western *Front* was able to break through the Polish defense and advance swiftly all the way to the gates of Warsaw in August. The larger Southwest *Front*, commanded by Egorov with Stalin as his commissar, fought on the left flank of the Western *Front* intending to sweep south of Warsaw. When it appeared that the Red Army was going to crush the Poles, Lenin spoke of continuing the Soviet offensive westward through Poland into Germany and simultaneously launching an offensive south through Romania into the lands of the former Austro-Hungarian Empire. The goal of both offensives was to ignite a Europe-wide revolution.[17] This fantasy lasted but a few weeks before the Poles regrouped and counterattacked.

The Red Army was routed when the Southwest *Front*, fighting on the Western *Front*'s left flank, failed to subordinate its actions to those of the latter, which was considered to be the main force against the Poles. Egorov and Stalin viewed their *front* as acting independently during the war and thus delayed in detaching two armies to serve with the Western *Front*. Without those two armies, Tukhachevskii was unable to decisively defeat the Poles during the advance on Warsaw. As a result, the Poles subsequently launched their war-winning counteroffensive against Tukhachevskii's weakened and worn-out forces. After the war, Tukhachevskii was blamed for failing to insist on a timely transfer of the armies in question. Commander in chief Kamenev was indirectly blamed for not making the relationship between the two *fronts* clear at the outset and directly faulted because, through incompetence in coding messages, his staff lost two days in ordering the transfer of the two armies. The outnumbered Red Army—which was fighting a full-scale war against anti-Bolshevik partisans in its rear—with the two *fronts* split one from the other, was forced back into Ukraine, in the process losing thousands of men to death, wounds, capture, and desertion. Mutinies erupted among the routed units. The two sides agreed to a truce in October and in March 1921 signed the Treaty of Riga ending the war.

The Initial Interwar Years, 1921–1928

The Bolsheviks recognized the need to come to terms with the question of what type of army to have in peacetime once their dreams of world revolution were dashed. During the civil war, a military faction had emerged within the party that had the goal of creating a standing professional army. Bolshevik idealists, however, clung to their hopes of creating a class-conscious citizens' militia army. The debate continued until 1925, when the party's Central Committee compromised, agreeing to create an army consisting of a standing force authorized at just over half a million men and a large territorial militia of several million citizen-soldiers serving part-time, to be trained and led by cadres of regular army personnel. Both forces were manned by conscription. The idealists hoped to eventually disband the regular army and leave the Soviet Union to be defended by a citizen's militia. Both the idealists and the military faction agreed that the army should cease to be used to suppress civilians; that task was handed over to the Ministry of Internal Affairs, which used ordinary police as well as its secret police (variously the Cheka, GPU, OGPU, and from 1934, the NKVD).

The precedent of imposing a universal obligation to serve, set in the imperial period, was embraced by the new Bolshevik regime during the civil war and carried over into peacetime. One important change was made, one that undermined the military's monopolies on the use of national manpower and the use of violence—and hence its institutional identity. Now the obligation to serve would unmistakably mean service to the party/state. Men were to serve not just in the military but also in the paramilitary forces of the border guards, gendarmerie, secret police, and special troops (OMON) of the Ministry of Internal Affairs. The border guards were organized into regiments and divisions and armed on the same basis as the army with tanks, artillery, and even aircraft. For the next one hundred years and beyond, the military had to compete for manpower with the Ministry of Internal Affairs and other independent police forces. Border guards acted as the first line of military defense of the border and in times of war were subordinated to the Ministry of Defense. OMON was tasked with rear-area security and during the civil war played a large role in suppressing anti-Bolshevik civilian uprisings.

Also affecting the military's corporate identity was the fact that, just as in the tsarist era, the military had no police force. Ordinary misbehavior and petty crime were dealt with by the chain of command, but serious crimes required the intervention of the secret police. To keep an eye on the military and ensure its loyalty to the regime, the party not only created PUR, but also assigned a secret police detail, called a "special section," to every regiment to deal with serious crime and root out political dissenters and traitors—especially among the officers. In wartime, the NKVD patrolled the rear areas looking for spies, saboteurs, and deserters. This arrangement would carry over into the post-Soviet period.

The new people's commissar of military and naval affairs, Mikhail Frunze, a full-time revolutionary before the October Revolution, proposed to end the dual command of officers and commissars and give officers sole authority over their units. Some army leaders wanted to abolish PUR altogether. The party insisted on keeping PUR but did agree to limit the commissars' role to political education and maintaining soldiers' morale.[18] With the decision to keep at least a modicum of a standing army, the People's Commissariat of Military and Naval Affairs, later to become the People's Commissariat of Defense, began the process of creating a rational organizational structure to manage manpower and matériel based largely on the model of the old Imperial Army and administered by thousands of former tsarist officers.

Mikhail Frunze took the first steps toward creating a new Bolshevik military doctrine. He borrowed from Mikhnevich, Neznamov, and other strategic thinkers of the late tsarist period and added Marxism, class consciousness, and egalitarianism. He introduced the idea of a unified military doctrine (UMD) to the 8th Party Congress in March 1918. His proposal coincided with the efforts of a party faction, the "military opposition," who wanted to displace Trotsky from his position of commissar of military and naval affairs. Trotsky subjected Frunze's ideas to withering criticism, causing the doctrine to be rejected.[19] After some revision, Frunze resubmitted the UMD to the 10th Party Congress in March 1921. Working within the context of Marx's dictum that war between capitalism and socialism was inevitable, Frunze cast a Marxist hue on many long-accepted ideas of war. Well-read, Frunze was an admirer of Suvorov, impressed by Engel's military writings, and influenced by Lenin's pragmatic policy of "peaceful coexistence," adopted in 1921, that sought to delay the inevitable armed conflict until the Bolshevik state was sure of winning. The gist of Frunze's thinking was, just as Engels and Neznamov each had independently concluded, that the military, political, and economic establishments should be unified in their outlook on what the military's tasks would be (what wars might be fought and how to prepare for them, but now based on a Marxist understanding of class warfare and social organization) and on how the political and economic establishments should organize the population (the working class) and socialist economy to support those tasks.[20] Above all, Frunze insisted that the offensive, conducted by a well-trained regular army, was the only way to victory.

Unity in preparing for and conducting war necessarily meant that the civilian political and economic leadership would be heavily involved in military affairs. Lenin had declared in early 1918 that the party would be the driving force behind the military in its organization, training, and supply and would define its strategic and operational goals. Manning the armed forces would also fall under the purview of the party, which would have a voice in deciding the class composition of the army as well as what kind of armaments would be produced and in what quantity. It was also taken as a given that the Red Army would be fundamentally oriented toward offensive action. The Marxist aspect of the UMD was to ignite class warfare in the rear of the enemy, suppress counterrevolutionary activity in "liberated" territory, and use the international communist movement to influence or disrupt the politics of Russia's adversaries.

Acquisition of modern technology dominated Frunze's thinking as well as that of those who followed him. In 1920, the People's Commissariat of Military and Naval Affairs created a "Commission for researching and applying the experience of the world and civil wars" chaired by Svechin. The commission advocated a deep appreciation for the potential of the new technologies that had emerged during the First World War—in particular the warplane, poison gas, motorized transport, and armored vehicles—to shape future war. Commissioners saw that aircraft could make the rear just as much a combat zone as the front line. They foresaw that combined arms warfare using motorization and mechanization would allow for fast, deep, and hard-hitting offensive operations. Mobilization of the economy would become more important than before because the scale of war could be so much larger, as 1914–18 had shown. Because a nation could not stockpile sufficient munitions and material in peacetime to sustain a long war, plans for industrial mobilization were by necessity part of war planning. To make the best use of new technology, a key concept of the unified military doctrine, Frunze and his successors recognized that the USSR needed a thoroughly educated officer corps.[21]

Trotsky, supported by Svechin and more practically minded albeit shortsighted party leaders, opposed a unified military doctrine on the same principles as conservative tsarist officers had. He considered that imposing a binding set of ideas on the leadership would limit creativity and innovation, yet a large number of Red Army leaders wanted a well-defined doctrine to guide their actions. Trotsky wanted the military leadership to focus on the fundamental task of turning peasants into soldiers, arguing that theory was no substitute for a well-trained army. He protested using the civil war experience as a model for Russia's future wars, arguing that it had been ad hoc in nature, with the Bolsheviks relying on whatever men and material it could lay hands on without much, if any, strategic or scientific thought.[22]

The party, however, decided in favor of Frunze. Appointed deputy commissar of military and naval affairs and chief of staff in 1924, he began to reform the army based on the premises of UMD. A year later, Trotsky's enemies in the party, led by Stalin, blamed him for the sorry state of the armed forces and ousted him from his military duties and promoted Frunze in his place. Frunze saw the military as the focus of social and economic redevelopment in the 1920s, writing: "In any new undertaking—economic, cultural or other—one must always ask the question: What relation does this undertaking have to the task of protecting the nation? Is there any possibility of letting it serve specific military purposes as well without impairing peaceful goals?"[23] This thinking reflected the lesson the Bolsheviks had learned from the First World War: that war planners needed to incorporate the capacity of the civilian economy into long- and short-term planning for war.

The Red Army leadership benefited from the secret German-Soviet partnership that, following the Treaty of Rapallo in 1922, allowed Germany to set up training bases in the USSR until Hitler closed them in 1933; it also included exchanges of officers between the two armies' staff academies. Senior German officers lectured at the Red Army's academy, and numerous prominent senior Soviet officers, including Tukhachevskii, Vladimir Triandifilov, Boris Shaposhnikov, Georgii Isserson, Ieronim Uborevich, Robert Eideman, Avgust Kork, Semen Timoshenko, and Grigory Kulik, attended the German staff academy, observed German maneuvers, or received other instruction from the German army. Scores of Red Army officers also trained together with Germans at the secret Kama armor training base near Kazan and the air base at Lipetsk. There is no doubt that these exchanges and joint training profoundly influenced these officers' vision of future war.[24]

One of Frunze's lasting legacies, besides the debate over the UMD, was to establish a general staff, first labeled the Red Army Staff, before it eventually changed its name to the Soviet General Staff. Appointing himself its first chief, Frunze, while operating loosely within Marxist ideology, intended its work to be intellectually rigorous, professional, and outside the influences of party politics. In the 1920s and 1930s, dozens of former tsarist colonels and generals, including Tukhachevskii, Shaposhnikov, and Svechin, served on it. As Trotsky feared, military theory and strategic issues soon dominated the work of the staff at the expense of the mundane yet essential operations of the troop units. Without explicitly referencing it, however, most accepted the UMD because coordination between the military and civilian leadership was essential to plan industrial production and military doctrine.[25]

During the interwar period, two factions of senior officers emerged. One comprised Bolshevik Party members who had earned their rank during the civil war. The most prominent were cronies of Stalin such as Kliment Voroshilov, who replaced Frunze as commissar of war in 1925, Semen Budenny, Filip Golikov, and Kulik. In a sense, these associates of Stalin's can be seen as "Bolshevik grand dukes." As favorites of Stalin, they were guaranteed prominent positions they seldom merited. The other faction consisted of prerevolutionary General Staff Academy–trained military specialists who had sworn loyalty to the Bolshevik regime and had also performed well during the civil war. The most prominent of these became the Red Army's prime military theorists after Frunze's death: Tukhachevskii, Svechin, Isserson, and Triandifilov. These four, and several others, came to have great influence over military thinking, which Bolshevik officers resented. The resentment was exacerbated because the former tsarist officers presented themselves as true professionals and treated the political as the dilettantes they were. The "Bolshevik grand dukes," having earned their spurs during the civil war, mistakenly believed they knew all they needed to know about the military arts and failed to keep pace with changes in technology and tactics. Courses designed to improve their military educations were established for them, but they did not take the instruction seriously, in part because the instructors were officers of the old army whom they detested. They contributed little in the way of strategic thinking and believed they served a higher purpose as the politically reliable guardians of the revolution, which they insisted was more important than military professionalism.

What the two factions had in common was dismay at the small size of the armed forces. Immediately following the war with Poland, the army and PUR were demobilized. Millions of peasants went home, and officers and commissars transferred to the burgeoning civilian bureaucracy and the secret police. The size of the regular forces was set at 562,000 men, primarily for budgetary reasons. In 1925, the army consisted of thirty-one cadre infantry and ten cadre cavalry divisions, and forty-six territorial infantry divisions and one territorial cavalry division. Throughout the 1920s, both factions incessantly lobbied for a larger active-duty force—to no avail. The country simply could not afford a larger standing military while the economy recovered from the devastation of war and revolution.[26] At times they had to defend what little they had. On several occasions during the 1920s, Voroshilov threatened to resign to keep the defense budget from being cut. Until 1937, the territorial divisions, each authorized between 600 and 1,100 cadre officers and men, and between 12,000 and 13,000 part-time serving soldiers, outnumbered the active forces. These forces constituted the reserve that would augment the standing army in wartime. Like the regular army, the number of territorial units expanded as the economy recovered. In 1935, at their peak, the territorial forces accounted for 74 percent of the army's infantry and cavalry divisions.[27]

Army and Society

Frunze and his successors made an honest effort to create an army of a new type with regard to the quality of life for the soldier. Because of economic difficulties, pay and the quality of life in the peacetime army was low, but enlistments were short—two years. The army succeeded in eliminating the brutal treatment of soldiers endemic to the tsarist army. The army made a sincere effort to minimize the social distance between officers and men to the point that the officers did not have rank but were identified by their command position and addressed as such—for example, "comrade company commander." Everyone was addressed as "comrade," regardless of job title. Despite the better treatment and egalitarian nature of the army, reenlistment numbers were insignificant and recruitment to the officer corps was anemic. Military service was still seen as onerous and to be avoided. Though young men still attempted to evade the draft, overall compliance was high, and few resorted to the drastic measures of their grandfathers' generation.

The army worked hard to create a positive image of itself. It contrasted its humane treatment of soldiers to the brutal treatment of the tsarist army. It highlighted the ideas that the Red Army was the people's army and not that of an autocrat and that it was an honor to serve in it—a privilege not allowed class enemies. The party actively recruited soldiers with the intent that they would go back to their families, farms, and workplaces and assume leadership roles that would strengthen the people's connection to both the party and the army. For practical purposes and to generate good will, the army sent soldiers to help collective farmers with the planting and harvesting. Much publicity was given to the help military units contributed to large construction projects. Civilian newspapers were filled with the exploits of military aviators. To further raise its profile, the military circulated its newspapers, *Krasnaia Zvezda* (Red Star) and *Krasnoarmeets* (Red Soldier), at libraries and sold them on newsstands.

To connect with Soviet youth, the Commissariat of Defense created Osoaviakhim (Society for the promotion of aviation and chemical defense), the purpose of which was to prepare youth physically and psychologically for military service. This voluntary paramilitary organization offered training in rifle marksmanship, close order drill, parachuting, glider piloting, and instruction in the customs and duties of military service, defenses against chemical attack, and so forth. In the countryside, teams of officers and men trekked to villages to give instruction to collective farm youth. In the urban areas, teams visited schools to recruit students to the organization. The Komsomol (Leninist League of Soviet Youth) promoted the glories of military service among its members, who consequently proved to be particularly active in Osoaviakhim.

Expanding the Armed Forces, 1928–1941

In 1928, once Stalin had defeated his main rivals for power, it became apparent that his priorities for the army were to (1) ensure the political loyalty of the officers and men, (2) expand the defense industry and upgrade military technology, (3) direct diplomacy and strategy to guarantee the defense of the USSR, and (4) take back territory lost in the war and revolution. In addition to the large questions that affected his personal power, and important ideological issues, Stalin took an active interest in strategic-level defense policy. Other than assiduously weeding out officers whose loyalties might lie with his political opponents (Stalin purged the officer corps and PUR of 16,000 men thought to be Trotsky supporters between 1923 and 1927), Stalin tended to trust his pal Voroshilov to manage the internal workings of the army. Like the tsars, Stalin had a hand in the promotion of generals and in making high-level assignments to the Commissariat of Defense and the General Staff.

With the advent of the First Five-Year Plan in 1928, which Stalin in part justified as a military necessity arguing that the USSR would either quickly make up for its backwardness or be crushed by the capitalists, the army did begin to grow modestly, having been previously held in check by the civilians controlling the purse strings. Before the success of the five-year plans, many in the army leadership had little confidence that the nation's military was adequately armed and equipped and they privately blamed Stalin.[28] When Stalin initiated the first of the five-year plans, he had already allowed the army to grow to 617,000 men, reaching 700,000 at the conclusion of that plan in 1932. During the second five-year plan, the active forces expanded to 930,000 soldiers, sailors, and airmen. Also in those years, the secret police mounted another purge of the army, this time arresting or dismissing some 3,000 former tsarist officers whose loyalty they considered suspect. The period 1936–37 saw the standing armed forces reach a strength of 1.5 million men. By lowering the draft age from twenty-one to nineteen and converting most of the territorial forces to regular divisions, the army doubled in size to 3 million by the end of 1939. On the eve of the Second World War, the army had grown to more than 4.5 million men and women (more than 5 million were under arms in the armed forces as a whole, counting the air force and navy). This growth was achieved by a process of increasing the intake of conscripts, transitioning the last of the territorial units to regular units, calling up 800,000 reservists in the spring of 1941, and extending the term of enlistment from two years to three. The Commissariat of Defense planned to have a fully armed and equipped force of 6 million men by the summer of 1942.[29]

With the recovery of the Soviet economy and the expansion of heavy industry, the army began to adopt more sophisticated weaponry, especially tanks and aircraft. The problem arose, however, of the army expanding faster than industry could produce arms and equipment, particularly in the period 1937–41. Even before the first of the five-year plans, defense production and its expansion involved a messy relationship between the Commissariat of Defense and General Staff, which generated requests; the State Planning Commission and the Main Industrial Administration, which decided what was possible to produce; and the Soviet government and Communist Party, which decided how much it was willing to spend.[30] At the end of 1938, the standing forces of the army had grown to about 150 infantry and cavalry divisions. In June 1941, it had increased in size to 303 infantry, armor, and motorized divisions, 81 of which were still in the process of forming. Not only did the defense industry struggle to arm and equip these new units, but it was also asked to field new model tanks and artillery pieces.

Interwar Military Thought after Frunze

The late 1920s to mid-1930s was a highly productive period for Soviet military thinking on strategy, tactics, technology, and the future of warfare. Sally Stoecker makes the point that "the military," even with the increased censorship associated with the advent of Stalinism, "was an independent institution that was capable of successful innovation during the First Five-Year Plan (1928–33) with the aid of budgetary resources, reform-minded officers, foreign expertise, indigenous R&D programs, and combat experience obtained in the Far East."[31] Some of the highlights of the era were the debates between Svechin and Triandifilov on whether the USSR would best fight the next war focusing on offense or defense. The army grappled with Isserson's and Tukhachevskii's concepts of deep battle that built on Triandifilov's work (combined arms operations of armor, artillery, motorized infantry, and tactical airpower); these ideas ran parallel with those of British (especially J. F. C. Fuller) and German (Hans Delbück is prominent) thinkers on mechanized war of which the Soviets kept themselves informed.[32] The general guidance on tactical doctrine expressed in the Field Regulations of 1929, despite all the thinking about the potential of armor, reaffirmed that infantry was the main arm of the service and that all other arms supported it. The military leadership continued to operate with the idea that war with the capitalist world was inevitable, though in the short-term Stalin adopted Lenin's outlook that it could and should be delayed until conditions favored the Soviet Union.

The debate between Svechin and Triandifilov centered on the latter's insistence—in line with Frunze's UMD—that the only way to victory lay in offensive battles of annihilation sustained by a militarized industrial economy and mobilized society. Those battles would be accomplished through what Triandifilov termed "deep operations," in which combined arms forces would penetrate the enemy front and drive deep into the rear, disrupting command, communications, and logistics and setting the enemy up for encirclement and ultimate destruction. He rejected the idea that World War I–type battles of attrition on either offense or defense would be repeated in future wars. Svechin, on the other hand, promoted his long-held position that offensive operations could also be attritional in nature and that defensive battles of attrition were highly desirable and could be an aspect of a strategy of annihilation. He insisted that conditions would not always be favorable to taking or remaining on the offensive; therefore, he proposed that the Red Army also train for and plan to employ defensive operations in order to wear down or even annihilate the enemy, and thereby create the conditions to transition to the offensive.[33] The Field Regulations of 1929 underscored the primacy of the offensive saying: "It is the task of all combat to inflict defeat on the enemy, but only a decisive offensive in the decisive sector culminating in persistent pursuit leads to the complete destruction of his forces and resources. Defense can only weaken an enemy, but not destroy him."[34] In the 1930s, Tukhachevskii and Isserson sought to build on Triandifilov's and Svechin's thinking by adding combined arms to the mix, as reflected in the Provisional Field Regulations for the Red Army (1936).[35]

The difference between the debates of the 1920s and those of the 1930s was that in the 1920s the idea of combined arms warfare was largely theoretical because the Red Army did not possess the means to conduct mechanized warfare. In the 1930s, with the progress of the First Five-Year Plan, in part influenced by Tukhachevskii's thinking on military-economic development, the Soviet economy began to develop the means to produce armored vehicles and aircraft in large numbers.[36] There were no armored units in the Red Army larger than a battalion until 1929, when the first, experimental mechanized regiment was formed using foreign-built tanks. In 1932, the Red Army formed its first two division-sized armored units, which it termed mechanized corps. These corps totaled just under 9,000 men each and were equipped with 463 light tanks and tankettes, 1,444 automobiles, and several battalions of motorized artillery. Tukhachevskii and Isserson intended for these corps to be the basis of an army capable of fighting "deep battles." As a result of the USSR's expanded industrial capacity, and the fielding of the armored units, greatly assisted by German investment related to the secret partnership, the Red Army General Staff Academy created an operations faculty to study combined arms operations. Forward thinkers, led by Tukhachevskii and Isserson, pressed for more mechanized corps every year but were thwarted by Voroshilov, who was not convinced of the merits of mechanized warfare and "deep battle" theory. He did support the production of thousands more tanks (at the end of 1935, the Red Army had more than 11,000 domestically produced tanks) but organized them into battalions, regiments, and brigades intended to support infantry units.[37]

In the late 1920s, Egorov weighed in on the offensive-versus-defensive debate promoting static defense. He proposed building a system of fortifications on the USSR's western border. Stalin agreed to implement the plan. It was not a continuous defensive belt like France's Maginot Line but was divided into fortified districts, which consisted of lengthy sections of trenches, pillboxes, bunkers, and roadblocks designed to hold key terrain and deflect the enemy to areas conducive to Soviet counterattacks. The underlying thought was that it would buy time for the Red Army to mobilize fully.[38] This line, which came to be called the Stalin Line, was continuously maintained and modernized until 1939, when the conquest of eastern Poland required the Red Army to deploy westward. At that point, the army stripped the fortifications of armaments and personnel and sent them west to equip a new defensive line (the Molotov Line).

Assessing the Threats, 1928–1939

In 1928, Tukhachevskii, as deputy commissar of defense, presented Stalin with his assessment of the threats to the USSR. He divided the nation's most realistic potential enemies into two camps: first and most threatening was a potential coalition of Great Britain, France, and all of the Soviet Union's European neighbors (Poland, Romania, Finland, Estonia, Latvia, and Lithuania), and fascist Italy; second were Germany, Czechoslovakia, Hungary, Bulgaria, Yugoslavia, Greece, Belgium, Japan, and the United States, any or all of whom might find a pretext to attack or join in a war against the Soviet Union.[39] One may legitimately question whether Tukhachevskii believed that the small and economically underdeveloped countries he listed posed an actual threat to the Soviet Union. It is plausible that Tukhachevskii was making the case for increased investment in the military industrial base as the First Five-Year Plan was being implemented. Stalin doubted that, in 1928 or the near future, these countries were contemplating war or could come together in an anti-Soviet coalition. For the time being, he was content to adopt a defensive posture while the Commissariat of Foreign Affairs succeeded in concluding treaties of nonaggression or neutrality with Germany, France, Italy, and all the states bordering the USSR other than Romania and China.[40]

In the mid-1930s, the Red Army Staff began to focus on a remilitarizing Nazi Germany as the most likely threat from the west, which it speculated could assemble a coalition of anti-Soviet allies. The Red Army Staff devised and updated mobilization and deployment plans to address changes in the diplomatic and military situations. When the Red Army Staff drew up plans in 1936–38, Stalin insisted that the army assume that the Germans' main attack would come south of the Pripet Marshes, whereas the army had been inclined to plan for a main attack from north of the marshes. Stalin assumed that Hitler would go for economic resources such as Ukrainian agriculture, Donbas coal mines, and Caucasian oil.

The Great Purge and Expansion

In the 1930s, Stalin became unsure of the army's loyalty to him, just as he feared for the loyalty of the party, the national minorities, and society at large. He reacted by unleashing the terror purge of 1937–38, the exact causes of which are varied and complex and may never be fully understood. Stalin's desire to ensure the armed forces were cleansed of those actively or potentially disloyal to him was likely a factor. What is clear is that the purge had a devastating effect on the higher levels of the Red Army officer corps and was used to resolve the feud between the military professionals and politicals. Arrested on false charges, Tukhachevskii and his faction of professional military intellectuals, with but few exceptions, were executed. In the weeks after the arrest of his rivals, Voroshilov, on Stalin's orders, drew up a list of three hundred more high-ranking officers to be purged. Definitive statistics on the number of officers denounced by their fellow officers or subordinates and arrested by the secret police's special sections are not available, and may never be, but at present historians agree that between 17,000 and 19,000 military officers and 5,000 PUR officials were made victims. A minority of them were arrested and shot; most were punished for supposed counterrevolutionary crimes or espionage by imprisonment in the Gulag or dismissed from the service. Within four years, several thousand of the purged officers and commissars were reinstated to the army.[41] The Great Purge marked a dramatic change in Stalin's relationship with the armed forces. Henceforth he became intimately involved in the internal dynamics of the military.

Even as the army and all Soviet society, government, and industry were being purged, Stalin expanded the armed forces. The army added thousands of tanks to its forces and created scores of armored units, which can be seen as major steps toward enabling the mechanized warfare theorists had envisioned for more than a decade. Fearing that war would soon break out with Nazi Germany or Imperial Japan, Stalin, in 1941, ordered that the army expand beyond the desires of the military high command. The pace of expansion between 1937 and 1941 increased the size of the army by two and a half times (five times what it had been in 1931). As noted above, men were drafted by the millions, and reservists were called up by the hundreds of thousands in such a short period that the defense industry could not keep pace with the army's needs. Lack of uniforms, equipment, and weaponry prevented the army from training the men expeditiously or thoroughly.

Wars with Poland and Finland, 1939–1940

Taken by surprise by the 1 September 1939 German attack on Poland only a week after the signing of the Nazi-Soviet Nonaggression Pact, which was an act of strategic diplomacy by which Stalin intended to buy time to rearm and regain the territories Russia lost after the First World War, the Soviet Army attacked Poland on 17 September. There appear to have been no contingency plans for an offensive, and the entire campaign was conducted in an ad hoc manner. Using infantry divisions in conventional form, the Red Army routed the valiant but overwhelmed Polish army. Despite the example of Germany's successful use of armored divisions, the Red Army, just weeks later, disbanded its few mechanized corps based on Gen. Dmitrii Pavlov's recommendations. Pavlov had been an adviser to the Republican Army during the Spanish Civil War and noted the ineffectiveness of large armored units. Taking the Spanish experience as universal, he advised Stalin that the Soviets' armor should be spread between the ever-increasing number of infantry divisions.

Only two months after the conquest of eastern Poland, the Soviets, falsely claiming they had been attacked, declared war on Finland with the goal of absorbing it into the Soviet Union. Planning the campaign against Finland, which began on 30 November 1939, was not addressed as a serious undertaking. The Commissariat of Defense left it to the Leningrad Military District to plan and conduct the war. The military district staff overestimated the capacity of the forces under its command and expected to conquer Finland with the resources at hand in only twelve days. The overly confident and inexperienced district staff gravely underestimated the preparedness, resourcefulness, and resolve of their Finnish adversaries.[42] When the initial assaults failed in a bloodbath for tens of thousands of Soviet soldiers who stumbled into the kill zones of the Mannerheim Line (Finland's scaled-down version of the Maginot Line) or froze to death in pockets isolated by Finnish ski troops, the army called a halt to the operation and started over.

Following the embarrassing failure, Stalin took charge of the war. He created a Stavka comprising himself, Voroshilov, General Shaposhnikov, and Adm. Nikolai Kuznetsov to direct the war from Moscow. During the pause, Stalin and Stavka made numerous personnel changes. Stalin reassigned the commander of the Leningrad Military District, Gen. Kirill A. Meretskov, to command an army in the field and replaced him with Marshal Semen Timoshenko. Besides Meretskov, Stavka demoted three commanders of armies and their chiefs of staff. Stavka also dismissed from their duties five division commanders, their artillery commanders, and their chiefs of staff. A handful of regiment commanders also got the axe. The command groups of two divisions and two regiments that the Finns encircled and destroyed were arrested, investigated, and executed for their failure.[43] After the war, Stalin dismissed Voroshilov from the post of commissar of defense and replaced him with Marshal Timoshenko.

A new offensive, under Timoshenko's leadership, begun in February 1940, showed no tactical or strategic ingenuity. A vastly reinforced group of armies employed massed infantry assaults supported by armor and heavy artillery. A willingness to accept huge losses of both tanks and infantry enabled the attacking forces to break through the Mannerheim Line and advance on Vyborg. In the meantime, the League of Nations condemned the Soviets for their aggression, foreign volunteers arrived by the thousands to fight for Finland, and there was talk of Britain and France declaring war on the USSR. Fearing foreign intervention, Stalin abandoned his goal of total conquest in favor of accepting concessions of border territory and the granting of air and naval bases on Finnish territory.[44] Finland agreed to a negotiated peace on 13 March 1940.

In the aftermath of the Winter War, the army held a "lessons learned" conference. Stalin attended, interjecting his opinions throughout the discussions. Obviously frustrated with the generals, he impatiently swept aside their excuses and attempts to shift blame among themselves. The talk focused on the nuts-and-bolts conduct of the war.[45] The participants failed to identify the combination of the Great Purge and the expansion of the army as causes of the abysmal performance of company- and battalion-level officers. In 1939, the army added 111 infantry divisions comprising 333 infantry regiments and 222 artillery regiments. It also created 692 new separate artillery battalions and sixteen tank brigades, as well as assorted corps, army, and higher headquarters. This required a 50 percent increase in the size of the officer corps in only fifteen months. In November 1939, a majority of company-level officers had been in the army only a brief time and had received limited training. Officer training, in 1938, had been cut from four years to only six months to provide officers quickly to replace those purged and to fill newly created units. Officers at the battalion level had been promoted to their duties with little time to gain experience at the company level, and without advanced instruction to command battalions. The senior ranks suffered the same problem but to a less severe degree.[46] The short duration of large and small unit training and lack of experience in command showed themselves on the battlefield and led to high rates of officer casualties, which further exacerbated the situation.

Voroshilov's dismissal from the post of commissar of defense stands as the first sign that the status of Stalin's cronies and those with revolutionary and civil war credentials was in decline, and that merit would outweigh political credentials in consideration for high promotion. Other casualties were the idea of brotherly relations between officers and the reliance on revolutionary consciousness for discipline. During the war, commanders took harsh measures against both officers and men for cowardice, desertion, and failure in battle. Division commanders, on their own, created penal battalions and had soldiers executed. After the war, the Commissariat of Defense enacted a stricter formal disciplinary code, one that allowed officers to shoot men for noncompliance.[47] The army officers blamed their failure in part on PUR and the commissars; Stalin agreed to again abolish dual command.

In the period between the Winter War and the Nazi invasion of the USSR in June 1941, the Red Army was used as a tool of Soviet imperialism in the takeover of the Baltic States, and the seizure of territory from Hungary (northern Bukovina) and Romania (Bessarabia) in 1940. The army continued to expand, which called for the promotion to high rank of both Bolshevik "grand dukes" and better-trained professional officers who had begun their careers in the immediate post–civil war era. PUR stopped using revolutionary and socialist ideals to motivate the soldiers and instead shifted to the use of traditional nationalist tropes. Heroic Russian history, rather than Marxism, came to dominate the political talks given by commissars. Also, in the autumn of 1940, following the Germans' success in using large, armored formations against the French and British, the Red Army reversed its stance on large armored units and hurriedly created nine mechanized corps (each consisting of two armored divisions and one motorized division). Stalin authorized the formation of twenty additional corps in February 1941, with 1,031 armored vehicles per corps.

Planning for War, 1939–1941

The new mobilization plan drawn up in 1939–40 more realistically identified the threats to the USSR as Imperial Japan, which had been seen as a likely threat since the late 1930s when it expanded into Manchuria threatening Siberia; and a German-led coalition of Italy, Finland, Romania, Hungary, and Turkey in the west. Shaposhnikov assumed that the main offensive would be launched north of the Pripet Marshes (as Stalin had previously argued) and wanted to assign the bulk of Soviet forces to meet that attack. Others, led by Gen. Matvei Zakharov, thought more forces should be assigned to defeat a likely strong thrust south of the marshes. In August 1940, Stalin replaced Shaposhnikov as chief of staff with General Meretskov, who instructed the staff to draw up new mobilization deployment plans that divided Soviet forces more evenly north and south of the Pripet Marshes. Stalin insisted that the plan be rewritten to assume that the Germans' main effort would come south of the Pripet Marshes.[48] The final Soviet plan called for the Red Army to take the offensive immediately after Germany declared war.

By late 1940, the Soviets had correctly identified the threat of a German-Finnish-Hungarian-Romanian coalition but incorrectly assumed that if the Red Army had material superiority south of the Pripet Marshes, it would prevail. The war games scenario for 1941 assumed an initial defensive posture for the Soviets, who would receive and blunt the Axis attack and then go over to the offensive. Historian Evan Mawdsley argues that, despite the provision for an initial defense, the war games in January 1941 focused only on the offensive aspect of the plan, indicating that Stalin and the army favored offensive action against Germany, giving defense lip service only.[49]

As tensions between the Soviet Union and Germany rose in the spring of 1941, the pair of Marshal Timoshenko and the new chief of the Red Army Staff, rising star Gen. Georgi Zhukov—both committed to an offensive doctrine— ordered Gen. Alexander Vasilevskii to update plans for a strike into Poland designed to disrupt a German attack and seize the offensive for the Soviet Union. When this attack would take place was not specified, but it is highly unlikely they thought it could be any time soon. The Red Army was far from ready in terms of manpower, weapons, and equipment. The attack was contingent on the perceived imminence of a German invasion. Implementing the offensive, as a form of "offensive defense," was predicated on the army first mobilizing the reserves, but the plan did not specify when this would begin. Stalin was shown a draft of the plan but was not ready to finalize it or order mobilization because, as argued by Mawdsley, he was not convinced that Germany was on the verge of attacking.[50]

The greatest failure in planning was Soviet thinking that the main German thrust would come *either* north *or* south of the Pripet Marshes. In fact, the Germans and their allies launched massive offensives *both* north *and* south of the marshes. In all the Soviet planning and war-game scenarios devised in the late 1930s, the forces the Soviets would need in order to defeat the Germans and Japanese were aspirational in nature: the more than three hundred infantry and cavalry divisions the planners projected they would need against a German coalition or Japanese attack did not exist. To support this plan, the military wanted 8.7 million men, 22,500 tanks, and up to 14,000 aircraft.

Planning for war in Asia followed the same pattern as that for war in the west. In 1938, the General Staff proposed to wait until a declaration of war was made by Japan and then attack. The planning identified waging war with two *fronts*: the Baikal *Front*, to be formed by the Transbaikal Military District; and the Far East *Front*, to be formed by the Special Red Banner Far East Army. The Baikal *Front* was to capture key terrain across the border and then advance down to the southern border of the Mongolian People's Republic. The Far East *Front* had the goal of seizing Harbin.[51]

As it prepared for war, the Red Army Staff worried that the Soviet rail network could not support the rapid movement of men and supplies westward, just as it had failed to do in 1914. Though it lobbied hard for the construction of new lines throughout the 1930s, the Red Army, like the tsarist army, was rebuffed by civilians who prioritized expanding the rail network to support economic growth over strategic military considerations. The few lines built on the western frontier increased capacity only marginally. Logistical support for the forces in the west was made more difficult after the conquest of Poland in 1939 extended the distance men and equipment had to be transported.

Like the tsarist army, to have the requisite number of divisions and brigades to support the war plans, units were manned at reduced numbers with most at between half- to three-quarters-strength. The Red Army, again following the example of the tsarist army, counted on having time to bring the divisions up to full wartime strength with reservists before hostilities broke out. The Red Army Staff was fully aware of the deficiencies of this manning policy, having closely studied the problems of 1914, yet chose to take their chances. The majority of units that engaged the Axis in June 1941 did so at reduced strength or with recently arrived reservists or conscripts who were neither fully trained nor integrated into their regiments.

As usual, the army went to war without enough leaders. The army failed to recruit enough officers to cover both the losses of the Great Purge and to fill the additional hundreds of newly created regiments, brigades, and divisions. At the end of 1938, the army was short 73,000 officers. The expansion of the army in 1938–39 created the need for another 203,000 officers, but the Commissariat of Defense was able to recruit only 158,000 new officer candidate. Like the tsarist army in 1914, the Red Army, rather than calling them ensigns, created the rank of junior lieutenant and trained these men in short courses of just six months at·most. Continued expansion in 1940 left the army undermanned by 125,000 officers. The party and Komsomol, like in the civil war, leaned on its members to volunteer to serve as officers. The officers who were recruited were rapidly promoted well above their level of training and experience. In June 1941, by intense recruiting, promoting noncommissioned officers, and commissioning party and Komsomol members from the ranks willing or not, the army had 439,143 officers, but 66,900 positions remained unfilled.[52]

The German Invasion as Catalyst for Change

The Second World War began on 1 September 1939, but the Great Patriotic War of the Soviet Union did not begin until 22 June 1941 when the Germans attacked the USSR. On the eve of the German invasion, Russia's army was the largest army in the world, though not all its forces were available to fight in Europe—more than a million men with their tanks, artillery, and aircraft were stationed in the Far East. Mobilization during the war brought in an additional 34 million men and women of all the Soviet Union's nationalities. Stalin, like Alexander I, took a hand in overseeing operations in the early part of the war, sometimes with disastrous outcomes. As the war progressed, those times when he refrained from direct participation in planning, he looked over his commanders' shoulders as Alexander II had.

During the calamitous first months of the war, hundreds of colonels and generals became casualties, some by ineptitude and others by skillful German tactics. The majority of Bolshevik "grand dukes" who had risen to high rank not on merit but on their revolutionary credentials, party loyalty, and performance during the civil war were lost along with many proficient officers. Incompetent survivors fell victim to administrative measures of transfer to lesser duties or being cashiered outright—often with Stalin's endorsement—after failing at the front. The German invasion led to a generational change in the leadership of the Red Army. These leaders took the final steps to transform the Red Army from a revolutionary people's army to a traditional national army.

Nazi Germany unleashed a war upon the Soviet Union completely different from the warfare the civil war generation had experienced. This war required rapid maneuver of large units across a wide and deep battlefield. It required commanders to maneuver infantry, tanks, artillery, and aircraft in combination using radio communications and to keep them supplied while learning from their adversaries' successes and their own mistakes–all things the civil war generation had never done or bothered to learn how to do. The rising post–civil war generation had studied the advances in technology and tactics, were more flexible in their thinking, and were waiting for their chance to take charge. Slowly, talent percolated upward. Men who proved capable rose as the incompetent slid downward. It was an uneven process, to be sure. Talented men who began their careers as junior officers in the civil war or shortly thereafter, such as Zhukov, were already on the rise. Finally, with the vacancies opened by the failures of the older generation, they got the opportunity to prove themselves. Officers who had earned their way to the top by sharpening their skills in peacetime and performing well in wartime welcomed the degradation or elimination of the Bolshevik "grand dukes."

Stalin's actions during the war followed the pattern set by the Romanov autocrats. On 30 June 1941, the State Committee of Defense (GKO) convened with Stalin as head. He intent was for the GKO to coordinate decision-making for all aspects of the war effort and mobilize the population and the economy. Eventually composed of eight party, government, and military officials, its resolutions had the force of law. Each member of the committee had a specific area of responsibility. Besides the army, there were representatives from heavy industry, the aviation industry, the secret police, transportation, and agriculture. The GKO oversaw the activity of all government departments and institutions in an effort to gain the maximum effectiveness of the USSR's material, human, and military resources. It directed the use of human resources for both the military and the economy. In line with the conception of unified military doctrine, the GKO dictated military and diplomatic strategy, adapted the structure of the armed forces, assigned men to command large units, and determined how the armed forces would be employed in the war—all in conjunction with the political goals and economic capacity of the nation. In addition to head of the GKO, Stalin assumed the post of commissar of defense and supreme commander in chief of the armed forces for the duration of the war.[53] He made himself the focal point of decision-making even to the extent of making operational decisions.

The Initial Disaster, 1941

In the opening phase of the Great Patriotic War of the Soviet Union (Hitler's Operation Barbarossa), Soviet officers and men alike found themselves overwhelmed by the ferocity of the German attack and the fast-moving pace of battle. Commanders of *fronts* and armies attempted to save their commands from destruction rather than take offensive operations. Despite their best efforts, whole armies became encircled. Their commanders neither knew how to break out, nor was permission to do so granted in timely fashion. Retreat followed retreat as Red Army units were overrun, annihilated, pushed back, or fled in fear of being surrounded. Minsk fell in early July with a loss of around 400,000 men taken prisoner. Smolensk fell in August with another 300,000 men captured. In September, Kyiv was encircled and captured with the loss of more than 525,000 men because Stalin had forbidden them to attempt a breakout until it was too late. Other vast encirclements took place at Viazma and Briansk, during the Germans' autumn drive on Moscow. With the Germans nearing the end of their logistical rope, Zhukov, bolstered by reinforcements from the Far East, was able to stem the Nazi advance at the gates of Moscow. Unlike in 1812, it had not been a planned withdrawal, also unlike in 1812, it would be a lengthy fight to clear the enemy from Russian soil.

Rather than blaming his generals' failures and penchant for retreat on incompetence or crediting them with well-intentioned motives to save their armies, Stalin jumped to the conclusion that the army leaders were either cowards or politically unreliable. He responded by imposing harsh penalties for failure in combat. On 29 June 1941, just one week after the start of the German invasion and the disintegration of the Western *Front*, Stalin ordered the arrest of the *front*'s commander, General Pavlov, and his staff for cowardice. After a quick investigation and short trial, Pavlov, his chief of staff, and three other generals were executed. Others were given prison terms. Their case was publicized as an example to the rest of the army. Three weeks later, on 17 July 1941, Stalin signed an order authorizing the secret police detachments in the army to shoot noncompliant men on the spot. One month after that, on 16 August, Stalin formalized coercion by introducing GKO Order No. 270. This decree provided for the arrest of families of officers or political workers who deserted the battlefield or allowed themselves to be captured. Furthermore, division commanders were to relieve immediately any officers not up to their tasks and, if necessary, to shoot them on the spot and replace them with capable junior officers or enlisted men.[54] From there, a veritable reign of terror began in the frontline units as obedience was enforced at gunpoint. Commanders and commissars alike shot hesitant and recalcitrant soldiers by the thousands and were in turn shot by soldiers. The situation got so out of hand that the generals, led by Zhukov, implored Stalin to countermand it. Stalin did not rescind the order; however, he did issue GKO Order No. 391 in October, which directed commanders and commissars to use restraint when deciding whether to use deadly force against their men.[55]

Stalin again resorted to coercion in the summer of 1942 to stem a second round of battlefield failures. The Soviet spring offensive to retake Kharkiv failed after only a few days in June 1942 and was quickly followed by the German spring offensive. This offensive drove the Red Army back to the Volga River at Stalingrad and culminated in the German occupation of the North Caucasus. Stalin, in his capacity as commissar of defense, issued NKO Order No. 227, his "not one step backwards" order, in July. It threatened death and disgrace to those who surrendered or retreated without good cause. It discouraged officers and commissars from shooting men out of hand, directing them instead to send cowards, deserters, or otherwise disgraced soldiers and officers to newly established combat penal battalions. It also called for regiments to create blocking detachments to round up men found away from the front without authorization and send them back to their units.[56] At the time, there was real doubt on the part of many soldiers and officers as to the efficacy of resisting the German onslaught; many questioned whether the Soviet regime merited defending. As in the First World War, instances of draft evasion, desertion, allowing oneself to be taken prisoner, and going over to the enemy numbered at least in the hundreds of thousands.

In July 1941, Stalin's questioning the political reliability of the officer corps led him to reinstate dual command. As in the civil war, armies and *fronts* formed military councils. No order of the commander was official until countersigned by the commissar. Commanders hated this arrangement, and commissars were none too pleased by it either, because if things went wrong, they were held jointly responsible. Even though the war was still going badly, the generals managed to persuade Stalin, in October 1942, that the political reliability of the officer corps was not an issue and that dual command only degraded battlefield efficiency. He agreed to restore unity of command under the officers.[57]

Soviet society responded in a variety of ways to the German attack. The recently conquered peoples in the Baltics received the Germans as liberators, as did many Ukrainians as far east as Kyiv. People in the North Caucasus also looked forward to the Germans' arrival. Anti-communists quietly hoped for a German victory. Peasants in the line of the German advance ignored mobilization orders. A far greater number responded either patriotically or simply out of conformity,: 2 million volunteered for the Red Army in the first six months, and another 2 million volunteered for the opolchenie, which Stalin ordered to be raised in July 1941, or for specially recruited communist shock battalions. The opolchenie and shock battalions were sent into battle underequipped, inadequately armed, and with scant training. Consequently, they typically suffered catastrophic casualties. Volunteerism petered out in 1942, though public support for the troops remained strong as evidenced by the many well-supported drives to send gifts to the soldiers and by the large number of subscriptions to the war loans.

During the war, there were more than 4 million cases of draft evasion and desertion; hundreds of thousands, if not millions, of Soviet soldiers went into captivity willingly; and hundreds of thousands more crossed the lines to surrender. A manpower crisis developed in 1943 due to two years of heavy losses. To fill the ranks, the Red Army took in more than 900,000 prisoners from the Gulag—and 100,000 guards as well—and in 1943 returned 800,000 soldiers to the ranks who had been trapped behind enemy lines in Belorussia and Ukraine during the retreats of 1941 but had not attempted to flee eastward to rejoin the army. All told, popular support for the war was a close run, but enough soldiers served faithfully and courageously for the Red Army to be ultimately victorious.

1942–1945

For the first six months of the war, the Red Army was unable to apply its concept of "deep battle" against the Axis powers. Offensive action by the Red Army was limited to small- and large-scale counterattacks. Soviet generals did attempt to employ combined arms in their attacks; however, due to poor communications (lack of radios or their ineffective use) and lack of experience or training in maneuvering formations larger than divisions, they often failed to coordinate the efforts of the various arms. With the Germans dominating the skies, tactical air support and air cover were practically nil. Coordinating artillery fire with attacking infantry was haphazard. The Red Army was also woefully unprepared to conduct the active defense, to maneuver promptly to the right place at the right time with the right stuff to stem the German assault or to avoid the massive encirclements of hundreds of thousands of soldiers at a time. Nonetheless, trading space for time and lives for bullets, the Red Army did wear down the German advance, stopping it in front of Moscow.

With the Axis forces exhausted, and waiting for their logistical trains to catch up, Stalin insisted on launching a counteroffensive in December 1941 to push the Germans back not just from Moscow, but along most of the front. General Zhukov, always self-confident and ever ready to speak truth to power, suggested a more limited, concentrated attack; Stalin overrode his objections. What transpired was an offensive involving five *fronts* conducted on a broad front of roughly six hundred miles from Kursk in central Russia northward to Lake Ladoga. Another *front* attacked south of Kharkiv along a thirty-mile front. The goals were not simply to lift the siege of Leningrad and push the Germans back from Moscow but to destroy the German army and seize the initiative for the Red Army as the first step in the drive to Berlin to end the war in 1942. Sure of success—a feeling not encouraged by Stavka—Stalin instructed the propaganda machine to declare that 1942 would be the year of victory.

Because Stalin had insisted on the broad front strategy, the Red Army's forces of hastily trained and inadequately armed men were spread too thinly to effect rapid and deep penetrations and turn them into encircling maneuvers in the manner of "deep battle." The German army skillfully fought on the defensive and tenaciously defended key terrain, and then counterattacked. After the Red Army had suffered well over 1 million casualties, Stalin called off the attacks. Across much of the battle area, the Red Army had forced the Germans back nearly sixty miles, but in all cases it failed to achieve the strategic breakthrough that might have been possible had Stalin allowed for a concentration of forces on a narrow axis. Because the Red Army had lost so many men and tanks, a large-scale summer offensive became problematic.[58]

Throughout the second half of 1941 and all of 1942, the GKO struggled to evacuate Soviet defense industry eastward to safety. Eventually 2,500 industrial enterprises were relocated to the Urals, the Volga region, western Siberia, and Kazakhstan along with nearly 10 million workers, engineers, technicians, and managers. With tremendous effort, coordination, sacrifice, and suffering, it took until 1943 before full production resumed.[59] In the meantime, frontline forces had to make do with less than their authorized amount of equipment and weapons. Training establishments also had to cope with shortages.

The Nazi summer offensive of 1942 carried the German army all the way to Stalingrad and the North Caucasus. Halting the Germans at Stalingrad led to the subsequent Soviet counteroffensive codenamed Operation Uranus (November 1942 to February 1943), conceived and directed by Generals Zhukov and Vasilevskii. This counteroffensive turned out to be the Red Army's first major offensive victory of the war. It was a textbook example of Svechin's argument for wearing down the enemy on defense as precursor to transitioning to the offense. While the German Sixth Army and Fourth Panzer Army were bogged down in and around Stalingrad, Stavka planned a massive encircling movement to capture those forces and trap the German forces in the Caucasus. The plan positioned several Soviet armies on either side of the city, specifically in the Don bridgeheads that the Romanian army had been unable to reduce. On 19 November 1942, the attack kicked off, catching the enemy by surprise. Two Soviet *fronts* punched through the Romanian and Hungarian lines and converged at Kalach on 23 November, trapping 300,000 Axis troops behind them. A simultaneous offensive on the Rzhev sector farther north, known as Operation Mars, was supposed to advance to Smolensk but failed, as Zhukov underestimated the Germans' ability to defend successfully with limited resources. Once the German forces at Stalingrad were surrounded, the plan called for the minimum number of Soviet forces necessary to be left behind to reduce the pocket while the rest of the attacking forces rapidly fought their way west to the Donets River and the city of Rostov, thereby sealing off the German forces in the Caucasus.[60]

The drive to the Donets took until February for several reasons: Zhukov had underestimated the number of Axis troops in the pocket, causing him to devote more men than originally anticipated to maintain the encirclement, thus weakening and slowing the westward attack; and the Germans reacted more quickly and with greater strength to stem the Soviet advance than Stavka anticipated. Overall, despite that fact that the best case did not transpire for the Soviets—the Germans were able to evacuate their forces from the Caucasus—and the Red Army suffered a significantly large number of casualties, it was a tremendous victory, highlighted by effective use of large, hard-hitting, fast-moving armored units. From this point on, Stalin, evidently trusting the loyalty and capacity of his senior leaders, allowed Zhukov, Stavka, and the *front* commanders much more leeway and independence in planning and conducting operations. As the Battle of Stalingrad wound down, the Casablanca Conference in January 1943 established the Allies' strategic goal of achieving the unconditional surrender of Nazi Germany.

July 1943 saw the next significant Soviet victory, at Kursk. As at Stalingrad, the Red Army began the battle on the defensive. Here the Red Army showed that with ample warning, time to prepare, an overwhelming superiority in men, artillery, and armor, and plentiful tactical aircraft, it could defeat the Germans' combined arms operation. Relying on defense in depth, the Soviets constructed three belts of trenches, strong points, minefields, and antitank ditches covered by artillery fire to grind down the attacking German forces. The Germans attacked simultaneously on the north and south shoulders of the Kursk salient. In the north, they were only able to break through the first line of defense before bogging down. In the south, the two German armies did manage to fight their way to the third line before being stopped when the Soviets threw in their reserve of armor to prevent a breakthrough. Hitler called off the offensive both in response to the losses and slow going and to withdraw the SS Panzer Corps so he could send it to Italy to counter the Allied invasion of Sicily.[61]

As the Germans withdrew from the battle, the Red Army launched attacks north and south of the salient to break through to the German rear and open the front for a general advance. As in the past, however, the Germans prevented a Soviet breakthrough, though at the cost of a fair amount of territory. Defeating the Germans in the summertime gave a huge boost to Soviet morale and confidence. From this point onward, the Red Army held the initiative. The rest of 1943 saw the Red Army steadily advance westward at considerable loss of life and equipment. Though it used combined arms operations in which masses of infantry rode into battle on tanks, the Red Army failed to make significant breakthroughs to engage in deep operations. The German army proved to be too skilled and resilient.

Not until nearly a year after the Battle of Kursk did the Red Army score its next significant victory, Operation Bagration, from 23 June to 19 August 1944. Intended to smash the Germans' Army Group Center, clear the Germans from Soviet territory, and open the way for a follow-on offensive into Germany, Operation Bagration fulfilled nearly all its objectives. Launched on a front even longer than that of the 1941–42 winter offensive, eight *fronts* of the Red Army attacked with overwhelming advantages in manpower and matériel, especially in armor, artillery, and close air support. With mobility enhanced by American Lend-Lease trucks, the Red Army advanced hundreds of miles westward to the gates of Warsaw, pushed the Germans out of all pre-1941 Soviet territory other than the Baltic States, and nearly obliterated Army Group Center. Historians generally credit the Red Army with having vastly improved its warfighting expertise and of making good use of its superior numbers.[62]

Frunze's Bolshevized UMD called for waging class warfare in the rear of the enemy, something the Soviets had been unable to do while the war was on their territory. Partisans, however, provided the means to disrupt the enemy rear. Operation Bagration employed tens of thousands of partisans in hundreds of detachments to destroy targets in the German rear area. The specific goal of the partisan attacks was to disrupt transport of troops and supplies. How effective the attacks were is still debated, but it is certain that the need to fight partisans and repair infrastructure made it that much more difficult for the Germans to hold the front lines.

The last eight months of the war saw Soviet success everywhere along the eastern front, but not dramatically, largely in part to Stalin's insistence on fighting on a broad front. Stavka suggested putting all Soviet resources into a concentrated drive through Poland, which they believed would shorten the war, but Stalin rejected this. Opting for a longer war that would end with the Balkans once more in the Russian sphere of influence, he directed more than a million men into resuming the offensive against Romania that had stalled in May. With their forces spread out, the Red Army steadily advanced into Europe, though without ever achieving another decisive breakthrough and ensuing battle of annihilation on the scale of Operation Bagration. The high rate of casualties (several millions from all causes from mid-1944 to May 1945) ensured a continuous inflow of raw recruits and inexperienced junior officers. Thus, a higher capacity at the top for planning and organizing campaigns and battles did not necessarily translate into efficient conduct of those battles at the division level. The official figure for deaths of Soviet soldiers during the war is 8,668,400, however, Lev Lopukhovsky and Boris Kavalerchik make a convincing case that the actual death toll is closer to 11,758,900.[63]

The Effects of the War on the Army

The war transformed the Red Army in ways both negative and positive. On the positive side, merit for promotion and command would henceforth carry more weight than political or revolutionary credentials. Even before the war, signs that the army was gradually becoming more traditional had become apparent during the 1930s. Stalin acquiesced to the army's repeated requests to reintroduce traditional titles of rank for officers. Officers were then addressed in reference to their rank, and no longer as comrade. On the negative side, officer-enlisted relations became excessively formal, to the point that they resembled those of the tsarist army. When the officers were given the power, and even duty, to shoot men out of hand after the Russo-Finnish War, a line was crossed from which they could never retreat. The army dispensed with all pretenses of revolutionary fraternity. Formal relations typical of traditional armies became the norm.

The war increased the professionalism of the officer corps. During the war, ten senior military officers including Ivan Konev, Meretskov, Konstantin Rokossovskii, Vasilevskii, and Zhukov who had been promoted to the highest military rank—Marshal of the Soviet Union—became prominent public figures, especially during the first two years of the war when Stalin kept a low public profile. None were Stalin's cronies. Some had served as enlisted men or ensigns in the First World War; none had participated in the revolutionary movement. All had proved they deserved their positions by merit. The officer corps emerged from the war with an enhanced, and to a degree inflated, self-image. It understood itself as a corporate body with specific interests that were not always aligned with the Communist Party's. Stalin feared the popularity of the army and its leaders, especially Zhukov. Indeed, the party's leverage over the military was diminished, especially after Stalin's death. Service as an army officer was now seen as an attractive career. Henceforth, volunteers for the officer corps were plentiful until the late 1980s.

Individual soldiers and junior officers also had been lauded in the press and held up as examples of ideal citizens and patriots. Before the war, workers, engineers, and party officials were held in highest esteem by the state-run media, but from 22 June on, army service was lauded and praised in ways it never had been before. Soldiers were portrayed as fighting not for the revolution or socialism but for Mother Russia (the *Rodina Mat'*). For the remainder of the Soviet period, the media elevated the image of the army.

The continuities between the tsarist and Soviet period were several and largely inevitable given that the leadership of the new Red Army was drawn from the old army and that the need for a strong national defense backed by a standing, professional military did not change with the revolution and the transition to socialism. The idea of the unified military doctrine became a reality in the 1920s and guided the integration of the armed forces with the government and economy in defense planning. Worries about the loyalty of the army transcended the two eras. In the minds of the Soviet political and military leadership, the Russian Civil War and Second World War validated the need for a large standing army. Heads of state continued to act as commanders in chief who assumed they had the right to participate in strategic planning and supervising major operations. The Second World War also highlighted the fraught choice of waiting to attack until the enemy declared war.

CHAPTER 5

THE COLD WAR, 1946–1991

The experience of the Second World War dominated strategic and tactical thinking for the rest of the Soviet period. It determined how the Soviet Army would organize, man, and prepare for war during peacetime until Mikhail Gorbachev came to power. All its efforts and thinking reflected a continuum of over a century of military thought and experience.

From the conclusion of the Second World War until the collapse of communism and the disintegration of the Soviet Union, the underlying psychology of Soviet strategic military and diplomatic thinking was that war with the West could threaten the very existence of the Soviet Union, just as the war with Nazi Germany had done. In the post–World War II era, however, Soviet political leaders struggled to decide whether war between the capitalist-imperialist camp and the socialist camp was truly inevitable. Both Lenin and Stalin had agreed that such a war was inevitable, but that it could be delayed for an indefinite period of what they termed "peaceful coexistence." Stalin maintained this outlook in the postwar years, but Khrushchev and his successors renounced the idea of inevitable conflict. Despite the politicians' renunciations, the Soviet armed forces prepared for war as though the capitalists were destined to attack.

In the years 1945–91, Soviet perceptions of the nature of future war passed through several phases. The first phase was the immediate postwar years, 1945–49, in which the Soviets envisioned a defense of Eastern Europe with conventional forces while considering that for the time being war was unlikely. The next phase, 1950–60, was shaped by the Soviet development of atomic weapons. Thinking shifted to include the potential of using aircraft-delivered nuclear weapons to deter aggression or using nuclear weapons on the battlefield if necessary while maintaining large armored and motorized forces to attack and seize enemy territory. The following phase, from 1960 to 1966, which saw the development of intercontinental ballistic missiles (ICBMs), led the Soviets to

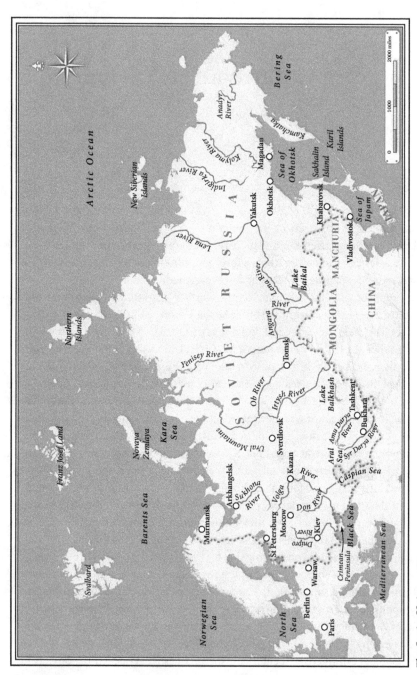

The Soviet Union, 1989

consider delivering nuclear strikes against the United States and Western Europe even if a conflict began as a conventional war. From 1966 to 1986, planning shifted to focus on fighting a conventional war in Europe, with the potential for it to escalate from the use of tactical nuclear weapons to the use of ICBMs. The final shift in outlook occurred between 1987 and 1991, when the Soviet military planned to conduct a conventional defense of Eastern Europe and avoid nuclear war if possible. There is no indication that the Soviet leadership thought a war with China would also be existential, yet the Soviet Army planned to conduct war with the Chinese in much the same way as with the West, to include the option of employing nuclear weapons.

The Postwar Years under Stalin

Within six weeks of the defeat of Nazi Germany, Stalin signed the first decree on demobilization of the armed forces, which released thirty-three classes of conscripts and 28,700 officers who were badly needed in the factories and on the farms. Thousands of soldiers deserted every month to go home, not waiting for official orders. By the end of 1948, having installed compliant communist governments in all the East European countries with the exception of Yugoslavia, the Soviet armed forces had been reduced from 11 million to 2.9 million men and women grouped into 175 armor and infantry divisions, a few score air force regiments, and a smattering of naval units. The armed forces had not been that small since 1938. The Soviet Army kept thirty-one of those divisions (few of which were at full strength) in Eastern Europe and Austria to perform occupation duties.[1]

The fact that Stalin so severely reduced the size of the military and limited the number of troops in Eastern Europe indicates that he neither intended to attack the West nor feared that an American-led coalition posed an imminent threat. Stalin withdrew all Soviet troops from Czechoslovakia in 1948. The majority of soldiers stationed in the USSR proper were, for about a decade, engaged either in suppressing armed nationalist movements in the Baltic Republics and Ukraine, or as labor in reconstructing destroyed infrastructure.[2] As for military efficiency, with much reduced manpower and a slashed budget, the first decade of peace was one of relative decline for the Soviet Army. Reminiscent of the 1920s, the Soviet economy was so devastated that the Soviets could neither afford to spend much on the military nor hope to project power for years. Once relations between the United States and the Soviet Union had become hostile, Stalin adopted a defensive posture. His thinking was that if the West, organized in 1949 as the North Atlantic Treaty Organization (NATO), attacked, the Soviet Army would blunt the attack and then take the war into central Europe using atomic bombs as necessary.

Stalin disbanded the GKO in 1945 and stepped down from the post of commissar of defense, but he remained involved in military affairs. He introduced a new military doctrine based on what he termed "permanently operating factors." These factors were stability of the rear, morale of the army, quantity and quality of divisions, equipment of the army, and the organizing ability of the commanding personnel of the army. This appears to have been a watered-down form of Frunze's unified military doctrine. All aspects of the permanently operating factors had been coordinated from the top through the GKO during the war and afterward through the Defense Council, which was headed by the general secretary of the Communist Party and included representatives from the party, the military, and industry. The Defense Council remained in existence until the disintegration of the USSR in 1991.

The Military under Khrushchev, 1956–1964

With the ascent of Nikita Khrushchev in 1956, the Soviet military underwent a significant modernization marked by the combination of nuclear weapons, missile technology, and nascent computerization. Khrushchev sought to reshape Soviet thinking on war with the West in light of the military's apparent transformation. He, unlike Lenin and Stalin, ceased to believe war with the capitalist-imperialist camp was inevitable. In his mind, the turning point was the Soviet production of atomic bombs, which made nuclear war a real possibility that he believed both camps wanted to avoid.

In addition, Khrushchev thought the socialist camp was ascending in economic power, having expanded into China and Eastern Europe while the capitalists were losing ground through decolonization. He saw the socialist camp as too powerful for the West to overcome and assumed the West saw it that way too. Khrushchev did not completely dismiss the possibility of war—neither he, the party, nor the army believed that the capitalist world had abandoned its fundamental hostility to socialism—but he trusted that the capitalists would not be so unwise as to start or provoke armed conflict. Khrushchev voiced his doubts about the inevitability of war with the West at the 20th Party Congress in 1956 and reiterated them at the 21st Party Congress in 1959. He embraced nuclear weapons as a deterrent and claimed that the USSR had no aggressive intent in Europe but reiterated Stalin's position that if attacked, the USSR would defend itself, even with nuclear weapons, and then counterattack. All evidence indicates that Khrushchev truly supported a defensive stance in Europe and believed that the chances of war with NATO were slim, to the point that he raised the potential of withdrawing Soviet troops from Hungary, Poland, and East Germany—to the horror of the military. To better manage the nuclear deterrent, Khrushchev created the Strategic Rocket Forces in 1959 as a separate branch of the armed forces. Khrushchev and his minister of defense, Zhukov, agreed that future war would be characterized by the mass use of air forces and missiles to deliver various weapons of mass destruction including atomic, thermonuclear, chemical, and bacteriological. Khrushchev disagreed with Zhukov and his successors that the role of ground forces would continue to be decisive.[3]

Marshal Rodion Malinovskii succeeded Zhukov in 1957. During his tenure, a team of army officers under the guidance of Chief of the General Staff Gen. Vasilii Sokolovskii wrote *Military Strategy* (1960), in which they challenged Khrushchev's confidence that there would be no war with the capitalist camp. The authors pointed out, whether likely or not, that the war the USSR needed to prepare for would be an Armageddon-like showdown between communism and capitalism. This third world war would include nuclear attacks in which the losers would be annihilated by rocket-delivered warheads. Even though nuclear weapons would inflict most of the destruction, Sokolovskii still believed that conventional forces would play an important role. Together Malinovskii and Sokolovskii unsuccessfully pushed back against Khrushchev's program of curtailing the production of conventional weapons, especially artillery and tanks.[4]

Given Khrushchev's contrary stand, the opinions expressed in *Military Strategy* cannot be considered to have been official policy, but only those of the authors. Many in the ground forces needlessly feared that they would take a secondary role to the Strategic Rocket Forces. In fact, armor and mechanized infantry remained the most career-enhancing branches. The officer corps resisted the downsizing imposed by Khrushchev, not only for reasons of national security but also for institutional reasons (careers and social status). Like Zhukov, they rejected the idea that nuclear weapons could or should be the ultimate defense of the USSR and argued (sometimes hysterically) that a smaller conventional force would leave them as vulnerable as they had been in June 1941. The Soviet nuclear delivery forces (the Strategic Rocket Force, navy, and air force) were never kept on the same footing of vigilance and preparedness as those of the US military, leading one to question whether the Soviet defense establishment truly had been serious about the possibility of nuclear war.

During his brief tenure as minister of war (1955–57), Zhukov presided over a second downsizing of the armed forces and began the process of making the Soviet Army fully mobile, turning all infantry divisions into motorized rifle divisions. He organized the ground forces into combined arms armies (which had more infantry than tanks) and tank armies (which had more tanks than infantry), making the Soviet Army a potent offensive weapon. On Khrushchev's orders, Zhukov began reducing the personnel and number of units in the armed forces, which had grown to 5.7 million men at the beginning of 1955. By 1959, the armed forces had been reduced to 3.6 million men. Tens of thousands of officers had their careers cut short. The number of tank and motorized divisions declined from 175 to 140.

As part of this downsizing, Zhukov, intending to avoid a repeat of the tsarist army's failure to cap the number of elderly generals, forcibly retired the oldest of the senior officers. Zhukov drew up two lists: one of older marshals and generals he wanted to retire, and another of younger colonels and generals he wanted to promote. Before acting, he asked Khrushchev and the Central Committee Secretariat to approve the lists. With the party behind him, Zhukov sent blunt telegrams to those to be retired to clean out their desks and turn over their commands to their deputies. The recipients, to a man, appealed to their party connections to overturn their retirements—all unsuccessfully. One, the sixty-six-year-old Marshal Andrei Eremenko, in a characteristically petulant fit, armed himself with a pistol and a box of ammunition and barricaded himself in his office and challenged anyone to come and take him out. It took a phone call from Khrushchev (who had served as his commissar during the Battle of Stalingrad), who promised him a job as an inspector general, to calm him down.[5]

Despite these cuts and Khrushchev's intent to redirect investment to the consumer sector, military expenditures remained almost unchanged. The military did not follow through with the planned reduction of a further 1.2 million men during 1960–61, possibly due to the crisis over the building of the Berlin Wall. Military expenditures rose in 1961 and again in 1962. Accepting Khrushchev's position that the initiative to start a war lay with the West, the military establishment, consistent with military thinking for the past 155 years, argued the need to be able to mount a successful invasion into Western Europe once war began. To succeed in invading Europe, they would need a huge army that could overwhelm the enemy and absorb losses while continuing to advance. They therefore vociferously resisted paring down the conventional forces. Khrushchev argued the contrary: that with the nuclear deterrent, only a small army was needed.[6]

In contrast to Khrushchev, who thought nuclear weapons would never be used but wanted them for their deterrent value, the military saw nuclear missiles as a sort of long-range artillery to hit concentrations of enemy forces and important political centers. Military leaders did not believe in the concept of limited nuclear war. Their differences in thinking about the use of nuclear weapons and opposition to any reduction of the conventional forces created tension between the military leadership and Khrushchev. Zhukov took the position that the military (under his leadership, not the party's) should be the arbiter of all things military. Khrushchev pushed back, asserting the power of the party over the army and forcing Zhukov to retire in 1957. By 1960, Khrushchev had manned all the high-level positions in the military with his supporters; he had served with many of them during the war. He thought he could trust these men to accept civilian control over the military and submit to party oversight of strategy and doctrine, which he saw as critically important in the nuclear age. In the end, the officer corps proved disloyal to Khrushchev. The Ministry of Defense and the General Staff conspired with the security organs and representatives of the party and government to oust Khrushchev from the general secretary position and into forced retirement under house arrest in 1964 citing his reckless foreign policy and irresponsible reduction of the armed forces.

In 1955, the Soviet Union oversaw the creation of the Warsaw Treaty Organization (WTO, usually referred to as the Warsaw Pact), consisting of Bulgaria, the German Democratic Republic, Czechoslovakia, Hungary, Romania, and Poland. The member nations signed the Treaty of Friendship, Cooperation and Mutual Assistance formally making the satellite states of Eastern Europe the USSR's military allies. The treaty created a joint military command, a political consultative committee, and various auxiliary organs. The signatories pledged to abstain from threats of violence in their international relations, to consult on international problems, and not to enter any coalition or agreement contrary to the Warsaw treaty.[7] In short, they were to subordinate their military and foreign policies to the Soviet Union. The postwar occupation followed by Romania's and Bulgaria's signing on to the WTO cemented Russia's long-sought hegemony over the Balkans (except for Yugoslavia).

A Soviet general or marshal always commanded the WTO. He presided over regularly held meetings in Moscow, where a permanent section of the Soviet General Staff that dealt with WTO affairs had its offices. The Soviets armed the WTO armies, but some of the member states also developed their own arms and ammunition manufacturing capacity. By 1960, the Soviets had troops only in East Germany and Poland. The size of the combined armies of the WTO, excluding the Soviet Army, in 1960 was about 1 million men. The Soviets gave the East Europeans up-to-date antiaircraft technology and weapons (air defense radar, antiaircraft missiles, and fighter interceptor aircraft), but not the most modern tanks and artillery. As the Soviets upgraded their forces with new weaponry, they passed off the older models to the East Europeans. The Soviets did not provide the WTO strategic offensive weapons such as long- or medium-range bombers and long- or medium-range missiles, nor did the Soviets give them nuclear weapons.

It is still not clear how much the Soviet military ever trusted the WTO, but it is known that no East European army was ever included in the forces intended to launch the first wave of an invasion into central Europe. One of the more problematic members of the WTO was Poland. The animosity between Poles and Russians is well known and did not end with the imposition of communism in Poland. In 1956, Khrushchev had threatened to invade Poland (as it had Hungary) if the Polish Communist Party did not get the striking and rioting population under control. The Polish army reacted by indicating it would side with the Polish people against the Soviets in such an eventuality. In the aftermath of the turmoil, the Soviet Army withdrew its officers from the Polish army, making it completely autonomous.

That same year, an anti-Stalinist reformist faction of the Hungarian Communist Party came to power, creating turmoil in the leadership that eventually spread to the population. The Hungarian people demanded radical change to reduce the power of the Communist Party, weaken the bonds of the command economy, and decrease Soviet influence over Hungary. The demand for change and the Hungarian premier's withdrawal of Hungary from the WTO on 1 November prompted Khrushchev to send in the Soviet Army—a move Zhukov advised against. Fighting erupted in Budapest in October that lasted for three weeks before it was suppressed. The conflict resulted in the deaths of more than 2,000 Hungarians and several hundred Soviet troops and the mass emigration of 200,000.

The Prague Spring of 1968, in which the Communist Czechoslovak government sought to reform socialism and become a neutral nonaligned state, threatened to destabilize the Eastern bloc and the WTO. After the Czechoslovaks ignored Leonid Brezhnev's repeated warnings to cease their activities, he ordered in the Soviet Army supported by Bulgarian, Hungarian, and Polish troops to occupy the country. Resistance was slight, resulting in several dozen civilian and military deaths. In the aftermath, Brezhnev proclaimed the Brezhnev Doctrine, which committed the Soviet Army and WTO to suppress any reformist movement within the bloc that threatened its stability. A large number of Soviet troops were then stationed in Czechoslovakia to support the new hardline regime and contain further unrest.

Trouble in Poland resurfaced in the 1980s with the Solidarity movement that eventually led to the imposition of martial law in 1981. During the turbulent months leading up to the Polish general Wojceich Jaruzelski taking control, the Soviet Politburo and Ministry of Defense discussed the feasibility of invading Poland and decided that armed intervention would be the option of last resort. The General Staff estimated it would need to call up 100,000 reservists to fill the number of divisions necessary to mount a successful invasion without reducing forces elsewhere in Europe, Asia, or from the war in Afghanistan. It also feared that the Polish army would turn against the invaders, leading to a protracted conflict that would make the USSR vulnerable to invasion by Western powers.

The Brezhnev Era, 1965–1982

During the Brezhnev era, the Soviet state considered nuclear war, or the threat of it, to be a rational instrument of foreign policy. From the military's point of view, victory in a nuclear war was possible, and strategic superiority in nuclear weaponry was obtainable and desirable. The Soviet military prepared to fight and win a conventional war in Europe, guided by the idea that whether it began a war on the offensive or not, taking the war into enemy territory was the key to victory. The military accepted that conventional war could and likely would escalate to nuclear war. Brezhnev adopted Khrushchev's diplomatic outlook—to avoid conflict and rely on nuclear deterrence—yet restored Khrushchev's manpower cuts to placate the military. From the civilian point of view, however, there could be no winners in a nuclear war. The Communist Party kept these conflicting outlooks from the public.

After the break with China in 1960, and with the WTO firmly established, overall Soviet military thinking consisted of the following elements: The military was to be prepared at all times to protect the territorial and political integrity of the "socialist camp"; to provide assistance in wars of national liberation; to conduct an "operational-strategic" offensive if threatened by imminent attack from the capitalist camp; and in the event, to defeat and disarm NATO and gain control of Western Europe, while at the same time defending the USSR against expected attacks by the People's Republic of China. The armed forces were also expected to maintain the internal security of the socialist camp against revisionism such as occurred in Hungary in 1956 and Czechoslovakia in 1968. The military also had an "internationalist duty" to defend the conquests of socialism everywhere, such as in Korea, Cuba, Vietnam, and eventually Afghanistan.[8]

The decision whether to employ nuclear weapons, both tactical and strategic, was the purview of the civilian, not the military, leadership. Both civilian and military leaders agreed that the purpose of strategic nuclear forces was to deter the enemy's use of nuclear weapons and, failing that, to not only win the war on the battlefield but also destroy the enemy's homeland. The civilian attitude from Khrushchev through Gorbachev was deterrence. Thoughts of how many missiles and how many warheads were necessary as deterrents fluctuated between parity and superiority. During the first half of the 1960s, when Soviet intercontinental delivery capability was limited, Moscow judged that if a nuclear exchange did occur, the damage to the USSR would be less devastating if it could strike first. Thus, the Soviet plan was—if war was imminent—to not only launch a ground offensive in Europe supported by nuclear strikes, but also make a massive preemptive nuclear attack on North America.[9]

The thinking of the Soviet leadership in the 1960s was that if the capitalist-imperialist camp initiated a war, then the USSR would first use nuclear weapons to destroy NATO's theater nuclear capability. Afterward, the Soviet air and rocket forces would launch attacks on large troop concentrations, fleets, and weapons storage sites to clear the way for a combined arms counteroffensive. The military emphasized that nuclear weapons were fully integrated into Soviet theater forces and would be used without hesitation. In 1971, Marshal Andrei Grechko identified medium- and short-range nuclear missiles as the main sources of firepower for the ground forces. Tactical weapons included Free Rockets Over Ground (FROGs), Scud and SS-21 short-range ballistic missiles, SS-20 medium-range ballistic missiles, and nuclear-capable artillery. The ground forces were to take advantage of the gaps in the enemy forces created by nuclear strikes by moving armored forces swiftly through the breaches to conduct encirclement operations. The Soviet military and government believed that there was a high probability of nuclear escalation once war started, and that even if a war began as a conventional war, they had to be ready to transition to nuclear war at a moment's notice.[10]

In December 1969, after several years of thoughtful debate, Soviet thinking changed in response to NATO's switch in 1967 to a position of "flexible response," which entailed dropping the strategy of massive retaliation. NATO no longer planned to rely on tactical nuclear weapons to stop a Soviet attack, thus reducing the chances of an escalation to all-out nuclear war—although the use of nuclear weapons was not ruled out to avoid defeat. Both the Soviet civilian and military leadership changed their war planning accordingly.[11] The new thinking was that war would occur in two phases. In the first phase, the Soviets, starting on defense, would defeat a NATO attack and then counterattack—without the use of nuclear weapons—to drive to the Rhine (in the late 1970s, they would aim for the English Channel and the Pyrenees), expel US forces from Europe, occupy Western Europe, and then seek to negotiate peace with the United States. If the United States would not come to terms, then the USSR would occupy the rest of Europe. The army planned to defeat NATO's main force in just three weeks and estimated that it could take three or four more months to mop up. If peace were not established, then phase two would be to prepare a defense against a US attempt to invade the USSR in the east, or to reenter Europe in the west. In this way, the Soviet military hoped to wage war with conventional forces and avoid the nuclear devastation of the USSR.[12] Fighting on the defensive was largely absent from strategic thought.

To support this new outlook, the Soviets created a huge conventional force that could strike hard and fast but also kept the capacity to launch preemptive nuclear strikes against NATO nuclear forces. In the early 1970s, the General

Staff estimated that a conventional offensive war against the West would necessitate, in the European theater of operations, a 3–5:1 advantage in infantry, 6–8:1 advantage in artillery, 3–4:1 in tanks and self-propelled artillery, and 5–10:1 in aircraft (helicopters and fixed-wing). Over the next ten years, Brezhnev restored Khrushchev's cuts in military manpower to 5.3 million men and expanded the military to 211 divisions, most of them armored or motorized infantry, with a handful of airborne divisions. Between 1968 and the mid-1970s, the military defense industry produced nearly 45,000 tanks and tens of thousands of armored personnel carriers. Just as before the First and Second World Wars, most of the divisions were manned below full strength with the idea that there would be time to bring them to full strength with reservists before hostilities broke out. Units stationed in East Germany were the exception: the army kept them manned at or near war footing.

Besides expanding, the armed forces upgraded its tanks, armored personnel carriers, and tactical aviation. The thinking was that NATO would be deterred by the Soviets' overwhelming conventional force, but if a war did break out, the Soviet military could win a conventional war and not have to resort to nuclear weapons. Though the armed forces retained the capacity to launch preemptive nuclear strikes, Brezhnev adopted the policy of "no first use" of either tactical or strategic nuclear weapons. The civilian Communist Party leadership no longer considered escalation inevitable.[13] The Soviets' switch to conventional war as the first option destabilized the international situation as their conventional buildup convinced some in the United States and NATO countries that the USSR was prepared to launch an invasion of Western Europe without needing to mobilize in advance. This made it more likely that NATO would resort to nuclear weapons defensively to buy time to mobilize and reinforce with conventional forces transferred from the United States.[14]

The expansion and upgrading fit with the Soviet General Staff's concept of the offensive-defense—that is, if attacked or threatened with attack, the Soviet military could counterattack or preemptively attack. The General Staff avowed that Soviet military doctrine was offensive in character. They were clear that they intended to win any war with NATO through offensive action.

In the 1960s and 1970s, the Soviets anticipated that there would be a two-week period of "high tension" before a war broke out. The military planned to use this time to mobilize reserves and deploy mobile nuclear-capable missile launchers. Just because the military's doctrine was offensive, however, did not mean the civilians were committed to firing the first shot. Both agreed to take the offensive once the first shot was fired. The General Staff wanted to start shooting sooner rather than later, thinking that seizing the strategic initiative in the first five minutes of a war would be decisive.

Coincident with the Soviet buildup of the 1970s, military thinking moved away from the strategy of intercontinental preemption to a strategy that abstained from nuclear strikes on North America, except in retaliation, and sought to avoid the use of nuclear weapons in Europe. This included deploying the next generation of medium-range ballistic missiles, such as the SS-20, as a deterrent. In response, the West developed and deployed its next generation of medium-range missiles, such as the Pershing II, a move the Soviet military had not foreseen.

China, after the break with the Soviet Union in the early 1960s, began to be seen as a threat and was factored into the military's recalculations that helped justify the costs of expansion and weapons development. Prior to 1970, war planners considered that attacking the United States with strategic nuclear weapons also required a nuclear attack on China to prevent China from being left as the dominant power. After 1969, the Kremlin decided to further deter China from taking advantage of a Soviet war with the West by beefing up its conventional forces in the Far East. In 1961, the Soviet Army had twenty divisions with 225,000 men and 200 aircraft along the border marked by the Amur River. By 1975, the number of armored and mechanized divisions on the Chinese border had risen to forty-five, with 375,000 men, 1,200 aircraft, and 120 medium-range missiles. Over the next ten years, this number increased to fifty-five divisions.[15] China had 1.5 million men stationed along the border and, as of 1969, possessed nuclear weapons.

US President Richard Nixon and Soviet General Secretary Brezhnev opened an era of détente in the early 1970s with visits to each other's countries. Brezhnev sought to use the reduction in tensions to limit spending on arms. Détente, and the civilian leadership's downplaying of the nuclear option, however, led to tension with the Soviet military. Brezhnev openly challenged the views that nuclear war was a rational instrument of policy, that victory in a nuclear war was possible, and that strategic superiority was desirable. He and the civilian leadership adopted the position that there could be no winners in a nuclear war. They successfully negotiated the Helsinki Accords, signed in 1975, which settled the postwar boundaries of Eastern Europe, relieving that as a source of friction. Later, in hopes of further reducing tensions, Brezhnev initiated the idea of a mutual pledge of no first use; getting no response from the West, he unilaterally pledged, in 1982 in a speech to the United Nations, that the USSR would not use nuclear weapons first in a military confrontation. Chief of the General Staff Marshal Nikolai Ogarkov did not publicly commit the military to this view until 1983. At that point, Ogarkov stressed the need for more-sophisticated conventional weapons to match the West's qualitative advantage. The civilians' shift on the use of nuclear weapons led the General Staff to abandon the idea that war would be decided early on with the massive use of nuclear weapons, as espoused by Sokolovskii in the 1960s. Rather, it anticipated a prolonged conflict conducted primarily with conventional weapons.[16]

"Deep battle" theory continued to guide the thinking of the Soviet Army. Nuclear war or no, once the main attack penetrated the enemy defenses, a maneuver element would enter the breach and drive deeply to attack enemy nuclear weapons sites and systems if they had not already been destroyed; other targets included headquarters, logistics capabilities, communication and transportation infrastructure, staging areas, key terrain, and airfields. The attacking maneuver unit could be either an air assault battalion or regiment, or an armored or mechanized infantry unit. The leading elements that penetrated the enemy lines were to avoid becoming decisively engaged and instead maneuver and drive forward until they reached their objectives. Tank regiments reinforced with mechanized infantry detachments were assigned objectives twenty to thirty miles in the enemy rear. Once the leading regiments had secured their objectives, the deep operation was to commence using operational maneuver groups (OMG). In the 1970s, Marshal Ogarkov, building on the army's Second World War experience, organized army-level OMGs comprising an armored unit, either a tank division or corps, heavily reinforced with self-propelled artillery; motorized rifle units; engineers; and motorized logistical support. A *front* OMG was based on a tank army with objectives up to ninety miles deep into enemy territory.[17] The primary objectives in a war in the European theater, using OMGs, were to deny NATO the ability to mobilize its resources or escalate the conflict with nuclear weapons, and, by rapidly occupying Western Europe, to exclude US forces from Europe.

Responding to an economic slowdown, Brezhnev refused to increase defense spending in 1977 and even proposed reducing it further, which heightened tensions between the General Staff and the Politburo. At the 26th Party Congress, in March 1981, Brezhnev announced there would be no further increases in military spending and that he planned to divert resources to the consumer sector. The high command protested so vigorously that in October 1982 Brezhnev, though in failing health, called a special meeting in the Kremlin to defend his policy to limit the growth of military spending to the same rate as the growth of the economy.

Meanwhile, the costs to the military for high-tech equipment rose just as the war in Afghanistan was eating into the military's funds. Minister of Defense Marshal Dmitri Ustinov supported the new spending plan, but Ogarkov argued the importance of both conventional and nuclear weapons in objecting to defense cuts. Ogarkov distrusted détente, which Brezhnev relied on to justify his spending limits.[18] Following Brezhnev's death in November 1982, Ogarkov continued to press for greater sums for the military even though the new general secretary, Yuri Andropov, followed Brezhnev's precedent of keeping military expenditures from rising. Probably as a sign of his displeasure, Andropov replaced Ogarkov in 1984 with Gen. Sergei Akhromeev.

The Chinese Threat

A potential war with the capitalist camp occupied most, but not all, of the attention of civilian policy makers and the General Staff; the Chinese threat and the potential for a two-front war was taken seriously. In March 1969, the USSR and China fought a two-week skirmish over Damanskii Island (Zhenbao Island to the Chinese). China disputed the Soviet Union's claim to the island, which it attempted to secure with border guards. The Chinese decided to make an issue of the island as part of their challenge to displace the Soviet Union as the leader of the world socialist movement. Chinese aggression caught the USSR by surprise, even though it was obvious China had strengthened its forces in the area as diplomatic tensions escalated.

In the end, fewer than a thousand soldiers were involved, and casualties were light; the Soviets kept control of the island. Several other smaller clashes occurred in the months that followed, the last being a company-sized fight in August at Lake Zhalanskhol in which Soviet border guards pushed an incursion by Chinese troops off Soviet territory. The clashes heightened Soviet fears of war with China, which increased dramatically after the US-Sino rapprochement in 1972. The USSR feared for its position in the Far East. The border cities of Vladivostok, Blagoveshchensk, and Khabarovsk were all vulnerable to Chinese attack. The General Staff did not believe the Soviet Army could beat the Chinese with just nuclear weapons but did not want to divert forces intended to fight NATO to the Far East.

The Afghan War

On 25 December 1979, the Soviet Union, contrary to the advice of both the General Staff and the Foreign Ministry, introduced ground troops into the Democratic Republic of Afghanistan (DRA). Two days later, Soviet special forces killed the communist ruler of Afghanistan, Hafizullah Amin. The Soviet Army and Brezhnev's government had supplied Amin and his Khalq faction of the communist People's Democratic Party of Afghanistan with armaments and thousands of advisers for several years, but a faction within the Politburo led by Andropov, then head of the KGB, had grown disenchanted with Amin's policies. Andropov feared that Amin, who had accepted economic aid from the United States, might switch sides. The Soviet Union preempted such a move, unlikely as it was, by allying with the other main faction of Afghan communists, the Parcham, led by Babrak Karmal, who replaced the murdered Amin. Karmal welcomed the Soviet forces.

When Chief of the General Staff Ogarkov was informed that the Politburo intended to send troops into Afghanistan, he furiously objected. Once Minister of Defense Ustinov overrode his objections, Ogarkov declared the army needed to commit between 400,000 and 500,000 troops, most of whom would be used to seal off the border with Pakistan. Ustinov and the Politburo dismissed these numbers out of hand. They hoped to keep troop strength to no more than 100,000 men, and preferably fewer in the specially created 40th Army. Furthermore, Ustinov forbade Ogarkov to use troops designated to support the defense of Eastern Europe, clearly signaling that, just as in tsarist times, defense in Europe took precedence. Therefore, the General Staff decided to use a handful of regular airborne regiments and several motorized rifle divisions manned by 50,000 reservists called up from the Turkestan and Central Asian Military Districts, many of whom were Muslim and sympathetic to the Afghans. They counted on the ability of a modern mechanized army to defeat lightly armed resistance fighters in short order. The strategic goal of the Soviet Union, reflected in the mission of the 40th Army, was not to conquer Afghanistan or turn it into a satellite state but to suppress the resistance movements long enough for Karmal's government to gain a secure hold over the population so it could survive on its own as a friendly neighboring socialist state.

Prior to the introduction of armed forces into Afghanistan, and throughout the conflict, the party leadership remained determined to limit the Soviet military commitment. The first acts of the 40th Army were to secure the single road into Afghanistan from the Soviet Union through the Salang Pass, as well as establish a bridgehead over the Amu Darya River on 25 December, two days before Red Army paratroops and a special KGB unit assassinated Amin and replaced him with Karmal. Soviet forces seized important posts in Kabul and attempted to neutralize the elements of the Afghan army loyal to Amin, which involved heavy fighting between Soviet airborne units and Afghan army units in Kabul.

From its entrance until the final withdrawal of the 40th Army in 1989, the Red Army's strategy centered on three major objectives. The first was to secure Kabul by keeping the roads open between that city and the cities of Kandahar and Herat and keeping the Salang highway open between Kabul and Termez in the USSR. The Soviet Army established outposts on these roads and devoted extra efforts to pacify the provinces north of Kabul as well as those bordering the USSR. The second objective was to take the war to the resistance in the form of sweeps of Mujahideen-held territory with large mechanized forces and aerial bombing of suspected rebel villages. After only a few years, these tactics compelled around 5 million Afghan civilians to flee to Iran or Pakistan. The army's third objective was to close the Afghan-Pakistani border to prevent foreign powers from supplying the resistance and to keep Pakistan from becoming a base of operations for the resistance movement. In this objective, the army failed utterly.[19]

In 1980, 1981, and 1982, the 40th Army conducted large-scale search-and-destroy missions into the hills and valleys. The Panjshir Valley, only forty miles from Kabul, received special attention. After the Mujahideen suffered heavy losses trying to fight conventionally, the rebels changed tactics. They, like the Poles in 1863, organized themselves into detachments of from twenty to two hundred men that ambushed and harassed Soviet troops using rifles, machine guns, mortars, and rocket-propelled grenades and then withdrew before the Soviet soldiers could bring their superior firepower to bear.[20] Throughout the war, the favorite targets of the Mujahideen were road-bound vehicular convoys. The guerrillas, like the Finns in 1939, would ambush the column, first disabling the rear and lead vehicles, thus bringing the rest to a halt, and then chopping it into isolated pieces.

In 1982, the majority of the reservists were withdrawn from the DRA and replaced by regulars in mechanized infantry and airborne units. The Soviet Army began to use battalion-sized helicopter-borne operations against the Mujahideen. These operations sometimes scored local successes but not on a scale that had a chance to change the course of the war. While in control of villages thought to be sympathetic to the resistance, the Soviet Army adopted a policy of laying waste to the infrastructure, crops, and livestock to make it worthless to guerrillas. Atrocities against civilians were common. This behavior contributed to the exodus of civilians to Pakistan and Iran, engendered greater hatred of the Soviet invaders among the people, emboldened them to see the war through to the end, and convinced them to send their sons to fight when they came of age.

Because the resistance had no aircraft, the Soviet Air Force had undisputed control of the air, but the Mujahideen could destroy both airplanes and helicopters with antiaircraft weapons such as heavy machine guns and Stinger antiaircraft missiles supplied by the United States. The Stinger missiles, particularly after 1986, reduced the effectiveness of Soviet airpower by forcing fighter-bombers to fly higher, thus reducing the accuracy of bombing, and forcing helicopter units to adopt less aggressive tactics. As pilots became more cautious, so did the ground troops they supported, thus reducing the pressure on the Mujahideen.

The Afghan War was essentially a counterinsurgency war; as such the 40th Army conducted three different levels of operations. Major operations using an airborne division supported by artillery and aircraft, accompanied by Afghan army units, sought to engage large groups of Mujahideen. These operations developed in stages and lasted for several weeks. The next level was smaller and usually consisted of one airborne regiment deployed in helicopters and/or armored personnel carriers with artillery and air support. They aimed to destroy a specific group of guerrillas whose location had been determined by Afghan intelligence. These operations lasted from around a week to ten days. As part of both types of operations, soldiers often combed villages in search of weapons caches or Mujahideen hospitals. Operations in areas far from bases conducted solely with helicopters lasted only three to five days because of difficulties of supply. Ambushes carried out by a few score soldiers constituted the third and smallest level of operations. Small units moving on foot conducted ambushes at night along roads and mountain trails thought to be frequented by the Mujahideen, and near villages suspected of harboring guerrillas. Combat had a seasonal rhythm. It was most intense in spring and summer but tended to slacken in the winter, when many Mujahideen went home to their villages or to Pakistan.[21]

Soldiers deployed in the combat zone for roughly eighteen months and then rotated home to be demobilized. Despite the myriad problems confronting the 40th Army and individual soldiers and officers, the Soviet forces gave a good account of themselves overall. Small unit leaders, particularly in the airborne and air assault units, devised innovative tactics to gain an edge over their adversaries. Men fought courageously, using personal initiative and ingenuity to accomplish missions and to survive.

Twice a year, the USSR sent replacements to the 40th Army: in the fall came the men called up in the spring, and in the spring came the men called up the previous fall. Despite continual reinforcements, units tended to operate below strength, with anywhere from one-quarter to one-third of the men on sick call or hospitalized.[22] The average number of Soviet soldiers in Afghanistan on an annual basis fluctuated between 80,000 and 115,000. Some additional helicopter-borne units sortied out of Termez in the Uzbek SSR. Many fighter and bomber units also operated from the USSR into Afghanistan. The peak total of Soviet troops operating in the conflict in any given year was approximately 150,000. Altogether approximately 642,000 Soviet servicemen served in the war during 1979–89.

At war's end, the Soviet Union claimed to have suffered a death toll of 12,854 soldiers and 1,979 officers, with 35,478 officers and men wounded in action. Some 330 servicemen, including 21 officers, were taken prisoner or declared missing in action. After the collapse of the USSR, the Russian Army announced that the true death toll was closer to 24,000 soldiers, when fatalities from all causes were included. The Soviet Army suffered 415,932 casualties from disease; especially prominent were jaundice, dysentery, hepatitis, typhus, and skin diseases endemic to the region. Combat wounds and disease resulted in 10,751 soldiers becoming invalids. The army's medical service was unprepared to tackle both combat casualties and the health requirements of a third world nation and did not rise to the occasion.[23] More than 26,000 Afghan Army soldiers lost their lives, and another 54,000 suffered nonfatal wounds.[24]

Equipment losses amounted to 332 helicopters, 147 tanks, 1,314 armored personnel carriers, 433 artillery pieces and mortars, 510 engineering vehicles, and 11,369 trucks.[25] The air force lost 114 airplanes. The Mujahideen resistance remained fragmented along tribal and ethnic lines, which prevented a coherent unified armed struggle that would have been even more costly for the Soviet Union.

In 1986, on orders from the Communist Party's new general secretary, Mikhail Gorbachev, and over the objections of the General Staff, the USSR began turning the war over to the Afghan army as the first step in the eventual Soviet withdrawal from the conflict. Gorbachev was unconvinced that the Soviet Army could win the war or that the Afghan people would ever accept the communist government. The General Staff argued the case for staying, fearing the loss of prestige from admitting failure. Nonetheless, the civilian leadership prevailed. The pullout, negotiated in Geneva between representatives from the Afghan government, the United States, the USSR, and the Mujahideen began in earnest in 1988 and was completed on 15 February 1989.

The Gorbachev Era, 1985–1991

The final years of the Soviet regime, the Gorbachev Era, from 1985 to 1991, saw the last shift in how the Soviet military thought it might fight a future war. From the beginning, there was tension between Mikhail Gorbachev, the armed forces, and the Soviet military-industrial complex. Gorbachev, elevated to the Politburo as a candidate member in 1980, observed that the party had taken a back seat to the Ministry of Defense and General Staff in formulating security policy and military doctrine since Khrushchev's ouster. He worried that the military and its considerations had been driving foreign policy for too long, and he intended to put the civilians in the Communist Party and Soviet government squarely in charge. Numerous things that had happened before he became general secretary in 1985 irked him, such as the deployment of nine hundred SS-20s to Eastern Europe, which had led to the US deployment in Western Europe of Pershing II missiles and cruise missiles. The SS-20 could hit London, but the Pershing II and US cruise missiles could hit Moscow. The deployment of the Pershing IIs had led to antinuclear protests in Western

Europe that were matched by antinuclear and overtly anti-Soviet protests in Eastern Europe. Gorbachev criticized the military for not considering the diplomatic issues involved. He dismissed the military leadership's claim that they could win in Afghanistan, a war the Ministry of Defense had promised would be short. He was also appalled at the Soviet Air Force's shooting down of Korean Air Lines Flight 007 in 1983 that led to international condemnation of the Soviet Union.[26]

By the end of 1987, exercising his prerogative as commander in chief, Gorbachev had replaced hundreds of generals, admirals, and marshals of the Soviet Union. These men were forced into retirement, most them in the aftermath of the May 1987 Matthias Rust affair, in which a young West German flew a civilian Cessna aircraft unopposed through Soviet airspace and landed in Red Square. Gorbachev used this incident to point out the incompetence of the senior leadership and question their use of the billions of rubles that had been spent on defense—particularly air defense. Most significantly, he was able to replace the hawkish minister of defense Marshal Sergei Sokolov with Gen. Dmitri Iazov. In the space of two years, Gorbachev replaced ten of the sixteen deputy defense ministers, the chief of the Strategic Rocket Forces, the heads of the Group of Soviet Forces in Germany, Poland, and Hungary, as well as the commanders of the Moscow and Belorussian Military Districts. These actions both enhanced civilian control over the military and furthered generational change whereby the World War II generation began to lose its dominance of military affairs. Gorbachev positioned the Foreign Ministry and the party to be more in charge of arms control negotiations at the military's expense.[27]

Gorbachev and his minister of defense, Iazov, like Brezhnev before them, sought parity with NATO rather than numerical superiority. The Soviet military began to recognize that quantitative superiority in conventional weapons had become less important than qualitative superiority. NATO had developed precision-guided munitions that could destroy targets that previously would have had to be attacked with nuclear weapons. Cruise missiles could strike deep targets with conventional warheads made of new and far more powerful explosives. While NATO was rearming with next generation weapons and technology, the Soviet bloc's arsenal fell behind: in 1987, the WTO reported that 49 percent of its aircraft and 19 percent of its naval vessels were obsolete. Most of the tanks and artillery pieces were aging.[28]

During the waning years of the Brezhnev era, the Soviet military gave more attention to strategic defense. In line with Svechin's thinking of the 1930s, the General Staff accepted that wars would transition between offense and defense. Staff officers wrote and talked in terms of offense still being the principal mode of operations; however, the need to prepare for defensive operations to counter a surprise attack by NATO and then transition to the counteroffensive as quickly as possible became more common. In the 1960s and 1970s, thinking had been predicated on the assumption of a war being started by NATO after escalating tensions and a buildup of forces in theater, which the Soviets could counter with their mobilization and preparations to attack; however, in the 1980s, with the advances in NATO's high-tech weaponry, the idea gained traction that a war could start as a surprise and the Soviets would be thrown on the defensive for an indeterminate length of time.[29]

Gorbachev's Reform of Doctrine

Gorbachev faced his greatest opposition from the military over the related issues of reducing military and defense industry expenditures and adopting a purely defensive military posture in Eastern Europe. By going over to a true defensive posture, Gorbachev hoped to vastly reduce Cold War tensions and the possibility of war, which would enable him to reduce the size of the military and the military budget. He wanted to redirect the savings to the failing consumer economy. At the 27th Party Congress in February 1986, Gorbachev not only renewed Brezhnev's no-first-use pledge, but he also unveiled his new defensive doctrine of "reasonable sufficiency," reminiscent of Khrushchev's thinking. In doing so, Gorbachev questioned how large the army needed to be. Gorbachev wanted the Soviet leadership to abandon the mindset that the capitalist-imperialist camp had to be destroyed. Instead, he adopted the policy that it would suffice merely to defeat an attack by the West. This, in a nutshell, was his "new thinking"; the army needed to be as large as reasonably sufficient to defeat a NATO attack. He dismissed the idea that a war with NATO would be existential to the socialist camp. Gorbachev, highly affected by the April 1986 Chernobyl nuclear accident, was convinced that a war could lead to the destruction of the entire human race, and thus the capitalist and socialist camps had to reconcile and together seek peace. Gorbachev's view was supported by Soviet public opinion (also affected by Chernobyl) as early as 1987.[30] Thus, if a NATO attack merely needed to be defeated and not followed up with a counterattack, then the USSR could make do with a smaller (but still large) armed force and a reduced arsenal of nuclear weapons. In essence, Gorbachev proposed a "defensive-defense" at the expense of the military's "offensive-defense." In May 1987, the WTO formally announced that its doctrine was now first and foremost geared to preventing war, both conventional and nuclear, and that half of all training time would be devoted to defensive operations. The Ministry of Defense and the General Staff did not take this pronouncement seriously; they, like their Western adversaries, thought, incorrectly, that it was part of the ongoing propaganda campaign to portray the capitalist camp as aggressive.[31]

Maintaining a large military was just as, if not more, burdensome to the Soviet Union as it had been to Imperial Russia. The economic burden was obvious when one considers that in 1987, when Gorbachev began contemplating the reduction of the Soviet military, the armed forces had 211 armored and mechanized divisions and seven airborne divisions distributed between at least five theaters of military operations. Those divisions had more than 53,000 main battle tanks, 48,000 pieces of artillery (including mortars and multiple-rocket launchers), and 4,600 surface-to-air antiaircraft missile launchers. The army had 4,500 attack and transport helicopters. Added to this was the cost of maintaining the Soviet Air Force, the air defense forces, the navy, and the Strategic Rocket Forces with all their aircraft, ships, submarines, and missiles. There were in excess of 5 million men and women on active duty and 55 million reservists.[32] To support this armed force, 40 percent of the Soviet workforce was employed in the military-industrial complex. To sustain and supply the military, the state, in the 1980s, devoted to it 49 percent of all new annual investment. In the words of Christopher Donnelly, "The Soviet Union did not have a military machine, it was a military machine."[33]

Gorbachev's announcement of his doctrine of "reasonable sufficiency" to the party and the world did not automatically translate into action. Military leaders and their allies in heavy industry resisted it successfully in the short term. Gorbachev put pressure on both camps by promising the Soviet people domestic economic reforms that could only come at the expense of the military. If the military balked, the public would blame it for the persistent lack of consumer goods. Many, if not most, of the replacements of the new military leaders were no more amenable to Gorbachev's reductions than their predecessors had been, but after 1987 they understood that opposition jeopardized their careers.

A public debate began thanks to Gorbachev's policy of glasnost, which dramatically reduced censorship. The core issue pitted the military versus civilians over the nature of the threat. The civilian-dominated party and government argued that the United States was not all that threatening and never had been, but that the military had exaggerated the threat for its own interests. Gorbachev's supporters believed that the Americans and Europeans did not want to be annihilated in a nuclear war any more than the Soviets did. Gorbachev came close to completely dismissing the ideological basis for the East–West conflict. Some antimilitary-minded party leaders went so far as to propose returning to the mixed cadre/territorial system of the 1920s (an idea that Khrushchev had flirted with). They also raised the idea of ending conscription in favor of a volunteer army.[34]

The military argued that the imperialists were as hostile and aggressive as they had ever been, citing President Ronald Reagan's modernization of the US arsenal and expansion of conventional forces. The General Staff was divided over whether to endorse "reasonable sufficiency." Those against reductions, led by the chief of the General Staff Marshal Sergei Akhromeev, argued that it was reasonable to have a military sufficiently huge to defeat or deter an attack. He called it "defense sufficiency." Minister of Defense Iazov, in 1987, claimed that nuclear parity equated to "reasonable sufficiency." Deputy minister for defense for armaments Gen. Vitalii Shabanov challenged Gorbachev's stance publicly, saying the USSR was prepared to launch a first strike if it proved to be a matter of necessity. The military hyped the threat from the United States even as Gorbachev downplayed it.[35] It took strong political pressure over several years for the Soviet military to accept "reasonable sufficiency" and reluctantly begin to implement it.

Following Through with "Reasonable Sufficiency"

In the course of 1987, numerous Soviet colonels and generals wrote articles favoring a doctrine that allowed a future war to start on either the tactical or the strategic defensive to wear down the enemy's attack before the Soviet armed forces went over to the offensive. This was in line with the refusal of the 27th Party Congress to raise military spending limits. In 1988, Gen. Vladimir Lobov wrote in support of Gorbachev's defensive mindset and rejection of war in the nuclear age in the military press: "In these conditions, and in conjunction with the defensive strategy of the Warsaw Pact, the main objectives of Soviet military strategy are to avert war and work out the means to repulse possible aggression."[36] Repelling aggression but without following it up by measures to destroy the enemy was a break from nearly two hundred years of military thinking. It did not go uncontested. "Dueling articles" appeared in the military press between 1986 and 1988 reminiscent of the debates in the 1920s and 1930s over the merits of offense versus defense. Both sides drew on the historical evidence from conflicts during 1938–45 to make their cases. It was a gut-wrenching exercise for the Soviet military to change its way of thinking.[37]

Gorbachev succeeded in negotiating the Intermediate-range Nuclear Forces (INF) Treaty with the United States in December 1987, which banned short- to medium-range land-based ballistic missiles, cruise missiles, and missile launchers with ranges of 300–600 miles, as well as intermediate-range missiles with ranges of 600–3,400 miles. Encouraged by this success, he stunned the military by proposing unilateral cuts in conventional forces to take them down to a "reasonably sufficient" size. On 7 December 1988, Gorbachev promised Reagan he would withdraw six tank divisions from the German Democratic Republic (GDR), Czechoslovakia, and Hungary, and disband them by 1991. He proposed reducing the overall Soviet arsenal by 10,000 tanks (5,000 from

Eastern Europe) and 8,500 artillery pieces, and 800 combat aircraft by the end of 1991. He also promised to eliminate one air-assault brigade and all assault-bridging formations deployed in Eastern Europe. Gorbachev looked to reduce the Soviet armed forces by discharging 400,000 soldiers and 100,000 officers. The WTO countries would also reduce their forces by more than 50,000 men and 2,000 tanks. He promised his next step would be to eliminate an additional 9,130 Soviet and WTO artillery pieces, and 930 combat aircraft. Gorbachev subsequently announced that he intended to eliminate or redirect to civilian consumer production 20 percent of all Soviet armament production capacity and to reduce defense spending by 14.2 percent.[38]

It came as no surprise to Gorbachev that the military objected to unilateral cuts. They complained that it would make the USSR less able to defend itself against attack than it had been in 1941.[39] Without these forces, the Socialist bloc could not respond to a NATO attack with a counteroffensive that could reach the English Channel, or even the Rhine—which was Gorbachev's point.

True to his word, and before the talks on reducing conventional forces in Europe (CFE) had concluded in an agreement, Gorbachev initiated the promised cuts. By December 1989, 265,000 military personnel had been discharged. Besides disbanding the promised six armored divisions, the army reduced the number of tanks in each remaining division in Eastern Europe from 328 to 260 and removed the tank regiments from motorized rifle divisions. Gorbachev, consulting with the Defense Council and the General Staff, ordered the operational maneuver groups disbanded.[40] The Strategic Arms Reductions Talks (START), which had been underway for most of the decade, made real progress in 1989 due to Gorbachev's unilateral reductions.

The reduction of Soviet troops in East Germany, coupled with Gorbachev's revocation of the Brezhnev Doctrine, encouraged unrest there, leading to the fall of the Berlin Wall in November 1989. The opening of the border between East and West Berlin, and shortly thereafter between East and West Germany, was the beginning of the end of the WTO. Domestic unrest, which contained anti-communist and anti-Soviet sentiments as well as pro-Western leanings, forced East European governments to decouple their militaries from their relationship with Moscow. To appease their people, in 1989, each of the Eastern bloc states announced reductions of its army by at least 10,000 men in the next draft cycle. Poland, which planned to reduce its military by 55,000 men, immediately released 22,000 men from duty early.

In negotiations between the WTO governments and the Soviet Union in 1990, the East European governments insisted that the withdrawal of 50,000 Soviet troops was not enough. Gorbachev then agreed to withdraw an additional 170,000 troops from Eastern Europe. Subsequently, the governments of

Poland, Hungary, and Czechoslovakia insisted on the complete withdrawal of Soviet troops. The GDR, however, did not call for the removal of all Soviet troops, which led popular pent-up anti-Soviet sentiments to burst out in violence.[41]

Later in the year, as East and West Germany began talks on reunification, it became clear to the East German government that to appease popular opinion, all Soviet forces would have to leave the GDR. This set in motion the removal of thirty-one Soviet divisions not only from East Germany, but also from Poland, Hungary, and Czechoslovakia. Some 350,000 enlisted men, 150,000 officers, and 150,000 family members relocated back to the USSR.

With the withdrawal of Soviet forces from Eastern Europe, WTO member states soon made it clear that they were not committed to maintaining the alliance. For all practical purposes, the Warsaw Pact ceased to function in 1990. All institutions of the WTO were officially dissolved in March 1991, throwing the General Staff's plans and doctrine for war into irrecoverable disarray.[42]

On 7 December 1990, Gorbachev announced his intent to reduce the military by a further 500,000 personnel. Marshal Akhromeev abruptly announced his retirement the same day. His loyalty was stronger to the military than to the politicians, even though the military had resisted him in implementing Gorbachev's reforms in the armed forces. Akhromeev was conflicted about Gorbachev's "new thinking" and "reasonable sufficiency." In this he represented much of the military leadership. Few were totally on board with Gorbachev, and many were dead set against him and his reforms.[43] The officers had spent their lives believing the Marxist-Leninist premise that the capitalists were implacable enemies of Soviet socialism and had internalized the idea that they could not be trusted, and now Gorbachev was taking their enemy away—the enemy that justified the militarization of the nation and gave the military such clout. While war may not have been inevitable, in their minds it was certainly possible and had to be prepared for, not just to defend the USSR but to destroy the West. Gorbachev's thinking and policies challenged their worldview with full force and proved wholly disorienting, making it hard for all and impossible for some to reorient their thinking.

Army and Society

The post–World War II Soviet Army was vastly different from the post–civil war army, as was the army's status and imprint on Soviet society. By the time Zhukov was through with his modernization efforts, the army was fully mechanized and motorized, utilized sophisticated radio communications, and possessed a growing arsenal of rockets, all of which required better-educated soldiers to serve effectively. As the Soviet Union became more urban and education more thorough, this requirement was met in the early 1960s. From 1946 to 1967, the term of conscript service in the Soviet Army was three years for the ground forces and four years each for the navy and air force. In the immediate aftermath of the war, young men generally had a positive outlook on service, as the army's prestige had risen considerably. For the first time in the Soviet era, the armed forces did not have trouble attracting officer candidates. Unlike the postrevolution generation of officers who were largely undereducated, the third generation of Soviet officers was well-educated; 75 percent had higher or special technical educations of from four to five years.[44] The image of officers as heroic leaders in combat shifted to that of officers being technologically sophisticated and able to manage complex weapons systems.

To maintain an armed force of several millions with relatively short terms of service, to condition the population to a potential nuclear war with the capitalist bloc, and to gain acceptance of a lower quality of life in order to support the military-industrial complex, the regime furthered the militarization of society, beginning with Soviet youth in primary school. The Little Octobrist organization was where political/military indoctrination for boys and girls seven to nine years old began. Next came the Young Pioneer organization, in which all schoolchildren were automatically enrolled. It operated in the schools to indoctrinate boys and girls ages nine to fourteen years old. At age fourteen, youths were highly encouraged to join the Leninist League of Soviet Youth (Komsomol) through age twenty-five. It was expected that all youths would participate in these organizations. Admission to higher education was contingent on Komsomol membership. Although these youth groups were established in the 1920s, it was not until after the Second World War that the military became active in the patriotic and military training of Young Pioneers and Komsomol members. Local military commissariats and military units sponsored such elective Young Pioneer and Komsomol clubs as "Young Soldier" and "Young Sailor," and ran summer camps associated with these clubs. They also sponsored military sports clubs and "corners of military glory" that honored heroic soldiers from local schools. Hundreds of thousands of schoolchildren were taken on field trips to army posts every year.[45]

With the introduction of the 1967 Law on Universal Military Service, which reduced the term of service to two years, preconscription military training for male youths became compulsory in secondary school, usually when they were fourteen to eighteen years old. This was the final step in their militarization before active service. The total instruction time amounted to 140 hours. Preconscription military training and the accompanying ideological indoctrination had been around in the USSR since the founding of Osoaviakhim in the 1920s, but it only became mandatory in 1970. The justification was that because the time in service had been reduced, the army needed the conscripts to arrive already in possession of basic military knowledge and skills.[46] A more likely rationale is that the Soviet regime had become insecure about the loyalty of the youth. The regime saw military service as the school of the nation and preinduction instruction as the "preschool" of the nation.

In the post-Stalin years, the Ministry of Defense created an updated version of Osoaviakhim, the All-Union Voluntary Society for Assistance to the Army, Air Force, and Navy (DOSAAF), to conduct mandatory preconscription instruction. With the 1967 military service law, the state required DOSAAF to expand its programs without prior notice or time to plan, and with insufficient funding and material resources. It took until 1972 to create basic military courses in nearly 80,000 schools. For youth who graduated school before completing the 140-hour program, DOSAAF struggled to create instruction points at tens of thousands of collective farms and industrial enterprises. The Ministry of Defense inadequately funded DOSAAF for its entire existence, thereby limiting its effectiveness.[47]

Shortly before the end of the Soviet Union, the Ministry of Defense considered the results of DOSAAF's work to range from unsatisfactory to barely adequate. After twenty years, the DOSAAF leadership admitted they could not claim that it was either well-organized or well-run. Each union republic ran its own DOSAAF organization. The Russian Soviet Federative Socialist Republic provided the most comprehensive training; the Central Asian and Baltic republics supplied the least. Officially, one had to finish the whole 140-hour program to graduate from high school and go on to higher education, but enforcement was lax. Responsibility for seeing to it that the young people received proper military instruction lay with the directors of schools, enterprises, and collective farms, but these institutions had other priorities and often ignored DOSAAF, leaving the instructors to their own devices. One Western source estimated in 1980 that only half of all youth had received the required DOSAAF experience.[48] The threat of nuclear war, the cult of the Great Patriotic War of the Soviet Union, and the pervasive presence of the military in most aspects of life and the economy served to militarize Russia to a degree greater than it had ever been under the tsars despite the inadequacies of DOSAAF.

Change in Public Attitudes toward the Military

The 1967 Law on Universal Military Service lowered the draft age from nineteen to eighteen and reduced the time in service by one year in each of the armed services. It changed the process of conscription from annual call-ups of all those registered to semiannual call-ups based on date of birth. Soviet youths registered for the draft when they turned seventeen. Men born in January–June reported for duty in June, and those born in the second half of the year reported for duty in December.[49] Being conscripted did not necessarily mean being sent to do military duty. The Soviet regime used the military draft system to recruit men to serve in the Ministry of the Interior (i.e., in various police forces), construction battalions, and border guards. Terms of service in these forces were the same as in the military and counted as military duty. With the expansion of the military above the 5-million-man mark in the 1960s and the shortened term, military service became the common denominator among males in Soviet society, with millions cycling through it every year.

By the 1960s, the positive feelings about military service generated by victory in the Second World War had worn off, and youths began to seek ways to avoid serving. The usual way to avoid service was to fake an illness as the imperial period; however, unlike their predecessors, few went so far as self-mutilation. Just as in the imperial period, it was common knowledge that medical exemptions could be had for a bribe, which in the 1970s amounted to the hefty sum of 1,000 to 2,000 rubles. The Soviet period saw the use of *blat* or *protektsiya* (influence of important people) to secure exemptions from service. Youths enrolled in higher education more to get an exemption than to get an education. Young men whose parents were educated, had white-collar jobs, and lived in big cities, especially Moscow or Leningrad, were more likely than were youths from peasant or working-class families to secure an exemption or serve a brief stint as an officer in the reserves. A study conducted in the 1980s noted that the desire and attempts to avoid service increased steadily as the distance from World War II grew. Generally, however, Soviet males considered service to be inevitable.[50] Draft evaders and those who refused to serve on religious grounds were subject to harsh punishment; they could be imprisoned for up to seven years.

An antiwar movement—Russia's third in the twentieth century—slowly emerged in reaction to the Soviet invasion of Afghanistan. When Gorbachev's glasnost policy reduced censorship and allowed for more freedom of expression, the antiwar movement exploded and spilled over into antimilitarism in both the USSR and Eastern Europe. The movement galvanized Soviet mothers to defend their sons from being drafted, increased the number of government and party elites who used their influence to exempt their sons from service, and demoralized future conscripts who saw how the Soviet state neglected its wounded veterans. Draft dodging became a problem during the Afghan War and increased once the war was over. Young men began to see evading conscription and desertion as acceptable behaviors, which many parents approved. In 1987, pacifist groups openly protested compulsory military service. Students, supported by faculty, staged protests against both the war and the lack of deferments for university students in 1988. Komsomol officials, disenchanted with the excessive militarization of the regime, gradually but unofficially endorsed draft evasion, and many law enforcement authorities tacitly accepted it.[51] Glasnost in many ways undermined the willingness of young Soviet men to serve their country. Gorbachev's opening to the West enabled the people of the Soviet Union to see how hollow the promises of socialism were. The threat of capitalist attack appeared to be minimal, and the idea of political liberty appealing. Societal support for conscription and preconscription training waned significantly. Many considered that basic military skills would be useless in a nuclear war.[52]

The use of the army to quell nationalistic domestic resistance further blackened the image of the army in the public's eyes. The most egregious use of the army against civilians was in 1989 in what became known as the "Tbilisi massacre." In the capital of the Georgia SSR, the army used paratroops to break up a nationalist rally of Georgians, resulting in the death of twenty-one protesters. Gorbachev blamed the army and allowed the generals responsible to be prosecuted, which further alienated the high command from him.

Another important aspect of the growing rejection of militarism in the Soviet Union was the practice of hazing, called *dedovshchina*, literally meaning the rule of the grandfathers. Dedovshchina was the harsh treatment of new recruits serving their first six months of service by the "grandfathers," or *stariki*—those serving their last six months. The soldiers serving their second or third six months laid low and looked forward to the day when they would become the "grandfathers." Hazing manifested in numerous ways: physical abuse to assert the authority of the stariki, followed by the theft of the new recruits' possessions; forcing the recruits to do all the menial chores, especially those assigned to the stariki; and theft of and extortion of money.

Dedovshchina was likely the result of a combination of factors. The rapid turnover of soldiers led to lack of cohesion among the rank and file and contributed to the vulnerability of the new recruits. Sergeants who also were short-serving conscripts and generally lacked authority sometimes became victims of hazing as well. The economy of shortages in the units resulted in theft as the only means of replacing one's worn-out uniform and gear. Officers' indifference and lax supervision over the enlisted men meant few stariki were punished. It was a war of the strong against the weak and produced units riven by hatred, which resulted in hundreds of suicides and murders each year.[53] The fear of being hazed contributed to draft evasion, and the publicity given the problem under glasnost gave the soldiers' mothers' movement more grounds for complaint while degrading the public's attitude toward the military. In 1989, the movement became institutionalized as the Committee of Soldiers' Mothers with branches in all the major cities.

Besides making the public aware of hazing, glasnost exposed massive corruption among the senior officers of the Soviet Army. Generals habitually diverted military funds and supplies to improve their personal quality of life. Most prevalent was their misallocation of military funds, materials, and the labor of soldiers to build dachas for themselves. Knowledge of this practice further eroded public respect for and trust in the Soviet military.

The August Coup

In 1991, Soviet military leaders' domination of politics, society, and the economy was eroding before their eyes. The General Staff's war-fighting doctrine and ability to defend the USSR were in shambles. The declining efficacy of the Communist Party disoriented the officer corps. Officers felt let down by both the party and the Soviet government, in part because Gorbachev's "new thinking," glasnost, and reductions of the military budget and personnel opened Soviet citizens' eyes to the extent to which their lives had become militarized, which led many to reject the military's dominance. Boris Yeltsin, the first president of the newly created government of the Russian Federation, in 1990 floated the idea that Russian general officers ought to think in terms of serving the RSFSR, which tested the loyalty of the officer corps to the USSR and to Gorbachev.[54]

National movements within the Soviet Union also posed a challenge to the military as soldiers and officers began to consider that their republics had more legitimate claims on their services. The independence movements under the now-overtly nationalist governments of Estonia, Latvia, Lithuania, Armenia, and Georgia demanded that conscripts serve only in their republics and, like Yeltsin in Russia, appealed to officers to put the interests of their republic ahead of those of the USSR. Estonia, Latvia, and Lithuania began to encourage draft resistance.

Russians' desire to serve also decreased. Military schools, the gateway to careers as officers, saw the number of applicants of all nationalities drop, while resignations of junior officers skyrocketed. These conditions led many officers to long for the "good old days" before Gorbachev began his reforms.

The Union Treaty, ratified in the spring of 1991, promised autonomy to each of the USSR's constituent republics. KGB chief Vladimir Kriuchkov initiated a plot to restore the Communist Party to power and prevent the treaty from going into effect. Kriuchkov recruited Minister of Defense Iazov to the plot, along with a six other high-ranking party and government officials. The poorly planned and executed coup attempt, which began on 19 August, failed after only three days. Gorbachev not only refused to go along with the coup but instead condemned it. Yeltsin took the opportunity to seize power from the Soviet government in the name of Russia as a sovereign country. Because of their need for secrecy, the plotters made only half-hearted efforts to garner support for the coup among the army units in and around Moscow. Furthermore, the coup plotters knew that not all officers would support them. As the coup unfolded, many officers condemned it as illegal, seeing the future of their careers in a Russian army under Yeltsin or were quite willing to see the USSR dissolve. The last act of the Soviet Army was one of disloyalty on the part of its highest leaders.

In the days and weeks following the failure of the coup, the union republics declared their independence. Yeltsin outlawed the Communist Party of the Soviet Union and confiscated its property within Russia. Slowly, the Soviet military broke up as the new nations bargained for weapons, equipment, and the return home of their soldiers.

After the Second World War, the Soviet Army became an ever-present and dominating factor not only in defense policy making, but also in economic decision-making and the life of society in the USSR. Soviet society became highly militarized with conscripted service being a normative experience for Soviet youth. Priority in material and resource allocation went to the military-industrial complex, which dominated industrial production. As the Second World War experience guided thinking on future war with the West, nuclear weapons were added to the now fully mechanized and motorized ground forces. War in Afghanistan, which the Soviet Army was unprepared to fight, undermined the popular image of the military. Gorbachev's reforms, especially that of ending censorship, opened the army to criticism, to nationalist reawakenings of the recalcitrant union republics, and to an antiwar/antinuclear movement in both the Soviet Union and the Eastern bloc. His "new thinking" undermined the military's influence in politics, the economy, and society, much to the dismay of many of its leaders.

CHAPTER 6

THE POST-SOVIET ERA,
1992–AUGUST 2022

Given that it has only been just over thirty years since the founding of the Russian Federation as a sovereign state, studying the Russian military in the post-Soviet period is more an exercise in current events than the object of true historical analysis. The archives of the Ministry of Defense are closed to foreigners, and even Russian researchers cannot access materials deposited since 1991. This chapter, therefore, will to a large degree be descriptive rather than analytical with no intent to draw firm conclusions.

The disintegration of the Soviet empire, along with its loss of control over Eastern Europe, ushered in a new era for the Russian military. In most respects, the change was not as radical as was the change from Imperial Russian to Soviet Army. Given that the high command of the armed forces intended to keep things as much the same as possible, there was significant, if not total, carryover of the military culture and thinking of the Soviet period, even more than from the imperial to the Soviet era. In the 1990s, the Russian army made only cosmetic changes, such as to uniforms and insignias. Tactics and doctrine remained anchored in the past. Weapons and equipment remained the same, and research and development stagnated as the economy imploded during the transition from socialism to capitalism.

As part of the disintegration of the Soviet Union, the new Russian Federation was awarded the former USSR's nuclear weapons, though it would take years to relocate them all to Russian territory. Most ethnic Russian officers who stayed in the service elected to serve in the Russian army, while most non-Russians left to serve their new nations' militaries. The army of the Russian Federation found itself having to adjust to an entirely new political and geographic landscape. With no threats from the west, and sufficient nuclear weapons to hold China at bay in the east, there was no basis for Russia to plan for a major war.

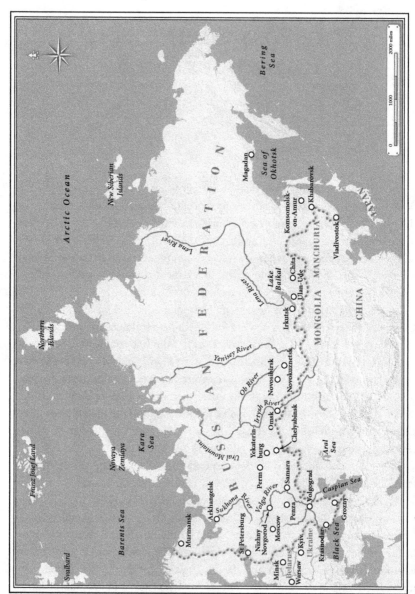

The Russian Federation, 2001

Russia had no need for a large army. Suppressing political unrest remained the exclusive domain of the police forces of the Russian National Guard (*Rosgvardiia*), a police force some 340,000 strong that answers to the president and the Ministry of the Interior. With Vladimir Putin's creation of an authoritarian state under his personal rule, by 2020 he seemed to have attained the same hold over the military that allowed tsars and Communist Party leaders to oversee the military's internal affairs and to direct wartime operations even below the strategic level.

Only slowly, and often unwillingly, did the army reform its doctrine and supporting force structure to match the new environment. Not until 2010 did the army shift the basis of tactical organization away from the division (of which it still had 203 of various strengths) to brigades and regiments made up of battalion tactical groups (BTGs). As of 2022, the armed forces had still not become a professional all-volunteer force. President Boris Yeltsin decreed in 1996 that the army would be fully professional by spring 2000, then Putin promised to achieve an all-volunteer force by 2010. The generals sought to maintain the system of conscription so the army could rapidly expand on short notice. For nearly twenty years after the disintegration of the Soviet empire, the Russian army floundered as it sought new ways of thinking about future war. A reassessment of the threats to Russia included economic and demographic decline, continued degradation of the environment, organized crime, and international terrorism, which far outweighed any large-scale conventional military threat. The focus of strategic thinking was no longer a major war with the West or China (though they were not completely ruled out) but the maintaining and expanding of Russian influence, if not outright hegemony, in the "near abroad" (all the former Soviet republics) by diplomacy, taking back territory through armed aggression, and somehow challenging the global dominance of the United States.

Although potential first use of nuclear weapons became part of doctrine in the decade after the disintegration of the USSR, this was the result of domestic infighting not a rethinking of strategy; civilian reformers promoted it to justify downsizing the army. Given the rhetoric of Vladimir Putin and his more extreme supporters during the war with Ukraine, it is unclear what the place of nuclear war is in current thinking on the practical application of force to ensure Russian domination in Eurasia and the near abroad. Although authorized 900,000 men, the size of the army fell, in 2010, to under 800,000 soldiers, a size it had not seen since the early 1930s. Since the 1990s, it has been manned by a mix of soldiers on three-year contracts and men serving only one-year terms of conscript service.

New Themes and Challenges

In the three decades since the collapse of communism and the disintegration of the Soviet Union, several new themes that characterize the army under the Russian Federation have emerged. The 1990s was a disastrous decade for the army. In the short term, there was a sense of disorientation, malaise, and general disassociation from society. The rapid downsizing of the enlisted ranks by the curtailing of conscription led to a vast surplus of officers. Young lieutenants with skills applicable to civilian work eagerly left the army, but mid- and senior-ranking officers clung to the army in hopes of a pension. It took more than a decade to reduce the number of officers to a reasonable level. As with Khrushchev's reduction in force in the 1950s, dismissed officers were denied a pension. Every budget cycle saw decreases in funding to mere survival levels of an ever-shrinking military. The high command was divided between those in the Ministry of Defense under Marshal Igor Sergeev, who wanted to focus efforts on strategic deterrence (nuclear forces) and tactical missiles, and those in the General Staff under Gen. Anatoly Kvashnin, who wanted to prioritize warfighting capabilities of ground troops through enhanced armored technology. The lack of consensus hindered the military's plea for more funding from the generally antimilitary State Duma under President Yeltsin. They offered no strategic vision to the government, while complaining bitterly about being downsized. No longer backed by the ruling Communist Party and supported by a vastly reduced military-industrial complex, the army lost its leverage over politics and the economy. The army's unpopularity in society fell to that of the Imperial Russian Army.[1]

Putin appointed Anatoly Serdiukov, a civilian, to be the minister of defense in 2007. Serdiukov began a reform program he labeled the "New Look," which included combating corruption in the Ministry of Defense and General Staff by transferring fiscal responsibility from the latter to the former. He also reduced the bloated military administration and vast surplus of officers, which earned him many enemies. Using the shortcomings of the army exposed by the Chechen Wars as leverage against the General Staff, he began the process of transitioning the army from a conscript force into a professional one. He was supported by the new chief of the General Staff, Gen. Nikolai Makarov, who advocated downsizing the armed forces by 200,000 to 1 million, increasing the number of contract soldiers (*kontraktniki*) to 425,000, and raising the pay of kontraktniki and junior officers.[2] In 2012, Putin replaced Serdiukov with Gen. Sergei Shoigu (elevated from the ranks of the security services, not the military), who eased off the scrutiny of finances but slowly pressed ahead with transitioning the enlisted ranks into a contract force and reducing the number of superfluous senior officers. Putin also promoted Gen. Valery Gerasimov to chief of the General Staff in place of Makarov. As annual levies of conscripts decreased, unit commanders pressured draftees to sign contracts.

Gerasimov has been credited with creating the "Gerasimov Doctrine" and has been proclaimed by some Western analysts to be the "father" of Russian hybrid warfare. Gerasimov endorsed the concept of nonlinear warfare, which combines both regular and irregular forces in the use of psychological, economic, and diplomatic means to weaken the enemy with deep operations all within a systematic and national effort that combines diplomacy, mobilized society, and the military—concepts whose origins predate Frunze. In practice, however, Gerasimov tended to promote ideas from the late Soviet era such as nuclear deterrence, the development of hypersonic missiles, and the maintenance of a large reserve force, rather than pursue Serdiukov's professionalizing reforms. His formal document on doctrine published in 2014 indicated the Russian military anticipated a long-term confrontational relationship with the West.[3]

Problematic for the army is the lack of a credible threat to justify it being large or to command a significant claim to the national budget. To address this situation, the Ministry of Defense, since the early 2000s, alternately in league with Presidents Putin and Dmitry Medvedev, chose to represent NATO as a threat even though there is no evidence that the General Staff ever drew up contingency plans to defend Russia from an attack from the west. Instead, Russia's military and diplomatic efforts focused on intimidating the newly independent states of the former Russian/Soviet empire by questioning their right to independence, mounting cyberattacks, engaging in economic warfare, and supporting right-wing opposition political parties and movements in Eastern Europe. This activity prompted Hungary to join NATO in 1999. Following suit, Estonia, Latvia, Lithuania, Bulgaria, Romania, Slovakia, and Slovenia joined in 2004. The Russian military reacted by claiming that NATO was positioning itself to threaten Russia. This "threat" then enabled the military to ask for more robust funding, particularly for research and development of high-tech weapons, but did not enable it to grow in manpower. The Russian Ministry of Foreign Affairs consistently worked to extend Russian hegemony and influence into the near abroad with military aid. In 2021, the Russian army sent troops into Belarus and Kazakhstan by invitation of their dictators, giving Russia leverage over Belarus's foreign policy but not Kazakhstan's.

Maintaining the strength of the armed forces became another new challenge. The Russian population has been in steady decline since 1990. Except for two years, deaths have exceeded births. Emigration is constant; millions of Russians have left the country since 1990, and the pace accelerated with the ongoing invasion of Ukraine. Russian women have one of the world's lowest fertility rates, and none of Putin's incentives have been able to raise it. The population is aging, with the average age being 40.3 years in 2022. The pool of military-age men shrinks annually.

Questions of manning also include a struggle between civilian policy makers and the military over the issue of ending the draft and going to an all-contract force—a struggle that originated in the waning days of the Soviet Union and continued into the Putin era. The conservative leadership of the army clings to the Petrine idea that the army, as an instrument of the state, needs to have the right to take men into the service whether they like it or not. They are also wed to the idea of using mandatory military service to inculcate patriotism in Russian youth. Further challenging the military's monopoly on calling up young men are, for the first time in Russian history, laws passed in 1993 and 2004 guaranteeing conscientious objection and alternative civilian service in lieu of military or other uniformed service.[4]

In 2022, an estimated 70 percent of the soldiers in the Russian army were contract soldiers serving three-year terms of enlistment for relatively decent pay (the equivalent of $600 per month). Although it looks like volunteerism was the primary method of recruitment, such is not the case. The majority of kontraktniki began their service as poorly paid conscripts earning 1,133 rubles monthly ($17).[5] In the 2020s, approximately 270,000 men have been drafted each year in two draft cycles; however, the army only gets about half of them. The air force, navy, Rosgvardiia, and the Ministry of the Interior get the other half. Once in uniform, commanders do their best to coax, pressure, trick, or coerce conscripts into signing contracts to stay on.[6] Those that do volunteer are generally from the less-educated, impoverished rural lower classes looking to get out of their small towns or villages. The army continued to be a multiethnic force with Russians dominating; however, like the tsarist army, the Ministry of Defense set limits on how many minority soldiers could be assigned to each unit. It also set a ceiling on the number of non-Russians to be drafted or allowed to take contracts. The army's reserve theoretically is 2 million men, but in the early 2020s only about 250,000 were considered sufficiently trained to be considered combat ready.

The armed forces also had to adjust to a reduction in funding. To support the armed forces, the state, between 1993 and 2019, committed between a low of 2.7 percent of GDP in 1998 to a high of 5.45 percent in 2016, which accounted for around 20 percent of the national budget.[7] Putin authorized a ten-year modernization plan in 2011 at the cost of 20 trillion rubles ($740 billion). To argue for more funding, the armed forces pled the need for ever-increasing investments to upgrade its technology to compensate for smaller numbers of personnel and to keep pace with NATO. They continually promised to roll out new weaponry but seldom got beyond prototypes. Mass production of high-tech weapons was limited, in part due to massive corruption in the design, procurement, and production process. Dozens of civilians and officers from colonels to colonel-generals have been prosecuted for malfeasance, fraud, and theft for a loss of tens if not hundreds of billions of rubles budgeted for defense.[8] During his tenure as minister of defense, Gen. Pavel Grachev somehow managed to amass a personal fleet of Mercedes automobiles on his salary, and Putin's longest-lasting minister of defense, General Shoigu, is widely thought to have enriched himself and his family (who own 4 billion rubles' worth of real estate) at the military's expense. Instead, the army mostly upgraded its old Soviet equipment and introduced new artillery, tanks, and armored personnel carriers and infantry fighting vehicles in limited numbers. The more sophisticated the designs, the fewer were produced—such as attack helicopters, precision-guided munitions, communication systems, and advanced aircraft—and the higher the failure rate in combat.

Uncertainty about where the military's loyalties lay has proved to be a constant across the centuries. Both Boris Yeltsin and Vladimir Putin felt a certain amount of insecurity about the loyalty of the army. Yeltsin kept his presidency thanks to the army. During the October 1993 constitutional crisis with the Duma, he called on the minister of defense, General Grachev, to send tanks to fire on his parliamentary opponents after the special forces unit Vimpel refused to attack. He did not ask the elite Alpha Group to help him, deeming them insufficiently loyal. Yeltsin for the most part kept aloof from his generals, several of whom became his political rivals. Putin, once the economy recovered in the 2000s, lavished as much money as he could on the military. The high command, when it realized Putin was working toward authoritarian rule, attached itself to him and the position of the presidency—a mutually agreeable proposition—to promote the interests of the army.[9] Common wisdom suggests that by 2022 the majority of generals owed their careers to Putin, and just as with Imperial Russian Army generals and the tsars, it was widely assumed that promotion to high levels depended on their subservience to him personally.

To bolster the loyalty of the rank and file, Putin, in 2019, created the Main Military Political Directorate modeled on the Soviet-era Political Administration of the Red Army (PUR). It assigned political instructors (analogous to the Bolshevik commissars) to teach patriotism and loyalty to soldiers. According to its chief, Col.-Gen. Andrei Kartapolov, the task of this organization "is to form a warrior-statesman, a reliable and loyal defender of the Fatherland, a bearer of the traditional spiritual and moral values of Russian society: spirituality and patriotism."[10] Putin succeeded in co-opting the Russian Orthodox Church. In service to him, it promoted traditional national patriotic values as it had in the Imperial Russian Army. He had the army recruit Orthodox priests to the regiments in 2009 and built a gigantic cathedral dedicated to the Russian army.[11] Putin did not revive Nicholas I's watchwords for the soldiers—"Orthodoxy, autocracy, nationality"—though they would be apt.

Army and Society

After the demise of the Soviet Army, Russian society continued to consider military service in the enlisted ranks to be low status. The length of service for conscripts is half what it was in the Soviet era—just one year, but still at a traditionally negligible rate of pay. Most educated urban youths seek to avoid conscription legally by performing alternative service or securing open-ended educational deferments that enable them to stay in school until they age out of the draft at twenty-seven, or illegally by bribing draft officials or ignoring their draft notice. The burden of service has largely fallen on the small-town and rural poor. From among them, the army has been able to attract or strongarm enough men to serve three-year contracts to meet its manpower goals. Female volunteers contribute to military numbers as well; in 2019, the 40,000 women in uniform made up 4 percent of the personnel of the armed forces.[12]

Dedovshchina and interpersonal violence among soldiers and against soldiers by superiors continued from the Soviet era hindering the army from improving its image and negatively affecting recruitment and retention. Suicides, murders, and desertion resulting from hazing and violence at the hands of superiors (which normally goes unpunished) occur regularly.[13] The Soviet-era Committee of Soldiers' Mothers (renamed the Union of Committees of Soldiers' Mothers of Russia, *Soiuz Komitetov Soldatskikh Materei Rossii*, UCSMR, in 1998) continued its activities into the post-Soviet years to hold the military accountable for its treatment of their sons. It organized protests against the First and Second Chechen Wars. In the latter half of the 1990s, the committee lobbied the Duma to pass legislation to force the military to respect the rights of servicemen, provide long-term care for veterans of regional conflicts, and provide support to the families of servicemen killed in the line of duty. The committee also sought to secure amnesty for deserters through the military procurator's office. Despite coercion by the Russian security services since 2014, the organization continued to support mothers' complaints and protests about the maltreatment of their sons and illegal use of conscripts in combat until it was finally shut down in February 2022 (it still operated on an unofficial basis afterward). In addition to UCSMR, *Prizyvnik* and a half dozen other legal organizations represented the rights of Russian conscripts and regularly sued the army. As a thorn in the side of the Ministry of Defense, the UCSMR was hated by abusive officers.[14]

To retain its connection to Russian youth, in December 1991, during the last days of the Soviet Union, the Ministry of Defense renamed DOSAAF the Russian Defense Sports-Technical Organization (ROSTO). In December 2009, ROSTO was renamed DOSAAF Russia and serves the same purpose of inculcating patriotism and preparing youth for military service. The main difference from the Soviet era is that DOSAAF Russia is truly voluntary. Fearing that post-Soviet youth had become increasingly unpatriotic, the Putin regime created another youth organization, the All-Russian Military-Patriotic Movement, or *Iunarmiia* (Youth army), sponsored by the Ministry of Defense. According to sociologist Jonna Alava, the regime's goal was for the Iunarmiia to "offer to the youth identities of a good citizen and a soldier." Additionally, it was to reinforce "Russianness, traditional gender roles, self-sacrifice, humility, hard work and the pursuit of heroism."[15]

Iunarmiia became affiliated with military units, military schools, DOSAAF Russia, and the Central Sports Club of the Army. Created in 2016, Iunarmiia recruited boys and girls ages eight to eighteen in the public schools. The Ministry of Defense claimed that the number of youths who participated in these organizations was a little more than 700,000 in 2020. Some children became members not by choice but due to pressure from school administrators, teachers, or their nostalgic parents who recalled fondly their days in the Young Pioneers (revived in 2022) and the Komsomol. Armed forces officers, public servants, and workers in defense industries were required to enroll their children in the Iunarmiia. Orphanages automatically enrolled their charges.[16] With military service no longer normative, Russians in general, and the urban educated younger generation in particular, viewed a desire or willingness to serve in the rank and file as aberrant behavior, with the exception being in the impoverished rural areas where it was seen as a mechanism of upward mobility. Some parents and teachers objected to the militarization of youth.

More than ever, public opinion regarding military affairs and war is of concern to Russian policy makers. During the 1990s, antimilitarism was the norm. People were more concerned about economic survival and resented any expenditures on the military they considered excessive. Young men took advantage of every loophole to avoid being drafted. The failure to take public opinion into account and a lack of control over the independent media undermined popular support for the First Chechen War and then fueled open opposition once the casualties mounted and the scale of civilian deaths in Grozny became widely known.[17] During the Second Chechen War, the army won the "information war" by keeping most reporters out of Chechnya and shaping the war's narrative through friendly media outlets. Even so, public support for the war was never great. Popular opinion began to turn in favor of the military in 2008 after the short victorious war against Georgia, which coincided with a general upturn in the economy. People's attention was further drawn to the military with the armed annexation of Crimea in 2014 and Russian military support for the insurgency in the Donbas region. Right-wing Russian nationalists overwhelmingly supported these actions, while anti-Putin liberals deplored them. The government launched a propaganda campaign that painted Ukraine's government as fascist and in the employ of NATO as part of the invasions of Ukraine's Crimea, Donbas, and then the rest of Ukraine. Putin squelched antiwar and antigovernment voices with laws forbidding "discrediting" the military and military operations. No foreign or anti-Putin reporters were allowed into the war zone. The war with Ukraine, officially labeled a "special military operation," begun in February 2022, polarized Russian society between those who supported Putin and the army and those who opposed them. Putin feared to declare war and mobilize the military and society for fear of popular resistance.

Wars of the Russian Federation

Since 1991, Russia has fought five wars: The First and Second Chechen Wars (1994–96 and 1999–2002/2009), a five-day war with Georgia (2008), a proxy war against Ukraine in the Donbas beginning in 2014 after a near-bloodless invasion of Crimea, and the current conventional war with Ukraine begun in 2022, which continues at the time of this writing. Russia was motivated to start every one of these conflicts by a desire to reassert its influence over or directly control territory lost as part of the demise of the Soviet Union. Some believe Yeltsin was motivated to use military force in Chechnya in 1994 in part to shore up his faltering domestic support with a short victorious war. There are strongly supported suspicions that Putin was behind the 1999 apartment bombings in Moscow, Buinaksk, and Volgodonsk, which he used to propel himself into power by insisting on a second war with Chechnya.[18] Putin's use of the military in the near abroad, especially to seize Crimea, Donetsk, and Luhansk, and to attempt to conquer Ukraine, was motivated both by Russian Great Power imperialism and his desire to consolidate authoritarian rule using the war as an excuse to finally shut down all civic and human rights organizations that support democracy and oppose his rule.

The First Chechen War

Lasting twenty-one months, from December 1994 to August 1996, the First Chechen War was a disaster for the Russian army. The initial invasion stands as its most inept foray into war in the past two hundred years. Given short notice to plan (as in the 1939-40 Winter War with Finland) by President Yeltsin, the General Staff together with the staff of the North Caucasus Military Region (NCMR) planned for a short campaign centered exclusively around the capture of the Chechen capital of Grozny. The planning was superficial at best, near criminal at worst. In an atmosphere of self-assured superiority, the planners assumed the invasion would be a cakewalk—Minister of Defense General Grachev boasted that the Russian army would take Grozny in two hours with an airborne regiment—and did not take their duties seriously.[19] They failed to gather sufficient intelligence to make informed decisions, communicate their ideas clearly, supervise subordinate units closely, and coordinate with those who would undertake the operation. The staff ignored the Russian generals with experience in Afghanistan who questioned the wisdom of the war. Col.-Gen. A. Mitiuchin, commander of the NCMR, led with an abusive command style; an after-action report noted that "all his 'instructions' were issued mostly in the form of uncensored curses and abuse."[20] The officer to command the assault on Grozny, Gen. Anatoly Kvashnin, was appointed only two days before the war started. Lax security enabled the Chechen leaders, many of whom had been trained in the Soviet Army, to prepare to resist.

On 11 December, the Russians attacked with three armored divisions. The soldiers, many of whom were native to the region and had ties to people in Chechnya, were not briefed as to why they were invading; the word "invasion" was not even used (reminiscent of the intervention in Afghanistan). Logistical support was poorly planned and chaotically managed. Soldiers went days without food. At times they were reduced to eating dogs. Morale plummeted as soldiers questioned the need for the war and the sacrifice of their lives.[21] Rather than flee the armored onslaught, the relatively well-armed Chechen forces conducted a rearguard action and engaged in guerrilla operations. In the first month of fighting, the invading forces lost 225 armored vehicles destroyed. The advance slowed and unit cohesion was disrupted because fuel for combat and resupply vehicles was contaminated with water (used to disguise theft by supply personnel). Because of that, vehicles, many taken out of storage where they had been since 1991, broke down by the score. In their fight against Chechen guerrillas, Russian soldiers committed atrocities—as they had in Afghanistan—and drove thousands of Chechens to join the resistance.

Reaching Grozny, the Russian army failed to surround it and sent 40,000 men into the assault with no training in urban warfare. Surprising the war planners, the Chechens ably defended Grozny destroying twenty of twenty-six tanks and 102 of 120 armored fighting vehicles in the first three days, mostly using rocket-propelled grenades. Chechen snipers took a heavy toll. Untrained in street fighting, the first assault into Grozny saw heavy Russian casualties, including the near-complete annihilation of the 131st Motorized Rifle Brigade in the fight for the train station in January 1995. The army then resorted to the use of massive firepower (particularly with multiple-launch rocket systems) on a scale that horrified the world, further alienated the civilian population, and energized the antiwar movement in Russia. In a well-planned counteroffensive, the Chechens recaptured Grozny and drove the Russians out in August 1996, which led to a formal negotiated peace and acknowledgment of Chechen independence. Russian personnel losses amounted to 7,500 dead, at least 13,000 wounded, and 700 deserters. Hundreds of Russian tanks and helicopters were lost.[22] Overall, it was a humiliating experience for the Russian army that hurt its image at home and abroad.

The Second Chechen War

In 1999, Yeltsin's prime minister, Vladimir Putin, as part of his bid to become president of Russia, decided it was time to attack Chechnya again to bring it back under Russian control. He launched the war in response to the apartment bombings in Moscow, Buinaksk, and Volgodonsk, which he blamed on Chechen terrorism. The war lasted from August 1999 to April 2009, though the role of the military in operations ended for the most part in 2002.

Without a doubt, the Russian army took to heart the lessons of the first failed Chechen conflict. This time, in advance of the war, soldiers were trained in urban warfare techniques. To motivate them, Putin told soldiers the goal was to "preserve the integrity of Russia."[23] The armed forces took charge of reporting the events of the war to the media, which served to keep the population ignorant of actual civilian casualties, atrocities, and Russian losses. There was more public support for the second war due to belief that Chechen terrorists were behind the apartment bombings. The progovernment media framed it as a war against international terrorism.

The General Staff's plan for the second war was, rather than race to Grozny, to commit 100,000 men to wage a protracted campaign to get to and then surround the capital. They brought weapons designed to help in street fighting, namely those capable of delivering thermobaric munitions. Rather than charge into the city in mass formations with armor as in 1995, the second battle for Grozny was preceded by weeks of artillery, rocket, and aerial bombing. Although this resulted in mass casualties of civilians, the Russian population remained largely ignorant of it as well as of the torture, beatings, and summary executions of suspected Chechen fighters and a raft of other human rights abuses and crimes committed by Russian soldiers. Russian reconnaissance forces along with pro-Russian Chechen forces entered the city in small, dismounted groups to locate enemy strong points. They then called in artillery or air strikes on the targets.[24] Not only were the soldiers tactically more prepared, but they also made better use of communications, artillery support, and snipers. Despite the improvements in combat techniques, the Russian army suffered large number of deaths—officially between 7,200 and 7,500 soldiers died—but the true toll is suspected to be almost double that.

Even with tight control over information, word of heavy losses and atrocities filtered back to Russia. Public opinion polls in the autumn of 2002 showed 60 percent of respondents supported a negotiated end to the war.[25] With Grozny secured, in 2002 the Russian army turned the war over to pro-Russian Chechen forces who continued low-intensity operations until 2017. In 2009, the last Russian military forces withdrew from Chechnya.

The Russo-Georgian War

In August 2008, in coordination with pro-Russian South Ossetian forces, the Russian armed forces launched a surprise attack on Georgia with the goal of seizing South Ossetia for Russia. The land, sea, and air campaign lasted only five days before an internationally brokered cease-fire was arranged. The result was Georgia's cession of South Ossetia to Russia. The balance of forces was so lopsided that no "lessons learned" or evaluations of the Russian military can realistically be made.

Although the victory boosted the esteem of the Russian high command, it exposed serious shortcomings. Of the 1.4 million men in the army, it could only scrape together 55,000 for the operation. The rest were scattered around the country with no way of quickly massing unnoticed. From this experience, the army began working on developing methods to mobilize swiftly numerous brigades and divisions to critical areas on short notice.[26]

Russian Aggression against Ukraine, 2014–2021

The Russian takeover of Crimea in February 2014 succeeded as a "special military operation" by well-prepared forces that achieved complete surprise against an unprepared adversary. Beginning in March 2014, Russian aggression in the Donbas took the form of a proxy war using pro-Russian separatists equipped and armed by Russia. The goal was to seize the Donbas and Luhansk regions and annex them to Russia. The Russian military supported the separatists by conducting a disinformation campaign, bringing in irregular fighters, and deploying regular Russian troops with tanks and artillery. Ukrainian armed forces were able to contest the separatist and Russian forces and turn the conflict into a stalemate that, over the succeeding eight years, cost thousands of soldiers, separatist fighters, and civilians their lives.

2022 Invasion of Ukraine (February–August)

One hundred years after its civil war in which Russian forces twice invaded Ukraine to secure it for the Soviet empire, Russia launched a third invasion as a war of choice by Vladimir Putin to expand Russian hegemony westward and to solidify his authoritarian rule in Russia. The Russian military has repeated many of the same errors it made during the Winter War in 1939 and the First Chechen War. Breathtakingly incompetent planning by the General Staff under General Gerasimov, under the guidance of Minister of Defense General Shoigu and President Putin, assumed a rapid victory over an outmatched opponent. Overestimating its own capacity, the Russian army assumed it would face token and ineffective resistance. Soldiers were told they would be welcomed as liberators. Intelligence provided by the foreign section of the Federal Security Service (FSB) failed to anticipate the unified, competent, and fierce resistance of a foe committed to preserving its territorial integrity and sovereignty. Military intelligence generated by the army's intelligence service (Glavnoye Razvedy-vatelnoye Upravlenie, or GRU) provided no useful information despite Russia's having been in a proxy war with Ukraine for eight years.

The Russians assembled a force estimated to number nearly 200,000 men. The initial invasion force consisted of 120 battalion tactical groups ranging from many understrength units with as few as 350 soldiers to a few overstrength battalions of 900 men supported by thousands of Rosgvardiia troops. The BTGs were drawn from eleven combined arms armies and one tank army. In addition to the mechanized units, the invasion forces included all the army's airborne and air assault units, naval infantry from four different fleets, and multiple helicopter and fixed-wing aviation units. The war began with attacks on four axes: south out of Belarus and Russia, southeast from Russia, north out of Crimea, and west from Russia, Luhansk, and Donbas.[27] According to Western intelligence sources, the Russian advance from Belarus was to divide with one force moving through Chernihiv east of the capital while the other flanked Kyiv on the west, pushing southward through the "exclusion zone" at the abandoned Chernobyl nuclear plant and surrounding marshland. The attack was timed for the winter so that the frozen earth would make the terrain trafficable for tanks. Using a pincer movement around the Ukrainian capital, Russian planners aimed to seize Kyiv in three to four days. The FSB's Spetsnaz was assigned the task of capturing President Volodymyr Zelenskyy, killing him if necessary, clearing the way for the Kremlin to install a puppet government. Forces moving west from Russia aimed to take Kharkiv in concert with an assault from the south out of Crimea to take Kherson and Mariupol, in order to link Crimea to Donetsk along the Sea of Azov. Proxy forces in Donetsk and

Luhansk, supported by the Russian army, were ordered to fight their way westward to clear those "republics" of Ukrainian forces so Russia could annex them.

The captures of Kyiv, Chernihiv, and Kharkiv were thwarted by determined and skillful resistance by Ukrainian regulars and territorial forces armed with sophisticated antitank missiles and short-range antiaircraft missiles and drones used to direct artillery fire or attack with onboard bombs. Chernihiv and Kharkiv were surrounded but Kyiv was not. The Ukrainian government, led by Zelenskyy, rallied the nation and appealed to the Western world for help, which soon materialized. Kherson was surrounded and then captured with almost no fighting because its pro-Russian mayor counseled against resistance. In contrast, the Russian army surrounded and bombarded Mariupol with missiles, artillery, and airstrikes that killed thousands of civilians but were met by stubborn resistance nonetheless. The defenders held out for three months refusing to surrender multiple times.

The causes of the army's failure to achieve in short order the maximum goals set it by Putin were many—and began before the shooting started. There was an astonishing disjuncture between Putin, General Shoigu, General Gerasimov, and the commanders in the field. Neither Putin, Shoigu, nor Gerasimov knew the true state of the units (their manpower issues, supply status, or weapons readiness) to be sent into war. Coordination suffered because there was no single commander of the invasion effort. Other problems were an inexplicable failure to secure air supremacy, lackluster battlefield performance due to ineffective senior leadership, poor training, low morale and lack of motivation, and insufficient numbers of replacements. Failure of equipment and weapons systems combined with foreign support for Ukraine compounded the army's woes. Attempts to disrupt the enemy rear (in line with Frunze's UMD) through a disinformation campaign and the use of spies and traitors within the Ukrainian government and armed forces had no significant effect on Ukraine's ability to resist. The reason for this, some in the army believe, was that highly placed individuals in the intelligence services embezzled large sums of money allocated to subvert Ukrainians in high places.

Organization of the opening campaign was flawed from the start. Each axis of attack had its own commander who acted independently of the others and reported to the General Staff. Road-bound spearheads aimed for deep objectives such as Kyiv, Kherson, and Mariupol along narrow sectors of advance that could easily be delayed or stymied by the destruction of bridges. When things began to go wrong, fearing for their jobs, some generals went to the front not to give advice or guidance, but to shout and scream at brigade and regiment commanders to deliver results. At lower levels, officers poorly supervised their men and seldom took the initiative to overcome obstacles.

The logistical preparation indicated that the army had learned nothing from its failures in the First Chechen War. Problems surfaced in the days before the war with men, in units assembled from as far away as Kamchatka, Murmansk, and Dagestan, already going hungry. During the initial assaults, too many units shared the same supply routes, which led to traffic jams. There was no provision for replacing blown-up bridges. Mechanical failures plagued convoys. Support services to repair trucks were inadequate to the task. There were not enough trucks on hand to replace destroyed vehicles, which forced the army to commandeer less sturdy civilian trucks. Corruption among logistics officers affected the delivery of supplies in quantity and quality (the deputy commander of the Southern Military District, Lt.-Gen. Viktor Voronov, was arrested on charges of corruption in July). Hungry soldiers resorted to stealing from civilians. In some units, for weeks at a time, three men had to share one prepackaged meal at each mealtime. Many of those meals had expiration dates of 2015. Vehicles ran out of fuel (often sold by soldiers for cash to buy food) or broke down and were abandoned by the score. Many found their way into the hands of the Ukrainian army, which refueled or repaired them and employed them against the Russians.

The Russian air force's surprise attack to destroy the Ukrainian air force on the opening day of the war was amateurish. The air force failed to destroy any air base; the majority of Ukraine's aircraft as well as its antiaircraft capabilities survived. Though diminished, the Ukrainian air force could still contest the airspace over the battlefield, thwart Russian air raids, and conduct raids of its own. Ukraine's antiaircraft forces, although weakened, remained intact and able to cause losses to Russian jets and helicopters and to intercept missiles and drones. The Russian air force then limited the use of helicopters and warplanes, resorting mostly to launching missiles from Russian airspace, with reduced accuracy. Especially deadly for Russian helicopters were the thousands of anti-aircraft missile systems given to the Ukrainian army by NATO.

The Russian military also failed in the electronics war. The army needed to, and expected that it would, dominate the electronic warfare aspect of the invasion. The military intended to disrupt Ukrainian command, control, and communications by manipulating the electromagnetic spectrum through jamming, intercepting, or altering communications, and jamming radar, GPS, and other signals. Russia's electronics warfare sections had done well in the 2014 invasion of Crimea, but apparently rested on their laurels. They did not improve their capabilities and underestimated or ignored the fact that Ukraine developed countermeasures in the intervening eight years. When sophisticated Russian communications equipment failed to work (it is rumored that half of the billions of rubles allocated to upgrading communications was embezzled), the Russians resorted to using cell phones on Ukrainian networks, which enabled the enemy to discover their plans and the locations of command posts and thus allowed precise attacks against key personnel. A notable casualty of a precision strike based on electronic intelligence was Maj.-Gen. Andrei Simonov, one of the Russian army's foremost electronic warfare specialists.

Troop-level problems with motivation and morale became manifest from the start. As in the First Chechen War and the intervention in Afghanistan, the army did not issue a uniform, definitive explanation or justification to the soldiers in advance of operations. That task was left to unit commanders, who gave a variety of explanations or none at all; this left the explanation to the pro-Putin media, which promoted Putin's claim that he wanted to denazify Ukraine and end the persecution of Russians in Ukraine. Some commanders told their men that grateful people would greet them with flowers and that the operation would be over in a matter of hours.

Soldiers deployed to Belarus, the Donetsk People's Republic (DNR), and the Luhansk People's Republic (LNR) were told they were there for maneuvers. Many soldiers discovered they were going to war when they were first shot at. Consequently, they were psychologically unprepared, especially those who were told they would be liberating the Ukrainians and the ethnic Russian minority from fascist oppression only to be confronted by a hostile populace that hastened to take up arms against them. Some soldiers rejected the claims of fascist repression, objected to fighting brother Slavs, and chose to desert or refused to fight.[28] An unknown number of officers refused to go to the front, and some that did go later resigned and were sent home. During the first six months of war, soldiers sabotaged their own weapons and vehicles or murdered their officers. Self-inflicted wounds among soldiers and junior officers sustained to get out of the fighting were noted in the first week of the invasion and increased in the months that followed.

More than a thousand soldiers in units not yet deployed or in uniformed service elsewhere in Russia, such as the Rosgvardiia, refused to be transferred to fight in Ukraine. Thousands of soldiers on contract who had been pulled out of combat to refit refused to return to the fighting. Soldiers were on solid legal ground to refuse to go into combat if they claimed conscientious objections to killing. Many refused to renew their contracts.[29] Especially alarming for the Kremlin were the men who defected to the Ukrainian side, a phenomenon last seen in the war with Nazi Germany. Enough soldiers defected for the Ukrainian army to form the Freedom of Russia Legion, composed of former Russian soldiers, Russians without military experience, and volunteers from Belarus. To combat the movement of soldiers to the other side, the Duma, in May 2022, introduced legislation to punish captured defectors with up to twenty years in prison and heavy fines.

A consequence of poor unit training was an unexpectedly large number of casualties, in the tens of thousands in just the first few weeks. In the ensuing months of combat, hundreds more soldiers died every week. Predictably, morale suffered. Frustration by soldiers and small-unit commanders at the losses, lack of success, and civilian resistance in the occupied areas contributed to large-scale atrocities, including mass murder of men, women, and children, and the torture and murder of civil authorities. The replacements for the first wave of losses fared even worse. A mercenary soldier of the Wagner Group, a private military company, fighting under contract with the army told a reporter: "I feel sorry for these 18-year-old kids who signed a contract believing in the state and their commanders, only to learn that the commander is just another dumbass with stars on his shoulders. They're sending people to their deaths for nothing."[30]

To make up the manpower shortages caused by the large number of casualties, and unsure of the depth of public support, the Ministry of Defense adopted a variety of extraordinary measures to increase the army's manpower. It introduced enlistment bonuses of between 170,000 and 250,00 rubles ($2,550 to $3,750) to any soldier who would serve in the "special military operation" for as few as three months, and up to 40,000 rubles ($600) to serve only in Russia. Soldiers were promised additional daily combat pay of 8,000 rubles ($120), and contract soldiers were credited with three days of service toward completing their contract for every day in Ukraine. Few volunteers came to the army, so the army went to them. It created mobile enlistment offices that set up at public events where they expected large numbers of youths to be present—the results were meager. And for the first time in Russian history, the Ministry of Defense hesitated to call up reservists, many of whom declared in advance they would not report for duty.

The government gave up trying to force Rosgvardiia men to participate in the "special military operation" and instead offered them short-term contracts to transfer to the army to fight in Ukraine for 200,000 rubles ($3,000) a month, which did generate some takers. These men complained that their high wages were eaten up by the need to purchase helmets and body armor out of pocket because either the army did not issue them or what was issued (old Soviet-era equipment) they considered worthless. In April, the army began contacting reservists individually and *asking* them to report for duty—few did. In May, the Duma passed legislation raising the age limit of voluntary enlistment from forty to fifty in hopes of attracting veterans of the Chechen Wars and technical experts, especially in the areas of information technology and electronics. In

June, the State Duma reduced the educational requirements for men to qualify to take contracts; young men no longer had to have a complete secondary education. No mention was made of making up the losses in officers. When all other measures failed, Putin ordered partial mobilization in September which generated street protests and renewed flight from the country of military-aged men.

To further augment manpower, the Ministry of Defense mandated conscription of men aged eighteen to sixty in Luhansk and Donbas to serve in the armed forces of those regions. Conscription was enforced with house-to-house searches for the thousands who attempted to evade it. The army lifted its quotas on non-Russians in an effort to pull in more men from the Caucasus and Central Asia; it even offered enlistment bonuses of 300,000 rubles ($4,500). Units on the Afghan border supporting Tajikistan and some from North Ossetia were deployed to Ukraine. Putin called on Syria and Chechnya to send volunteers and contracted with the Wagner Group to send men to fight in Ukraine. In July, the Wagner Group, to replace its losses, began to recruit from Russian penal colonies with the promise of good pay (200,000 rubles or more) and the expungement of their criminal records after six months. Later the army too would recruit from prison colonies. Putin curtailed Russian operations in Syria, Abkhazia, and South Ossetia to allow relocation of several thousand troops to Russia.[31] In June, Putin ordered the governments of all eighty-five regions to form four-hundred-man-strong volunteer battalions (much like Stalin had in 1941) that would then be given one month of training before being sent to fight in Ukraine. The governors had to pay the enlistment bonuses out of their own budgets. The number of volunteers for these units fell short of expectations. Most volunteers were over forty years old. Many had experience in the Chechen Wars.

On the eve of the Ukraine invasion, it was estimated that contract soldiers made up 70 percent of the Russian army, yet it is likely that thousands of the soldiers in the war zone during the initial invasion were conscripts. These men, serving only one year of service, were poorly trained and unmotivated. Their presence contributed to high casualties and poor unit performance. In one artillery battery of the 252nd Motorized Rifle Regiment, twenty-six of forty soldiers were conscripts with only the most rudimentary training. Russian law prohibited sending conscripts to war involuntarily in the first four months of service, yet none had been asked. This led to backlash by soldiers' mothers, whose protests led Putin to promise that the practice would stop.[32] As for many of the volunteers, whose ages ranged from eighteen to forty, poverty and joblessness rather than patriotism drove them to join the army.

Even the best-trained troops experienced failure. The 31st Guards Air Assault Brigade sent to capture the Kyiv airport on the first morning of the war failed to take it. The Russian army needed the cargo airport and military base fifteen miles northwest of downtown Kyiv to serve as the principal staging ground and logistics hub for a decisive thrust into the heart of the capital. The unit had not rehearsed taking the airfield, and the men were not even told that they were going to war until they were already in the air. Only the officers knew the mission and objectives on the ground. After several days of fighting and heavy losses, the Russian paratroops controlled the airfield proper, but planes could not fly in tanks and heavy equipment because it remained under Ukrainian artillery fire. Without use of the airport, the Russians could not quickly advance into Kyiv to capture the government. After several weeks, the brigade withdrew in the face of Ukrainian counterattacks.

An astonishing one-third of the estimated 120 BTGs on hand for the initial invasion were so depleted that they had to be withdrawn from the fight to refit, rearm, and take in replacements at the end of March. Of these, 28 were thought to be so mauled that they were no longer combat effective. An egregious failure of a BTG was the Battle of Voznesensk in early March. On 2–3 March, a force of Ukrainian regulars and local territorial defense members turned back a four-hundred-man-strong BTG. During two days of fighting, the BTG lost around a hundred soldiers killed or captured and unknown numbers wounded. The Ukrainian force destroyed or captured thirty of forty-three armored vehicles and trucks (the Ukrainians salvaged fifteen armored vehicles for their use) and shot down an attack helicopter. A second Russian unit arrived several days later and took the town but was thrown out for good after four days of fighting and heavy losses.[33] They failed their mission to seize a river crossing. In May, two other BTGs were mauled by artillery in a matter of minutes, leading to the possible loss of at least seventy vehicles, including numerous tanks, and nearly five hundred soldiers killed and wounded in a failed attempt to cross the Siverskyi Donets River near the town of Bilohorivka. Part of one BTG got across the river then was cut off and annihilated after the Ukrainians destroyed the pontoon bridge. The Russian army's ability to fight a combined arms war that required the coordination of the efforts of armor, infantry, artillery, and tactical air support appeared to be on the level of that in 1941.

Like Stalin in 1939, Putin misjudged and discounted the potential reaction and response of the international community. Putin's war became especially costly because he underestimated the resolve of NATO to support Ukraine, a nonmember state. The European Union, NATO, and other Western countries all saw through Putin's nonsensical "denazification" justifications and united to resist his aggression. Their main economic tools to oppose Russia were massive and deep sanctions against the banking system and curtailing trade—including Russian oil, which Putin had hoped to use as leverage against the European Union—and the export of sophisticated technologies that Russia's military-industrial complex desperately needed. NATO's initial military response was to ship hundreds of tons of antiarmor and antiaircraft weapons and share real-time military intelligence with the Ukrainian armed forces. Once the Ukrainian defense proved to be viable, NATO began sending armored vehicles and advanced artillery systems including mobile long-range missile systems.

As in 1939, foreign volunteers—male and female, with and without prior military experience—came from much of the English-speaking world, Western Europe, the former Soviet bloc, former Soviet states such as Belarus, Georgia, and Chechnya, and even from as far away as Brazil, to help a victimized country fight Russia. Belorussian railway workers sabotaged the rail network to disrupt Russian army logistics. Activist hackers and criminals came to see Russia as fair game, which they generally had not before the war, and set to work disrupting internet capabilities of government ministries, agencies, civilian entities doing business with the government, and random economic targets. Numerous attacks on television and social media networks broadcast antiwar messages. Such cyberattacks barely degraded Russia's war-making capabilities but exacerbated domestic economic hardship and uncertainty.

Putin's reorientation of the army's efforts to eastern and southern Ukraine in April led to attritional tactics reminiscent of the First World War and the Winter War, as the army switched to relying on artillery to batter the enemy's positions before sending in tanks and mechanized infantry. The Russian army suffered tens of thousands of casualties in these attacks, but Putin, Gerasimov, and Shoigu willingly accepted them to move forward even incrementally. Such tactics inflicted heavy losses on the Ukrainians, as they had the Finns.

In Ukraine, as in both Chechen Wars, the Russian military alienated the civilian population and drove upwards of 100,000 men and women to join the Ukrainian army and territorial defense forces. As they had first practiced in Syria while supporting the Assad regime, the Russian armed forces used cluster bombs and thermobaric bombs against civilians. Using missiles and artillery, the army bombarded areas obviously civilian, specifically targeting apartment buildings, hospitals, train stations, and places known to shelter noncombatants. They targeted emergency services by shelling an area again after rescuers arrived. The torture and mass murder of civilians stiffened Ukrainian resolve. Following Frunze's dictum in his UMD that occupied territory must be secured against resistance and copying Stalin's methods following the conquest of Poland in 1939 and the Baltic States in 1940, the Russian military and secret police brought with them lists of Ukrainians to be killed. They tortured and murdered hundreds of local officials, anti-Russian activists, and those

Ukrainians they suspected might organize resistance. They ruthlessly and wantonly killed and tortured civilians whom they suspected of supplying intelligence to the Ukrainian military.[34] Thousands of Rosgvardiia police patrolled the occupied towns and cities to suppress anti-Russian activity and to look for saboteurs and deserters. The result of such terror united the Ukrainian people behind their government, reinforced their determination to defend themselves, and led Ukrainians in occupied areas to engage in partisan warfare, which in Crimea was particularly effective.

The Russian home front was another weak point. Putin's attempt to rally support by declaring his intent to "denazify" Ukraine and protect supposedly persecuted Russians divided rather than united Russia. Support for and opposition to the war cut across all age groups; however, by far, most supporters of the war were members of the older generation born before the collapse of the USSR who were less educated and struggled financially, and less-educated youth who knew only Putin as president of Russia. Most of those against the war were in the ages of thirty to forty, educated, worldly, and economically successful. A considerable portion of educated, well-traveled eighteen- to twenty-nine-year-olds (military age), especially those connected to the world through the internet, also opposed the war.[35] Antiwar protests emerged spontaneously on the first day of the war and were met with massive and brutal police repression. Even though the last of the free press and many humanitarian NGOs were shut down within a week, antiregime and antiwar reporting on the internet remained active. Russians who knew where to look could still find the truth about the war using VPNs to evade the government's attempt to control online access to information. Independent journalists continued reporting and submitting their stories to online platforms outside Russia. Antiwar graffiti and the tying of green ribbons on trees and poles showed that the regime's efforts to eliminate freedom of speech could not extinguish the expression of antiwar sentiments both in street demonstrations and in social media. Soldiers called home on their cell phones conveying the horror of the war to their friends and family. More than twenty-five recruitment centers and Rosgvardiia buildings across Russia, including in Moscow, were firebombed with Molotov cocktails in the first six months of the war. The regime also suffered the ire of prowar hard-line nationalists who called for the army to escalate the fighting and crush Ukraine utterly and openly expressed their disappointment in the army's performance.

From the start, the war became a referendum on Putin and the future of Russia. Hundreds of thousands of prodemocracy anti-Putin Russians fled the country, leading to a "brain drain" of intellect, entrepreneurship, and high-tech skills necessary for a modern economy to flourish. Capital flight was measured in the trillions of rubles. Hundreds of thousands of military-age men, including army reservists, emigrated to avoid being pressed into service. Widows and bereaved mothers publicly mourned the loss of their men and questioned the war. Families of the missing clamored for news—mostly not forthcoming—of their men. Non-Russian minorities claimed their men were callously sent to their deaths and suffered a disproportionately large number of casualties. The 20,000-man force of the proxy DNR suffered a casualty rate above 50 percent in just twelve weeks. The similarly equipped, trained, and employed forces of the LNR likely suffered the same catastrophic level of losses, which generated complaints from officials and the population of those regions that their men were being used as cannon fodder.[36] Once Luhansk was "liberated," the soldiers refused to fight beyond the region's borders. People scoffed at Moscow's typical underreporting of casualties. To be sure, millions blindly supported the war in the name of Russian nationalism and exceptionalism, uncritically accepting the line promoted by the state and pro-Putin media outlets. Patriarch Kirill of the Russian Orthodox Church proclaimed his support for the war, but some priests openly opposed the war and called for its end.[37]

In his role as commander in chief, Putin behaved more like Lenin and Stalin than the tsars. He decided on war without consulting his government or his oligarch supporters. He adjusted the timing of the invasion of Ukraine to accommodate the wishes of China. When his maximum goals proved to be unrealizable, Putin, like Stalin in 1939, revised his war aims and ordered the military to reorient the focus of the campaign to accept lesser goals, to the dismay of some generals and far right milbloggers who wished for general mobilization and an intensification of the war. In April 2022, Putin claimed—likely insincerely—that the aim of the war was no longer to capture Kyiv and arrest the government, but to secure Luhansk, Donbas, and other areas of eastern Ukraine with Russian populations. Foreign Minister Sergei Lavrov officially renounced Russia's goal of regime change in May. After that, Putin was consistent in his messaging regarding war aims.

Putin had a hand in making operational and tactical-level decisions from the outset. In February, he forbade the army from destroying bridges behind the Ukrainian lines—much to its dismay—because he wanted the infrastructure to be intact when he seized all of Ukraine. In April, he began to consult directly with the generals on the conduct of operations in the main areas of activity, bypassing Shoigu, who had fallen into disfavor, and Gerasimov. Reaching down into the conduct of a battle, when it appeared that storming the Azovstal steelworks in Mariupol would incur heavy losses, Putin ordered the army to contain the Ukrainian forces "so tightly that not even a fly can get through" but not to attempt to overwhelm them. Two weeks later, he ordered a renewed assault.[38] In July, he mandated an "operational pause" to reduce the tempo of fighting while he and Shoigu sought ways to replenish manpower losses.

Like Stalin in 1941, Putin in April began to make high-level personnel changes. He appointed Gen. Alexander Dvornikov, "the Butcher of Syria," formerly commander of the Southern Military District, to take charge of a renewed effort to win the war. At the beginning of the war, Dvornikov commanded the operation in southeast Ukraine and presided over the destruction of Mariupol. In his new post, Dvornikov failed to rapidly secure Donbas and Luhansk and incurred ever larger losses. Putin then, in July, replaced him with Col.-Gen. Sergei Kuzovlev, assigned Col.-Gen. Alexander Lapin to command the "Center" groupings of troops, and put Gen. Sergei Surovikin in command of the Southern Group of Forces. Putin relieved Lt.-Gen. Sergei Kisel of command of the 1st Guards Army for its poor performance. Vice Adm. Igor Osipov, commander of the Black Sea Fleet, kept his post despite the sinking of the guided-missile cruiser *Moskva* in April but was relieved in August following numerous highly successful acts of sabotage in Crimea that destroyed half the number of aircraft supporting the fleet and several ammunition dumps. In June, Putin replaced the commander of the airborne forces, Col.-Gen. Andrey Serdyukov—reportedly for poor performance and high casualties—with Col.-Gen. Mikhail Teplinsky, chief of staff of the Central Military District. In Stalinist fashion, Putin had Col.-Gen. Sergei Beseda, chief of the FSB's intelligence operations in Ukraine, arrested and briefly imprisoned for his flawed assessment of Ukrainian defense capabilities, striking fear into both the intelligence service and the military high command. A few weeks later, Putin pulled the FSB out of Ukraine entirely and gave the GRU sole responsibility for intelligence operations. For unknown reasons, in July he replaced Col.-Gen. Gennady Zhidko, his handpicked deputy minister of defense and head of the Military Political Directorate, with Col.-Gen. Viktor Goremykin.

Like the tsars, Putin personally awarded generals for battlefield success. In July, he awarded Col.-Gen. Lapin the "Hero of Russia" medal for completing the takeover of Luhansk. He announced that Maj.-Gen. Esedulla Abachev would also be made a "Hero of Russia" for his leadership in southern Ukraine. He suggested to Shoigu that he award medals to the soldiers who took part in the capture of Lysychansk. At the same time, he kept his generals out of the headlines to avoid any one of them becoming popular and potentially a political opponent.[39] Putin made several trips to military hospitals to have publicity photos taken of him presenting medals to wounded soldiers. Like Stalin, he awarded units Guards status for outstanding performance in the war including several that were accused of committing war crimes.

In six months of war, while inflicting heavy losses on the Ukrainian army and territorial defense forces, it is estimated that Russia lost at least 1,200 tanks and 2,500 armored personnel carriers and infantry fighting vehicles (more than during the entire Afghan War), either destroyed or captured. Hundreds of towed and self-propelled artillery and antiaircraft systems were either abandoned, destroyed, or captured. So many tanks and artillery pieces were put out of action that the army began to bring older-model tanks and artillery out of storage to replace them. Nearly 150 aircraft (jets, helicopters, and drones) were shot down or destroyed on the ground with the loss of scores of pilots. Western intelligence agencies estimated the Russian army and its auxiliaries to have suffered approximately 75,000 casualties—between 15,000 and 20,000 killed and three times that many wounded, missing, or captured. Ukraine claimed to have killed more than 40,000 Russians. Possibly ten Russian generals were killed by enemy fire along with several hundred lieutenant-colonels and colonels—including a regiment commander who buckled under pressure and committed suicide—and more than a thousand lieutenants and captains, who were already in short supply. In sum, thirty years after the demise of communism and the Soviet Union and the transition from the Soviet Army to the army of the Russian Federation, neither the Russian government, military, nor society were ready to conduct modern conventional warfare efficiently and effectively—they either had not learned from their experience in the twentieth century or were for some reason unable to build on those lessons.

CONCLUSION

What this survey of the history of Russia's army across three centuries has shown is that to meet the challenges posed by the changes in the European balance of power, diplomacy, politics, economics, and society, the history of the Russian state and its army reveals several recurring themes that bridge the late imperial period, Soviet, and post-Soviet eras. The themes are the adoption of a strategy to maintain a defensive posture in the west, an offensive strategy against the Ottoman Empire until its demise, and an expansionist policy to the east until defeated in the Russo-Japanese War; the maintenance of a large standing army; the practice of heads of state exercising their prerogative as commanders in chief to make operational as well as strategic decisions; and a consistent unease about the loyalty of the national minorities to the army and of the army to the state. With the creation of the Russian Federation, Russian foreign and military policies became focused on reestablishing hegemony over the former states of the USSR. Military leaders still want forces as large as they can possibly persuade the civilian government to allow, and although it is now far more homogeneous, the Russian army still distrusts and mistreats ethnic minorities. Having established authoritarian rule, Vladimir Putin, like several of the tsars and Communist Party leaders, actively involved himself in strategic and operational decision-making, especially in the Second Chechen War and the war with Ukraine.

When it came to whether to begin a war by attacking or by defending, the Russian leadership often engaged in debate but generally determined to go on the offensive at the earliest time feasible. How long that might be varied. In the cases of war with Napoleon and Hitler, the Russian and Soviet armies ceded the initiative to their enemy although some generals suggested a contrary approach. In these cases, the Russians were not able to mount major, planned offensives for months. Only after lengthy retreats were they able to wear down the invaders and eventually turn the tables on them. There was unanimous agreement to initiate the Russo-Turkish Wars of 1828–29 and 1877–78. The Ottomans took the initiative at the start of the Crimean War. There was no debate about starting on the defensive against Japan in 1904. Circumstances dictated that an outnumbered Russian army would have to buy time for reinforcements to come from European Russia before it could consider going on the offensive. Plans for war with Austria-Hungary and Germany changed from, in the 1880s, starting on the defensive to, in 1912, seizing the initiative to attack two weeks after the onset of mobilization. During the Cold War, there was a strong inclination among Soviet military planners to strike first against NATO if rising tensions signaled war was imminent; however, the policy set by the civilian party leadership from the late 1940s was to let the capitalists be the aggressors, a policy that remained unchanged with the advent of nuclear weapons. Official Soviet pronouncements always referred to responding to Western provocations, though it was not clear if that meant an actual attack or an imminent attack. The civilian leadership clearly meant for it to be an actual attack, whereas the military thought in terms of preemptive attack as a defensive measure. Only when Gorbachev, in the late 1980s, forced his doctrine of "reasonable sufficiency" on the military did the high command come around to unequivocally supporting a defensive outlook without concrete plans for a counteroffensive. Since the creation of the Russian Federation, the Russian army has initiated every conflict in which it has engaged.

Russia maintained a large army, sometimes the largest in Europe, across the centuries. As long as the empire's boundaries required defending, it would need an outsized army. The extensive borders implied the potential for war on several fronts. During the wars with the Ottomans, Russia had to maintain a strong defense in Europe. The same held for the years of the Russo-Japanese War. During the First World War, the army had to be large enough to fight along a western front that stretched from the Balkan Mountains to the Baltic Sea, as well as in the Caucasus. The Russian Civil War saw the Bolsheviks engaged on five fronts simultaneously, which necessitated a multimillion-man army. Before the German attack on 22 June 1941, besides manning the border with the Third Reich with millions of soldiers, the Red Army kept more than a million men in the Far East to guard against Japanese attack. During the Cold War, the armed forces also kept a large portion of their strength in the east to defend against China while also keeping substantial forces in the west to confront NATO. How large was large enough was subject to debate. Some Soviet policy makers factored in the ability to expand based on reserves as part of the equation, whereas others counted standing forces only. Once the credible threats to Russian security dwindled to only China, the defense establishment still argued for as large an army as it could get, primarily out of institutional self-interest.

For most of its history, the number of troops Russia's adversaries could pit against it also supported the argument for a large army. Napoleon brought nearly half a million men against Russia in 1812. The Germans and their Austro-Hungarian allies deployed millions in 1914–18. Nazi Germany and its allies also sent millions against Russia in 1941. The potential, though highly unlikely, of having wars simultaneously with NATO and China encouraged the maintenance of a huge military establishment during the Cold War.

Until the present, the need for troops to maintain domestic order also necessitated a large army. In both the imperial and Soviet periods, the state needed to put down and keep down restive populations with intimidating military forces. Before the emancipation of the serfs, the army's local battalions answered calls to put down peasant revolts. After emancipation, they were often used to break up strikes and suppress riots, in addition to suppressing peasant disturbances. Combating the Revolution of 1905 diverted tens of thousands of soldiers to pacification duties. During the First World War, the army put down a Kazakh uprising. The Soviet period saw the Red Army used to put down worker and peasant uprisings and nationalist movements during the civil war. Despite the militarization of the police forces during and after the civil war to suppress dissent, in the aftermath of the Second World War, the army was employed to repress nationalist movements in Ukraine and the Baltic Republics for nearly a decade. As late as 1989, the army found itself pitted against civilians agitating for independence from the USSR. The Russian Federation relies on the Russian National Guard and special troops of the Ministry of the Interior to suppress dissent; these institutions in effect take the burden from the military, but also compete with it for manpower.

Imperial Russia's expansionist policy in Central Asia contributed to the army's large size; as did Russia's efforts to extend its hegemony over the Balkans. Soviet Russia's takeover and occupation of the Baltic States in 1940 also relied on a large army, as did its occupation of Eastern Europe after the Second World War.

Although Russia always had a large standing army, that was not always seen as desirable. Throughout the nineteenth century, the tsars, the Ministry of War, and the Main Staff worked consistently to reduce the size of the standing army to the lowest feasible level. The quest to create a reserve system was in part driven by that goal. During the Soviet period, the military leadership's desire for a huge standing army put them in conflict with the political leaders who sought to keep the armed forces to a smaller, less economically and socially burdensome size.

From Alexander I to Putin, Russian heads of state have done their best to exercise decisive control and direction over their militaries. In peacetime, they strove to force the military to conform to their domestic and diplomatic agendas, often through key personnel assignments. In wartime, the tsars, heads of the Communist Party, and Russian presidents exercised their powers as commanders in chief to make high level personnel assignments, direct strategy and sometimes even operations. Alexander I, Nicholas I, Alexander II, and Nicholas II all either took command of operations or went to the theater of operations to exert personal influence. Lenin and Stalin both exercised their power over the military with regard to wartime strategy, priorities, and operations. Khrushchev and Gorbachev imposed aggressive downsizing on their reluctant militaries. Gorbachev forced the military to quit the Afghan War and to revise its war-making doctrine. Yeltsin initiated the First Chechen War. Putin, as prime minister and Yeltsin's heir apparent, orchestrated the Second Chechen War, ordered the army into Georgia, and directed it to seize Crimea and begin a proxy war in Donbas before finally sending the army to invade Ukraine in 2022.

The relation between the army and society no doubt affected the military in a variety of ways. Enlisted service was normally seen as unattractive except for a brief window after the Second World War. Men attempted to avoid the draft with the use various subterfuges and behaviors ranging from bribes to self-mutilation. Draft evasion has been a constant. Under the tsars, military service as an officer was attractive for the status it offered. Uniformed service elevated the social status of commoners. The post–World War II Soviet officer corps had high social status until the war in Afghanistan. The rise of Russian nationalism under Putin seems to have revived the status of the officer corps—at least in conservative circles.

With the exception of the fight against the Ottoman Turks, Russian public opinion and national sentiment did not support wars of aggression. After the emancipation of the serfs, if a war was longer and costlier than anticipated, the tsars ignored public opinion at their peril. The Russo-Turkish War in 1877, while it did not fire the public's imagination, did not produce opposition, perhaps because the fighting lasted only nine months. Not only did the war with Japan in 1904–5 fail to elicit popular support, but after nearly a year of battlefield reverses, an antiwar movement emerged and public protests mounted. Attacking the Central Powers on behalf of their "brother Slavs," the Serbs in 1914 likewise failed to resonate with the Russian people. From the start of the First World War, desertion and draft evasion plagued the army. The prospect of war with NATO, given the potential for nuclear Armageddon, was distinctly unpopular with Soviet society, especially in the wake of the 1986 Chernobyl nuclear accident. The war in Afghanistan—widely seen as either an act of aggression or unnecessary interference—led to a troublesome antiwar movement, increased draft evasion, and a fall in the prestige of the Soviet Army. Both Chechen wars were unpopular: the first galvanized soldiers' mothers to create an antiwar movement. Putin's near-bloodless seizure of Crimea received wide popular support, but the 2022 invasion of Ukraine sharply divided Russian society with many opposed to it.

NOTES

Chapter 1

1. L. M. Val'kovich, "Polevoie upravlenie russkoi armii v 1812 godu," *Voprosy istorii*, no. 11 (1982): 184.
2. Kagan, *Military Reforms of Nicholas I*, 4.
3. Fuller, *Strategy and Power in Russia*, 134; Curtiss, *Russian Army under Nicholas I*, 234.
4. Hartley, *Russia*, 25–35.
5. Curtiss, *Russian Army under Nicholas I*, 177, 234; Fuller, *Strategy and Power in Russia*, 239.
6. Curtiss, *Russian Army under Nicholas I*, 239, 246, 250, 273; Fuller, *Strategy and Power in Russia*, 254.
7. Wirtschafter, "Peacetime Regimental Economy," 52–59.
8. Wirtschafter, "Peacetime Regimental Economy," 44, 45, 50.
9. Wirtschafter, "Peacetime Regimental Economy, 40, 42–43; Curtiss, *Russian Army under Nicholas I*, 99, 100.
10. Curtiss, *Russian Army under Nicholas I*, 182. Curtiss cites SVP, Pt. I, Bk. III, *Obrazovanie Voenno-Uchebnykh Zavedenii*, art. 850.
11. Curtiss, *Russian Army under Nicholas I*, 176, 179, 186–90.
12. Curtiss, *Russian Army under Nicholas I*, 192, 193–95.
13. Keep, *Soldiers of the Tsar*, 344, 345.
14. Frederick W. Kagan, "Russia's Wars with Napoleon, 1805–1815," in Kagan and Higham, *Military History of Tsarist Russia*, 109–11.
15. Kagan, "Russia's Wars with Napoleon," 113.
16. Yermolov, *Czar's General*, 89.
17. Epstein, "Patterns of Change and Continuity," 375–88; Kagan, "Russia's Wars with Napoleon," 114.
18. George Nafziger, *Napoleon's Invasion of Russia* (Novato, CA: Presidio, 1988), 69–70, 107.
19. N. A. Troitskii, "O chislennosti Russkikh armii v nachale otchestvennoi voiny 1812 goda," *Voprosy istorii*, no. 11 (1987): 171–73.
20. Fuller, *Strategy and Power in Russia*, 177–212.
21. Fuller, *Strategy and Power in Russia*, 177–212; Yermolov, *Czar's General*, 107.

22. Curtis Cate, *The War of the Two Emperors: The Duel between Napoleon and Alexander: Russia, 1812* (New York: Random House, 1985), 158–59, 165–66, 176–77.

23. Cate, *War of the Two Emperors*, 182.

24. Cate, *War of the Two Emperors*, 207; Val'kovich, "Polevoie upravlenie russkoi armii v 1812 godu," 187–88.

25. Epstein, "Patterns of Change and Continuity," 381; Kagan, "Russia's Wars with Napoleon," 118; Phillipe de Segur, *Napoleon's Expedition to Russia: The Memoirs of General de Segur* (New York: Carroll & Graf, 2003), 69–87.

26. Kagan, "Russia's Wars with Napoleon," 118–19; William C. Fuller, "The Baleful Consequences of Victory: Russian Strategy and the War of 1812," in Fuller, *Strategy and Power in Russia*, 183–86; Nafziger, *Napoleon's Invasion of Russia*, 211.

27. Yermolov, *Czar's General*, 202.

28. I. Iu. Lapina, "Zemskoe opolchenie v zagranichnoi pokhode russkoi armii (1813–1814 gg.)," *Voprosy istorii*, no. 12 (2007): 93–99; Leggiere, "From Berlin to Leipzig," 39–84.

29. Richard Stites, *The Four Horsemen: Riding to Liberty in Post-Napoleonic Europe* (Oxford: Oxford University Press, 2014), 240–321; Hartley, *Russia*, 64–66.

30. Bitis and Hartley, "Russian Military Colonies," 321–30; Bitis, "Reserves under Serfdom?, 186; Hartley, *Russia*, 192–98.

31. Hartley, *Russia*, 190–91.

32. Hartley, *Russia*, 207; Bitis and Hartley, "Russian Military Colonies," 326; Fuller, *Strategy and Power in Russia*, 258–59; A. De Gurowski, *Russia as It Is* (New York: Appleton, 1854), 93–94.

33. Fuller, *Strategy and Power in Russia*, 234.

34. Kagan, *Military Reforms of Nicholas I*, 78–84, 85–86, 98, 99, 100.

35. Kagan, *Military Reforms of Nicholas I*, 77, 96, 97, 103–5, 120, 126.

36. Kagan, *Military Reforms of Nicholas I*, 128.

37. Kagan, *Military Reforms of Nicholas I*, 87, 89.

38. Frank S. Russell, *Russian Wars with Turkey: Past and Present* (London: King, 1877), 98, 99, 101, 102, 104, 105.

39. Tadeusz Stachowski, "Between Waterloo and the Alma: The Polish-Russian War of 1831, Part I: Grochow," *History Today* 29 (May 1979): 310–17.

40. Kagan, *Military Reforms of Nicholas I*, 215–16, 219, 222.

41. Fuller, *Strategy and Power in Russia*, 243–44, 254.

42. Fuller, *Strategy and Power in Russia*, 255, 275.

43. Kagan, *Military Reforms of Nicholas I*, 4–5, 138.

44. Curtiss, *Russian Army under Nicholas I*, 102–7, 114–15.

45. Roberts, *Russian Intervention in Hungary*, 121.

46. Shishov, *Russkie General-Fel'dmarshaly Dibich-Zabalkanskii, Paskevich-Erivanskii*, 464, 465, 466; Roberts, *Russian Intervention in Hungary*, 138.

47. Shishov, *Russkie General-Fel'dmarshaly Dibich-Zabalkanskii, Paskevich-Erivanskii*, 465; Roberts, *Russian Intervention in Hungary*, 124, 125, 134, 135.

48. Shishov, *Russkie General-Fel'dmarshaly Dibich-Zabalkanskii, Paskevich-Erivanskii*, 468, 470; I. S. Chirkov, "Bude mozhno, bez prolitiia dorogoi russkoi krovi': Vengreski pokhod 1849 g. v perepiske velikogo kniazia Konstantina Nikolaevicha s imperatorom Nikolaem I i tsesarevichem Aleksandrom Nikolaevichem," *Istoricheskii arkhiv*, no. 3 (2011): 129–30; Roberts, *Russian Intervention in Hungary*, 145.

49. Roberts, *Russian Intervention in Hungary*, 148–49; Shishov, *Russkie General-Fel'dmarshaly Dibich-Zabalkanskii, Paskevich-Erivanskii*, 470.
50. Roberts, *Russian Intervention in Hungary*, 142, 167, 168–69, 183, 198, 199.
51. Aleksei Krivopalov, "Russia's Military Strategy and Lessons of the War," in Candan Badem, ed., *The Routledge Handbook of the Crimean* War (London: Routledge, 2022), 34–53; Vladislav I. Grosul, "Russian Society and the Crimean War," *Russian Studies in History* 51, no. 1 (2012): 39, 41–42, 46–52; Fuller, *Strategy and Power in Russia*, 260–63.
52. Kersonovskii, *Istoriia russkoi armii*, vol. 2: *Ot vziatiia parizha do pokoreniia srednei azii 1814–1881 gg.*, 176.
53. Curtiss, *Russian Army under Nicholas I*, 120–24, 126; Fuller, *Strategy and Power in Russia*, 262–63.
54. Badem, *Ottoman Crimean War*, 99–101, 104–9.
55. Badem, *Ottoman Crimean War*, 183–87.
56. Badem, *Ottoman Crimean War*, 169–70, 177, 255.
57. Figes, *Crimean War*, 208–29.
58. M. A. Rakhmatullin, "Voiny Rossii v krymskoi kampanii," *Voprosy istorii*, no. 8 (1972): 107.
59. Baumgart, *Crimean War*, 137–41.
60. Baumgart, *Crimean War*, 141–48.
61. Smolin, "Veshchi omundirovaniia i snariazheniia ves'ma," 173–88.

Chapter 2

1. Persson, *Learning from Foreign Wars*, 107, 114.
2. Rich, *Tsar's Colonels*, 226.
3. Walter Pintner, "Russian Military Thought: The Western Model and the Shadow of Suvorov," in Peter Paret, ed., *Makers of Modern Strategy from Machiavelli to the Nuclear Age* (Princeton, NJ: Princeton University Press, 1986), 366–67.
4. Peter von Wahlde, "A Pioneer of Russian Strategic Thought: G. A. Leer, 1829–1904," *Military Affairs* 35, no. 4 (Dec. 1971): 151.
5. Persson, *Learning from Foreign Wars*, 73–74, 80–81.
6. Brooks, "Reform in the Russian Army," 68; Miller, *Dmitrii Miliutin*, 26.
7. Kersonovskii, *Istoriia russkoi armii*, 2:176–77, 182.
8. Miller, *Dmitrii Miliutin*, 182–93.
9. Zaionchkovskii, *Voennye reformy 1860–70*, 125–34.
10. Keep, *Soldiers of the Tsar*, 376.
11. Keep, *Soldiers of the Tsar*, 378.
12. Reese, *Imperial Russian Army*, 122.
13. Arslanov and Sheptura, "Provedenie mobilizatsii i mobilizatsionnaia rabota v russkoi armii. Vtoriia polovina XIX veka," 7.
14. Kersonovskii, *Istoriia Russkoi armii*, 201–2.
15. Arslanov and Sheptura, "Provedenie mobilizatsii i mobilizatsionnaia rabota v russkoi armii," 5.
16. Arslanov and Sheptura, "Provedenie mobilizatsii i mobilizatsionnaia rabota v russkoi armii," 6.
17. Persson, *Learning from Foreign Wars*, 110, 124–25.

18. Keep, *Soldiers of the Tsar*, 378.
19. Volkov, *Russkii ofitserskii korpus*, 162, 166.
20. Beliaev, *Russko-Turetskaia voina*, 51–53, 55–57.
21. Bruce W. Menning, "War Planning and Initial Operations in the Russian Context," in Hamilton and Herwig, *War Planning 1914*, 85.
22. Reese, *Imperial Russian Army*, 84–86, 112–13.
23. Keep, *Soldiers of the Tsar*, 364–67.
24. Fuller, *Civil-Military Conflict*, 13–15, 49; Theodore H. von Laue, *Sergei Witte and the Industrialization of Russia* (New York: Atheneum, 1974), 32.
25. Marian Kukiel, "Military Aspects of the Polish Insurrection of 1863–64," *Antemurale 7–8* (1963): 364–65, 383, 386.
26. Kukiel, "Military Aspects," 390, 391.
27. Kersonovskii, *Istoriia Russkoi armii*, 199.
28. Keep, *Soldiers of the Tsar*, 358–59, 363.
29. Persson, *Learning from Foreign Wars*, 120–23, 125–26, 131, 134–35.
30. Persson, *Learning from Foreign Wars*, 43–44.
31. Robert F. Baumann, "The Russian Army, 1853–1881," in Kagan and Higham, *Military History of Tsarist Russia*, 146; John S. Bushnell, "Miliutin and the Balkan War: Military Reform vs. Military Performance," in Eklof, Bushnell, and Zakharova, *Russia's Great Reforms*, 139–45, 152.
32. Gokov, "Ofitsery rossii'skogo genshtaba v Russko-Turetskoi voine.," 142–44, 146, 147; Beliaev, *Russko-Turetskaia voina*, 106.
33. Beliaev, *Russko-Turetskaia voina*, 102–3.
34. V. M. Khevrolina, "Russko-Turetskaia voina 1877–1878 gg. i obshchestvennoe dvizhenie v Rossii," *Voprosy istorii*, no. 9 (1978): 23–25, 26–27.
35. Alena Eskridge-Kosmach, "The Russian-Turkish War of 1877–78 and the Attitude of Russian Society (Based on Memoirs, Diaries, and the Epistolary Heritage of Contemporaries)," *Journal of Slavic Military History* 29, no. 2 (2016): 439.
36. Bushnell, "Miliutin and the Balkan War," 139.
37. John Posey, "From the Diary of A. A. Polovtsov: Leadership during the Russo-Turkish War, 1877–1878," *Southern Quarterly* 7, no. 3 (1969): 287, 290.
38. Barry, *War in the East*, 159–69, 263–79.
39. Frederick V. Greene, *Sketches of Army Life in Russia* (New York: Charles Scribner's Sons, 1881), 10.
40. Frederick A. Wellesley, *With the Russians in Peace and War: Recollections of a Military Attaché* (London: Eveleigh Nash, 1905), 282–83.
41. Menning, *Bayonets before Bullets*, 64–66; Bushnell, "Miliutin and the Balkan War," 142; S. A. Zalesskii, "Russkie voiny na Balkanakh v 1877–1878 godakh," *Voprosy istorii*, no. 12 (1972): 115, 116.
42. Alexander Statiev, "The Thorns of the Wild Rose: Russian Ordeals at the Shipka Pass during the Russo-Turkish War of 1877–1878," 370–86.
43. Menning, *Bayonets before Bullets*, 74–78; Beyrau, *Militär und Gesellschaft im Vorrevolutionären Russland*, 394; *The War Correspondence of the "Daily News," 1877–8, Continued from the Fall of Kars to the Signature of the Preliminaries of Peace with a Connecting Narrative Forming a Continuous History of the War between Russian and Turkey* (London: Macmillan, 1878), 196–97.

44. Menning, *Bayonets before Bullets*, 79–81; Amedée le Faure, *Histoire de la Guerre D'Orient*, vol. 1 (Paris: Garnier Freres, 1878), 163; Greene, *Report on the Russian Army*, 386.

45. Beyrau, *Militär und Gesellschaft im Vorrevolutionären Russland*, 390.

46. Nikolai Epanchin, *General Gurko's Advance Guard 1877*, trans. H. Havelock (London: Kegan, Paul, Trench, Trübner & Co., 1900), 3.

47. Gokov, "Ofitsery rossii'skogo genshtaba v Russko-Turetskoi voine 1877–1878 gg.," 145.

48. Wellesley, *With the Russians*, 219–20, 221.

49. Eskridge-Kosmach, "Russian-Turkish War," 451; Posey, "Diary of A. A. Polovtsov," 291.

50. Posey, "Diary of A. A. Polovtsov," 292–93.

51. *Spectator*, 20 October 1877, 3, 4.

52. Zalesskii, "Russkie voiny na Balkanakh v 1877–1878 godakh," 109.

53. General Staff, War Office, *Handbook of the Russian Army* (London: Imperial War Museum, Dept. of Printed Books, n.d.; Nashville: Battery Press; Skokie: Articles of War, 1996), 25.

54. Richard von Pfeil, *Experiences of a Prussian Officer in the Russian Service during the Turkish War of 1877-78*, trans. C. W. Bowdler (London: Edward Stanford, 1893), 54; Posey, "Diary of A. A. Polovtsov," 285.

55. Wellesley, *With the Russians*, 219.

56. Fuller, *Strategy and Power in Russia*, 354–57.

57. Fuller, *Strategy and Power in Russia*, 358, 359; Menning, "War Planning," 82.

58. Wirtschafter, *From Serf to Russian Soldier*, 3.

59. Wirtschafter, *From Serf to Russian Soldier*, 36, 38; Hartley, *Russia*, 39–42.

60. Hugh D. Hudson, "'Even If You Cut off our Heads': Russian Peasant Legal Consciousness in the First Half of the Nineteenth Century," *Canadian-American Slavic Studies* 35, no. 1 (Spring 2001): 1–3, 6.

61. Hartley, *Russia*, 109–12, 120, 121, 122, 138–39.

Chapter 3

1. Fuller, *Strategy and Power in Russia*, 377–80, 384.

2. Fuller, *Strategy and Power in Russia*, 386–87, 389.

3. Bruce W. Menning, "The Offensive Revisited: Russian Preparation for Future War, 1906–1914," in Schimmelpenninck van der Oye and Menning, *Reforming the Tsar's Army*, 222.

4. R. S. Avilov, "'Blizhaishim povodom k stolknoveniiu nashemu s Iaponiei mozhet posluzhit' imenno Koreiskii vopros . . .': Zapiska general-leitenanta N. I. Grodekova o mobilizatsionnoi gotovnosti Priamurskogo voennogo okruga, 1900 g.," *Istoricheskii arkhiv*, no. 4 (2018): 159–83; Schimmelpenninck van der Oye, *Toward the Rising Sun*, 185–95.

5. Jacob, *Russo-Japanese War*, 15–29.

6. Menning, *Bayonets before Bullets*, 158.

7. Menning, *Bayonets before Bullets*, 158–63.

8. Dmitrii V. Krupnitskii, "Otsenka boevykh deistvii vysshego komandnogo sostava armii protivoborstvuiushchikh storon," *Voenno-istoricheskii arkhiv*, no. 2 (Feb. 2009): 11, 23.

9. Jacob, *Russo-Japanese War*, 23–26; Denis Warner and Peggy Warner, *The Tide at Sunrise: A History of the Russo-Japanese War, 1904–1905* (New York: Charterhouse, 1973), 320–32, 457–71; I. I. Rostunov, ed., *Istoriia russko-iaponskoi voiny 1904–1905 gg.* (Moscow: Nauka, 1977), 165–258.

10. Menning, *Bayonets before Bullets*, 171–79; Connaughton, *Rising Sun and Tumbling Bear*, 153–204.

11. Menning, *Bayonets before Bullets*, 179–84.

12. Rostunov, *Istoriia russko-iaponskoi voiny*, 293; Connaughton, *Rising Sun and Tumbling Bear*, 258–90.

13. Montgomery M. Macomb, "Notes on the Russian Infantry Soldier," *Journal of the United States Infantry Association* 2, no. 4 (April 1906): 31.

14. Menning, *Bayonets before Bullets*, 185–86; Rostunov, *Istoriia russko-iaponskoi voiny*, 297–302.

15. Mul'tatuli and Zalesski, *Russko-iaponskaia voina*, 76, 199; Sedgwick, *Russo-Japanese War on Land*, 115–29.

16. Rostunov, *Istoriia russko-iaponskoi voiny*, 365; Gushchin, *Russkaia armiia v voine*, 139; Mul'tatuli and Zalesski, *Russko-iaponskaia voina*, 76, 199; Sedgwick, *Russo-Japanese War on Land*, 63–84.

17. Bobryshev et al., *Peterburgskii, Petrogradskii, Leningradskii voennyi okrug*, 52–53, 110.

18. Bezugol'nyi, Kovalevskii, and Kovalev, *Istoriia voenno-okruzhnoi sistemy v Rossii*, 290; Bobryshev et al., *Peterburgskii, Petrogradskii, Leningradskii voennyi okrug*, 110.

19. Wallscourt Hely-Hutchinson Waters, "Reports on the Campaign in Manchuria in 1904," Arnold-Forster Papers, vol. 60 (ff. 111) (London: British National Library), 199.

20. Bushnell, *Mutiny amid Repression*, 38, 82, 91.

21. Vladimir A. Petrov, *Ocherki po istorii revoliutsionnogo dvizheniia v russkoi armii v 1905 g.* (Moscow: 1964), 323; Bezugol'nyi, Kovalevskii, and Kovalev, *Istoriia voenno-okruzhnoi sistemy v Rossii*, 301; Shatsillo, "Poslednie voennye programmy Rossiiskoi imperii," 227.

22. Beryl Williams, "1905: The View from the Provinces," in Smele and Heywood, *Russian Revolution of 1905*, 44, 47.

23. Reese, *Imperial Russian Army*, 237–41.

24. Bezugol'nyi, Kovalevskii, and Kovalev, *Istoriia voenno-okruzhnoi sistemy v Rossii*, 300.

25. Kieth Armes, "French Intelligence on the Russian Army on the Eve of the First World War," *Journal of Military History* 82, no. 3 (2018): 763.

26. Fuller, *Strategy and Power in Russia*, 415, 416; Bruce W. Menning, "Mukden to Tannenberg: Defeat to Defeat, 1905–1914," in Kagan and Higham, *Military History of Tsarist Russia*, 212–13.

27. Fuller, *Strategy and Power in Russia*, 428–33.

28. Menning, "Pieces of the Puzzle," 793–96; Menning, "War Planning," 115–20.

29. Menning, "Mukden to Tannenberg," 219–21.

30. Valerii A. Avdeev, "V. A. Sukhomlinov i voennye reform 1905–1912 godov," in Rybachenok, *Rossiia*, 247–84.

31. Menning, "Mukden to Tannenberg," 203, 224.

32. Bezugol'nyi, Kovalevskii, and Kovalev, *Istoriia voenno-okruzhnoi sistemy v Rossii*, 325; Avdeev, "V. A. Sukhomlinov i voennye reform 1905–1912 godov," 260.

33. Menning, "Mukden to Tannenberg," 205, 215.

34. Reese, *Imperial Russian Army*, 249–51.

35. Menning, *Bayonets before Bullets*, 208–9, 210.

36. Neznamov, *Sovremennaia voina* (1911 ed.), cited in Pintner, "Russian Military Thought," 369.

37. Menning, *Bayonets before Bullets*, 215–16.

38. Anton Ivanovich Denikin, *The Career of a Tsarist Officer: Memoirs, 1872–1916*, trans. Margaret Patoski (Minneapolis: University of Minnesota Press, 1975), 181, 182.

39. Rediger, *Istoriia moei zhizni*, 2:191.

40. Menning, "Mukden to Tannenberg," 218; Menning, "War Planning," 107.

41. Avdeev, "V. A. Sukhomlinov i voennye reform 1905–1912 godov," 253–54.

42. Aleksei A. Brusilov, *A Soldier's Note-book 1914–1918* (1930; repr., Westport, CT: Greenwood, 1976), 20, 21; Robinson, *Grand Duke Nikolai Nikolaevich*, 90–91.

43. Rediger, *Istoriia moei zhizni*, 147–49.

44. Reese, *Imperial Russian Army*, 288.

45. Reese, *Imperial Russian Army*, 288–89.

46. Menning, "War Planning," 126.

47. Stone, *Russian Army in the Great War*, 69–80.

48. Stone, *Russian Army in the Great War*, 69–80, 86–100, 107–12.

49. Golovin, *Russian Army*, 219, 222; Stone, *Russian Army in the Great War*, 146–77.

50. Tunstall, "Austria-Hungary and the Brusilov Offensive," 34.

51. Tunstall, "Austria-Hungary and the Brusilov Offensive," 35–37.

52. Golovin, *Russian Army*, 244; Stone, *Russian Army in the Great War*, 232–57.

53. "Description of General Headquarters, March 1916," in Daly and Trofimov, *Russia in War and Revolution*, 19.

54. Gatrell, *Russia's First World War*, 188–92; Sanborn, *Drafting the Russian Nation*, 35–36, 77.

55. Robert S. Feldman, "The Russian General Staff and the June 1917 Offensive," *Soviet Studies* 19, no. 4 (April 1968): 526–30.

Chapter 4

1. Rex A. Wade, *Red Guards and Workers' Militias in the Russian Revolution* (Stanford, CA: Stanford University Press, 1984), 329–31.

2. John Erickson, *The Russian Imperial/Soviet General Staff*, The College Station Papers No. 3 (College Station, TX: Center for Strategic Technology, 1981), 61.

3. Benvenuti, *Bolsheviks and the Red Army*, 27–37; "Spravka Upravleniia delami NKVM po istorii organizatsii tsentral'nogo apparata voennogo upravleniia v 1917–1928 gg.," in Anderson, *Reforma v Krasnoi Armii*, 319–43; Erickson, *Soviet High Command*, 25–53.

4. Reese, *Red Commanders: A Social History of the Soviet Army Officer Corps, 1918–1991*, 24–26; Erickson, *Russian Imperial/Soviet General Staff*, 63.

5. Trotsky, *How the Revolution Armed*, 1:313; 2:75; Benvenuti, *Bolsheviks and the Red Army*, 109–18.

6. Reese, *Soviet Military Experience*, 9–11.

7. Iurii Petrov, *Stroitel'stvo politorganov partiinykh i komsomol'skikh organizatsii armii i flota (1918–1968)* (Moscow: Voenizdat, 1968), 244; von Hagen, *Soldiers in the Proletarian Dictatorship*, 37.

8. Reese, *Soviet Military Experience*, 11.

9. Trotsky, *How the Revolution Armed*, 2:115–20; Babel, *1920 Diary*, 18.

10. Bubnov et al., *Russian Civil War*, 93, 103, 111, 132, 165.

11. Bubnov et al., *Russian Civil War*, 89, 96.

12. V. V. Ovechkin, "Dezertirstvo iz Krasnoi armii v gody grazhdanskoi voiny," *Voprosy istorii*, no. 3 (2003): 108–14.

13. G. F. Krivosheev, ed., *Soviet Casualties and Combat Losses in the Twentieth Century* (Mechanicsville, PA: Stackpole, 1997), 37.

14. Bubnov et al., *Russian Civil War*, 192–93, 274–76.

15. Bubnov et al., *Russian Civil War*, 326–27.

16. Bubnov et al., *Russian Civil War*, 267, 268.

17. B. N. Petrov, "Ot 'Revoliutsionnoi chesotki' k voennoi katastrofe: Evoliutsiia voennoi doktriny sovetskogo gosudarstva (1918–1941 gg.)," *Voenno-istoricheskii arkhiv*, no. 3 (2001): 18–19.

18. Benvenuti, *Bolsheviks and the Red Army*, 168–75; von Hagen, *Soldiers in the Proletarian Dictatorship*, 137–52.

19. S. S. Voitikov, "Voennaia oppozitsiia," *Voenno-istoricheskii arkhiv*, no. 1 (2014): 85–104; S. S. Voitikov, "Voennaia oppozitsiia," *Voenno-istoricheskii arkhiv*, no. 2 (2014): 84–102.

20. Frunze, "Edinaia Voennaia Doktrina i Krasnaia Armiia," in *Izbrannye Proizvedeniia*, 30–51.

21. Odom, "Soviet Military Doctrine," 120.

22. Leon Trotsky, *Military Writings* (New York: Merit, 1979), 106–8; Condoleezza Rice, "The Making of Soviet Strategy," in Paret, *Makers of Modern Strategy*, 654–57.

23. Timothy Sosnovsky, "The Soviet Military Budget," *Foreign Affairs* 42, no. 3 (April 1964): 491–92.

24. Ian Ona Johnson, *Faustian Bargain: The Soviet-German Partnership and the Origins of the Second World War* (Oxford: Oxford University Press, 2021), 80, 81–82, 101, 115–16, 119, 143–44, 148.

25. Rice, "Making of Soviet Strategy," 660, 661, 662; "Polozhenie o Narodnom Komissariate po voennym i morskim delam SSSR, priniatoe III sesiei TsIK Soiuza SSR 12 noiabria 1923 g.," in Anderson, *Reforma v Krasnoi Armii*, 56–57.

26. S. A. Tiushkevich, *Sovetskie vooruzhennye sily: Istoriia stroitel'stva* (Moscow: Voenizdat, 1978), 150–51; Erickson, *Russian Imperial/Soviet General Staff*, 86.

27. Tiushkevich, *Sovetskie vooruzhennye sily*, 150–53; Reese, *Stalin's Reluctant Soldiers*, 26–33; Stoecker, *Forging Stalin's Army*, 36–38.

28. K. A. Abramian, "'Vse perputalos', verit' nikomu nel'zia': Vypiski iz Dnevnika Komkora I. S. Kutiakova, 1927–1937," *Istoircheskii arkhiv*, no. 2 (2019): 66, 68.

29. Bushueva, *Krasnaia armiia est' nechto besprimernoe v mirovoi istorii*, 91–94; Reese, *Stalin's Reluctant Soldiers*, 32–33.

30. Samuelson, *Plans for Stalin's War Machine*, 29–62.

31. Stoecker, *Forging Stalin's Army*, 8.

32. Habeck, *Storm of Steel*, x, 94, 105–14; Mikhail Mints, "Predstavleniia voenno-politicheskogo rukovodstva SSSR o budushchei voine s Germaniei," *Voprosy istorii*, no. 7 (2007): 85–96.

33. Stone, "Misreading Svechin," 690–93; Mints, "Predstavleniia voenno-politicheskogo rukovodstva SSSR, 97, 100; Dmitry Plotnikov, "Still Misreading Svechin: Annihilation, Attrition, and Their Strategic and Operational Implications," *Journal of Military History* 86, no. 3 (July 2022): 670–87.

34. "Field Regulations of the Red Army, 1929," *USSR Report, Military Affairs* (Springfield, VA: Foreign Broadcast Information Service, *JPRS-UMA-85-019*, 1985), 3.

35. David M. Glantz and Jonathan M. House, *When Titans Clashed: How the Red Army Stopped Hitler* (Lawrence: University Press of Kansas, 1995), 6–10.

36. Samuelson, *Plans for Stalin's War Machine*, 92–98; N. S. Simonov, "*Mobpodgotovka*: Mobilisation Planning in Interwar Industry," in Barber and Harrison, *Soviet Defence-Industry Complex*, 205–21.

37. Harrison, *Russian Way of War*, 176–77.

38. Mints, "Predstavleniia voenno-politicheskogo rukovodstva SSSR," 98.

39. Harrison, "Soviet Planning for War," 771.

40. R. A. Savushkin, "Zarozhdenie i razvitie sovetskoi voennoi doktriny," *Voenno-istoricheskii zhurnal*, no. 2 (1988): 19–26; Petrov, "Ot 'Revoliutsionnoi chesotki' k voennoi katastrofe," 22–23.

41. Whitewood, *Red Army and the Great Terror*, 264; Reese, *Soviet Military Experience*, 85–89; Reese, *Red Commanders*, 126–33.

42. O. Manninen, "Pervyi period boev," in *Zimniaia voina 1939–1940: Kniga pervaia; Politicheskaia istoriia* (Moscow: Nauka, 1998), 145–47; Irincheev, *War of the White Death*, 5–7.

43. Roger R. Reese, *Why Stalin's Soldiers Fought: The Red Army's Military Effectiveness in World War II* (Lawrence: University Press of Kansas, 2011), 51, 52.

44. Reese, "Lessons of the Winter War," 825–52.

45. Kul'kov, Rzheshevskii, and Shukman, *Stalin and the Soviet Finnish War*, 95, 41–42, 78, 163.

46. Reese, *Red Commanders*, 136–47.

47. Van Dyke, "Timoshenko Reforms," 84–85.

48. Harrison, "Soviet Planning for War," 771.

49. Mawdsley, "Crossing the Rubicon," 825, 827.

50. Mawdsley, "Crossing the Rubicon," 844–60.

51. Petrov, "Ot 'Revoliutsionnoi chesotki' k voennoi katastrofe," 28–29.

52. Reese, *Stalin's Reluctant Soldiers*, 132–62; Reese, *Red Commanders*, 136–37, 163.

53. Mawdsley, *Thunder in the East*, 64.

54. "Prikaz Stavki verkhovnogo glavnogo komandovaniia krasnoi armii no. 270, 16 avgusta 1941 goda," *Voenno-istoricheskii zhurnal*, no. 3 (1988): 26–28; I. A. Basiuk, "General armii D. G. Pavlov i tragediia iiunia 1941 g.," *Voprosy istorii*, no. 5 (2010): 46–48; Merridale, *Ivan's War*, 112–13.

55. N. P. Patrushev, *Organy gosudarstvennoi bezopasnosti SSSR v Velikoi Otechestvennoi voine: Sbornik dokumentov*, vol. 2, bk. 2: *Nachalo, 1 sentiabria–31 dekabria 1941 goda* (Moscow: Rus', 2000), 164–65; Rodric Braithwaite, *Moscow 1941: A City and Its People at War* (London: Profile, 2006), 165.

56. Patrushev, *Organy gosudarstvennoi bezopasnosti SSSR v Velikoi Otechestvennoi voine: Sbornik dokumentov*, 2/2:20.

57. "Polozhenie o voennykh komissarakh Raboche-Krest'ianskoi Krasnoi Armii" and "Ob ustanovlenii polnogo edinonachaliia i uprazdnenii instituta voennykh komissarov v Krasnoi Armii," in *KPSS o Vooruzhennykh Silakh Sovetskogo Soiuza: dokumenty 1917–1918* (Moscow: Voenizdat, 1969), 307–8, 318–19.

58. Hill, *Red Army*, 265–95.

59. John Barber and Mark Harrison, *The Soviet Home Front, 1941–1945: A Social and Economic History of the USSR in World War II* (New York: Longman, 1991), 127–32; Mark Harrison, "Industry and the Economy," in Stone, *Soviet Union at War*, 15–34.

60. Mawdsley, *Thunder in the East*, 149–82.

61. Mawdsley, *Thunder in the East*, 249–72.

62. Mawdsley, *Thunder in the East*, 299–309; Hill, *Red Army*, 562–73.

63. Lev Lopukhovsky and Boris Kavalerchik, *The Price of Victory: The Red Army's Casualties in the Great Patriotic War*, trans. Harold Orenstein (Barnsley, UK: Pen & Sword, 2017), 142–43.

Chapter 5

1. Matthew A. Evangelista, "Stalin's Postwar Army Reappraised," in Lynn-Jones, Miller, and Van Evera, *Soviet Military Policy*, 283–88, 297–98.

2. Evangelista, "Stalin's Postwar Army Reappraised," 300–301, 304.

3. Sergei Khrushchev, "Defense Sufficiency and the Military-Political Conception of Nikita Khrushchev (1953–1964)," in Otte and Pageda, *Personalities, War, and Diplomacy*, 216–17, 221–22, 224.

4. Khrushchev, "Defense Sufficiency," 226–27.

5. Reese, *Red Commanders*, 186.

6. Khrushchev, "Defense Sufficiency," 226, 229.

7. Holden, *Warsaw Pact*, 9–10.

8. Lee and Starr, *Soviet Military Policy*, 50–51.

9. MccGwire, "Soviet Military Objectives," 669.

10. Gouré, Kholer, and Harvey, *Nuclear Forces in Soviet Strategy*, 19, 126, 128.

11. Zisk, *Engaging the Enemy*, 47–49, 55–76.

12. Odom, "Soviet Military Doctrine," 125.

13. MccGwire, "Soviet Military Objectives," 671–75, 678; Richard N. Lebrow, "The Soviet Offensive in Europe: The Schlieffen Plan Revisited?" in Lynn-Jones, Miller, and Van Evera, *Soviet Military Policy*, 319.

14. Lebrow, "Soviet Offensive in Europe," 312–46.

15. MccGwire, "Soviet Military Objectives," 678, 682.

16. Larrabee, "Gorbachev and the Soviet Military," 1020–21.

17. Grau, "Russian Deep Operational Maneuver," 25; Bluth, *Collapse of Soviet Military Power*, 70.

18. Larrabee, "Gorbachev and the Soviet Military," 1003; Bluth, *Collapse of Soviet Military Power*, 70.

19. Robert F. Baumann, *Russian-Soviet Unconventional Wars in the Caucasus, Central Asia, and Afghanistan* (Ft. Leavenworth, KS: Combat Studies Institute, 1993), 136; Sarin and Dvoretsky, *Afghan Syndrome*, 101.

20. Liakhovskii, *Tragediia i doblest' Afgana* (1995), 174–78, 180–85.

21. Vladislav Tamarov, *Afghanistan: Soviet Vietnam* (San Francisco: Mercury House, 1992), 20.

22. Baumann, *Russian-Soviet Unconventional Wars*, 149; Grau, *The Bear Went over the Mountain*, xiv, 202.

23. Grigori F. Krivosheev, *Soviet Casualties and Combat Losses in the Twentieth Century* (London: Greenhill, 1997), 285–89; Borovik, *Hidden War*, 134, 135.

24. V. Izgarshev, *Pravda*, 17 August 1989, 6; *Argumenty i fakti*, no. 4 (4–10 November, 1989): 7; Liakhovskii, *Tragediia i doblest' Afgana* (1995), Appendix 14.

25. Liakhovskii, *Tragediia i doblest' Afgana* (1995), Appendix 14.

26. Larrabee, "Gorbachev and the Soviet Military," 1005–7.

27. Larrabee, "Gorbachev and the Soviet Military," 1007–9.

28. Bluth, *Collapse of Soviet Military Power*, 72, 76.

29. Bluth, *Collapse of Soviet Military Power*, 79.

30. Garthoff, *Deterrence and Soviet Military Doctrine*, 160.

31. Baev, *Russian Army*, 20.

32. Odom, "Soviet Military Doctrine," 114–15.

33. Baev, *Russian Army*, 53. The author cites Christopher Donnelly, "Evolutionary Problems in the Former Soviet Armed Forces," *Survival* 34, no. 3 (Autumn 1992): 30.

34. Patrick Cronin, "Perestroika and Soviet Military Personnel," in Green and Karasik, *Gorbachev and His Generals*, 137, 139.

35. Thomas Nichols and Theodore Karasik, "Civil-Military Relations under Gorbachev: The Struggle over National Security," in Green and Karasik, *Gorbachev and His Generals*, 33–38; Bluth, *Collapse of Soviet Military Power*, 86–90.

36. Vladimir N. Lobov, "Strategiia pobedy," *Voenno-istoricheskii zhurnal*, no. 5 (May 1988): 11.

37. Mahoney, "Defensive Doctrine," 402–4, 408.

38. Nichols and Karasik, "Civil-Military Relations under Gorbachev," 43, 44, 46–47.

39. Cronin, "Perestroika and Soviet Military Personnel," 129.

40. Bluth, *Collapse of Soviet Military Power*, 96, 98.

41. Ray Moseley, "In East Germany, Soviet Soldiers Pay for Overstaying Welcome," *Chicago Tribune*, 20 September 1990; Prokop Tomek, "Life with Soviet Troops in Czechoslovakia and after Their Withdrawal," 106, https://doi.org/10.7592/FEJF2017.70.tomek.

42. Odom, *Collapse of the Soviet Military*, 274–75.

43. Fred Wehling, "Old Soldiers Never Die: Marshal Akhromeev's Role in Soviet Defense Decision Making," in Green and Karasik, *Gorbachev and His Generals*, 68.

44. Odom, "Soviet Military Doctrine," 115.

45. Hornsby, "Soviet Youth on the March," 418–45; David M. Gist, "The Militarization of Soviet Youth," *Naval War College Review* 30, no. 1, Special Issue (Summer 1977): 121, 123, 124–25.

46. Gist, "Militarization of Soviet Youth," 125; Simes, "Military and Militarism," 136–37; *The RUSI Soviet Warsaw Pact Yearbook 1989* (Surrey, UK: Jane's Defence Data, 1989), 57–59.

47. Ellen Jones, "Manning the Soviet Military," *International Security* 7, no. 1 (Summer 1982): 115; Robert G. Wesson, "The Military in Soviet Society," *Russian Review* 30, no. 2 (April 1971): 139; William E. Odom, "The Soviet Military-Educational

Complex," in Dale R. Herspring and Ivan Volgyes, eds., *Civil-Military Relations in Communist Systems* (Boulder, CO: Westview Press, 1978), 93, 94; Herbert Goldhammer, *The Soviet Soldier: Soviet Military Management at the Troop Level* (London: Leo Cooper, 1975), 41, 42.

48. Simes, "Military and Militarism," 140; Raymond E. Zickel, *Soviet Union: A Country Study* (Washington, DC: Library of Congress, 1991), 742; *RUSI Soviet Warsaw Pact Yearbook 1989*, 57–59; Gist, "Militarization of Soviet Youth," 126.

49. Goldhammer, *Soviet Soldier*, 4, 20.

50. William Zimmerman and Michael L. Berbaum, "Soviet Military Manpower Policy in the Brezhnev Era: Regime Goals, Social Origins and 'Working the System,'" *Europe-Asia Studies* 45, no. 2 (1993): 285, 287, 288, 290, 296, 297; Ellen Jones, "Social Change and Civil-Military Relations," in Colton and Gustafson, *Soldiers and the Soviet State*, 256; Tamarov, *Afghanistan*, 1.

51. Simon, *Warsaw Pact Forces*, 157–63; Natalie Gross, "Youth and the Army in the USSR in the 1980s," *Soviet Studies* 42, no. 3 (July 1990): 483; Bruce Porter, *Red Armies in Crisis* (Washington, DC: Center for Strategic and International Studies, 1991), 39; *RUSI Soviet Warsaw Pact Yearbook 1989*, 60.

52. Robert English, "Europe's Doves," *Foreign Policy*, no. 56 (Sept. 1980): 47–50, 51, 56; Julian Cooper, "The Military and Higher Education in the USSR," *Annals of the American Academy of Political and Social Science* 502, no. 1 (March 1989): 115–17.

53. Reese, *Soviet Military Experience*, 149–51.

54. Baev, *Russian Army*, 53–54.

Chapter 6

1. Pavel K. Baev, "The Plight of the Russian Military: Shallow Identity and Self-defeating Culture," *Armed Forces & Society* 29, no. 1 (Fall 2002): 137.

2. Elisabeth Braw, "Russia's Conscription Conundrum: The Obstacles to Modernizing the Country's Armed Forces," *Foreign Affairs*, 25 August 2015.

3. Eugene Rumer, *The Primakov (Not Gerasimov) Doctrine in Action* (Washington, DC: Carnegie Endowment for International Peace, 2019), 5–15.

4. Jonna Alava, "Russia's Young Army: Raising New Generations into Militarized Patriots," in Pynnöniemi, *Patriotism and Militarism in Russia*, https://doi.org/10.33134/HUP-9-9, 249–84; Peter D. Waisberg, "The Duty to Serve and the Right to Choose: The Contested Nature of Alternative Civilian Service in the Russian Federation," *Journal of Power Institutions in Post-Soviet Societies*, no. 1 (2004), https://doi.org/10.4000/pipss.224.

5. By comparison, teenage workers at McDonald's in Russia were making 25,000 rubles ($420) per month for a thirty-five-hour week. (The dollar to ruble calculation is based on the March 2022 rate of one ruble equaling $.015.)

6. James Beardsworth, Yanina Sorokina, and Irina Shcherbakova, "Born under Putin, Dead under Putin: Russia's Teenage Soldiers Dying in Ukraine," *The Moscow Times.com*, 8 April 2022.

7. https://www.macrotrends.net/countries/RUS/russia/military-spending-defense-budget (accessed 7 April 2022).

8. "Kak korruptsiia v rossiiskoi armii i VPK sorvala blitskrig Putina v Ukraine," *The Moscow Times.com*, 10 May 2022.

9. Baev, "Plight of the Russian Military," 137–39.

10. Ray C. Finch, "Ensuring the Political Loyalty of the Russian Soldier," *Military Review* (July–Aug. 2020), 53.

11. Sergey Mozgovoy, "Vzaimootnosheniia Armii i Tserkvi v Rossiiskoi Federatsii," *Journal of Power Institutions in Post-Soviet Societies*, no. 3 (2005), https://doi.org /10.4000/pipss.390; Nikolai Mitrokhin, "Liubov' bez Udovletvorenniia: Russkaia Pravoslavnaia Tserkov' i Rossiiskaia Armiia," *Journal of Power Institutions in Post-Soviet Societies*, no. 3 (2005), https://doi.org/10.4000/pipss.401.

12. Elena Lysak, "To Serve or to Fight? What Do Women Seek in the Russian Army?" *Journal of Power Institutions in Post-Soviet Societies*, no. 17 (2016), https://doi.org /10.4000/pipss.4187.

13. Dale R. Herspring, "*Dedovshchina* in the Russian Army: The Problem That Won't Go Away," *Journal of Slavic Military Studies* 18 (2005): 607–29; Anton Oleynik, "*Dedovshchina* as an Element of the 'Small Society': Evidence from Russia and Other Countries," *Journal of Power Institutions of Post-Soviet Societies*, no. 1 (2004): 22–29, https://doi.org/10.4000/pipss.136; Aleksandr Baklanov, "Riadovoi, ubivshii vosem' sosluzhivtsev v Zabaikal'e, rasskazal o poborakh i ugrozakh iznasilovaniia: Ego otets govorit o dedovshchine, Minoborony vse otritsaet," *Meduza.io*, 7 November 2019.

14. Liliya Yapparova, "'The State Isn't Interested': The NGO 'Soldiers' Mothers of Saint-Petersburg' has defended the rights of Russian servicemen for 30 years. Now it can no longer work with them," *Meduza.io*, 7 October 2021.

15. Alava, "Russia's Young Army," 253.

16. Evan Gershkovich, "Russia's Fast-Growing 'Youth Army' Aims to Breed Loyalty to the Fatherland," *The Moscow Times.com*, 17 April 2019; Alava, "Russia's Young Army," 262.

17. Lieven, *Chechnya*, 119–21; B. I. Kagarlitskii, "Chechnya—Preliminary Results: The Chechen War and Public Opinion," *Russian Social Science Review* 40, no. 4 (July–Aug. 1999): 30–47.

18. David Satter, "The Bloody Czar: Did an Act of Terrorism Carry Putin to Power?" *National Review*, 15 August 2016, 24–27.

19. Lieven, *Chechnya*, 102–19; R. Garwood, "The Russo-Chechen War: The Second Russo-Chechen Conflict (1999 to date): A 'Modern Military Operation'? *Journal of Slavic Military Studies* 15, no. 3 (2002): 67–68.

20. Knezys and Sedlickas, *War in Chechnya*, 81.

21. Dmitry Shlapentokh, "The Chechen War and Russia's Identity Crisis," *Contemporary Review* 270, no 1573 (Feb. 1997): 72–77; Babchenko, *One Soldier's War*, 22–23.

22. John B. Dunlop, "How Many Soldiers and Civilians Died during the Russo-Chechen War of 1994–96?" *Central Asian Survey* 19, nos. 3–4 (2000): 331, 338; Hodgson, "Is the Russian Bear Learning?," 67.

23. Hodgson, "Is the Russian Bear Learning?," 79.

24. Timothy L. Thomas and Lester W. Grau, "Russian Lessons Learned from the Battles for Grozny," *Marine Corps Gazette* 84, no. 4 (April 2000): 45–48; Anna Politkovskaya, *A Dirty War: A Russian Reporter in Chechnya*, (London: Harvill, 2001), 110, 111, 145, 183.

25. Andrei Piontkovsky, "Why Russia Lost the Chechen War," *Globe and Mail*, 24 February 2003, A13.

26. Alexander Golts, "Modernization versus Mobilization," in Blank, *Russian Military in Contemporary Perspective*, 265–68.

27. Ekaterina Reznikova and Julia Balakhonova, "Some Fight to the Last Ditch While Others Get Rich: A Guide to the Ukrainian War," *Proekt.media*, 23 May 2022.

28. Sasha Sivstova and Igor Zimin, trans. Sam Breazeale, "'Nobody Understood What Was Happening': *Meduza* tells the story of Albert Sakhibgareyev—a Russian contract soldier who deserted from the war in Ukraine," *Meduza.io*, 25 March 2022.

29. Vladimir Sevrinovsky, "'Refusing to Kill People Isn't a Crime': The Russian National Guard is firing officers who refuse to join the war in Ukraine," *Meduza.io*, 29 March 2022; Alexander Ermochenko, "Rossiiskie voennye massovo otkazyvaiutsia vystupat' protiv Ukrainy," *The Moscow Times.ru*, 29 March 2022; "300 soldat iz Iuzhnoi Osetii otkazalis' voebat' v Ukraine i vernulis' domoi," *The Moscow Times.ru*, 31 March 2022; "60 Russian Paratroopers Refuse to Fight in Ukraine—Reports," *The Moscow Times.com*, 7 April 2022; "Kontraktniki massovo otkazybaiutsia idti na reshaiushchuiu bitvu za Donbass," *The Moscow Times.ru*, 15 April 2022; Sofia Sandurskaia, "Iz Pskova otkazalis' ekhat' na voinu s Ukrainoi," *The Moscow Times.ru*, 4 June 2022.

30. Lilia Yapparova, "A Mercenaries' War: How Russia's invasion of Ukraine led to a 'secret mobilization' that allowed oligarch Evgeny Prigozhin to win back Putin's favor," *Meduza.io*, 14 July 2022.

31. Iulia Krasnikova, "ChVK 'Vagner' verbuet zakliuchennykh kolonii Petgerburga dlia poezdki na Donbass 'idti v avangarde, pomogat' obnaruzhivat' natsistov,'" *Vazhnye istorii*, 4 July 2022, https://istories.media/reportages/2022/07/04/chvk-vagner-verbuet-zaklyuchennikh-kolonii-peterburga-dlya-poezdki-na-donbass-idti-v-avangarde-pomogat-obnaruzhivat-natsistov/; Vladimir Sevrinovsky, trans. Sam Breazeale, "'Who Caused This Unemployment—Nazis or Our Government?': The Dagestani soldiers dying in Putin's war," *Meduza.io*, 11 April 2022.

32. "U menia panika. Gde moi rebenok?," https://meduza.io/feature/2022/02/24/u-menya-panika-gde-moy-rebenok; Larisa Deriglazova, "To Fear or to Respect?: Two Approaches to Military Reform in Russia," *Journal of Power Institutions of Post-Soviet Societies*, no. 3 (2005), https://doi.org/10.4000/pipss.415; Irina Shcherbakova, "'This War Is a Vampire': Buryat Activists Protest Ukraine Invasion," *The Moscow Times.com*, 27 April 2022; "'Proekt' Rasskazal o total'noi Negotovnosti Rossii k Voine s Ukrainoi," *The Moscow Times.ru*, 4 May 2022.

33. Yaroslav Trofimov, "A Ukrainian Town Deals Russia One of the War's Most Decisive Routs: In the Two-Day Battle of Voznesensk, Local Volunteers and the Military Repelled the Invaders, Who Fled Leaving Behind Armor and Dead Soldiers," *Wall Street Journal*, 16 March 2022.

34. Thomas Grove, "Russia Turned a Bucha Building into an Execution Site and Underground Prison," *Wall Street Journal*, 23 April 2022.

35. Nadezhda Svetlova, trans. Eilish Hart, "'When the Blitzkrieg Failed, He Started to Have Doubts': The Kremlin's invasion of Ukraine put some Russians at odds with their loved ones. For others, it brought them together," *Meduza.io*, 10 March 2022; Evgeniia Al'bats, "Banderovskaia Shavka," *Novye Vremena*, 5 May 2022; "A Social Portrait of Russians Who Are For and Against the War in Ukraine," *The Moscow Times.com*, 18 May 2022.

36. Kirill Platov, "Pushechnoe miaso Kremlia: kak zhitelei LDNR sgoniaiut na voinu s Ukrainoi," *The Moscow Times.ru*, 30 June 2022.

37. Dar'ia Kozlova, "(Ne)svobodnye liudi Sibiri: Kak zhiteli Novosibirska i ego Akademgorodka vstretili 'spetsoperatsiiu' v Ukraine," *Novaya gazeta.eu*, 26 March 2022; "Dozens Detained on May Day in Russia," *The Moscow Times.com*, 3 May 2022; Georgi Kantchev, Evan Gershkovich, and Yulia Chernova, "Fleeing Putin, Thousands of Educated Russians Are Moving Abroad," *Wall Street Journal*, 10 April 2022; Anna Fillipova, "'Putinskai Rossiia—Zhivoi Zakoldovannyi Trup': Odnoi iz Samykh Zametnykh antivoennykh Organizatsii v Rossii Stalo 'Feministskoe soprotivlenie,'" *Meduza.io* 22 March 2022; "5 Russian Recruitment Offices Hit by Arson Attacks," *The Moscow Times.com*, 22 April 2022; Pervyi mitropolit RPTs prizval ostanovit' voinu v Ukraine, *The Moscow Times.ru*, 4 July 2022.

38. "Putin Changes Tack in Mariupol," *Meduza.io*, 21 April 2022; "Kto upravliaet rossiiskimi voiskami v Ukraine?" *Vazhnye istorii*, 23 August 2022.

39. "Putin prisvoil zvanie Geroia polkovniku, vziavshemu Lisinchansk," *The Moscow Times.ru*, 4 July 2022.

Bibliography

Books

Anderson, Kirill. *Reforma v Krasnoi Armii: Dokumenty i materialy 1923–1928 gg.* Moscow: Letnii sad, 2006.

Babchenko, Arkady. *One Soldier's War.* Translated by Nick Allen. New York: Grove, 2006.

Babel, Isaac. *1920 Diary.* New Haven, CT: Yale University Press, 1995.

Badem, Candan. *The Ottoman Crimean War (1853–1856).* Leiden, Neth.: Brill, 2010.

Baev, Pavel K. *The Russian Army in a Time of Troubles.* London: Sage, 1996.

Barber, John, and Mark Harrison, eds. *The Soviet Defence-Industry Complex from Stalin to Khrushchev.* New York: St. Martin's Press, 2000.

Barry, Quintin. *War in the East: A Military History of the Russo-Turkish War 1877–78.* Solihull, UK: Helion, 2012.

Baumgart, Winfried. *The Crimean War: 1853–1856.* London: Bloomsbury Academic, 2020.

Beliaev, Nikolai I. *Russko-Turetskaia voina 1877–1878 gg.* Moscow: Veche, 2019.

Benvenuti, Francesco. *The Bolsheviks and the Red Army.* Cambridge: Cambridge University Press, 1988.

Beyrau, Dietrich. *Militär und Gesellschaft im Vorrevolutionären Russland.* Cologne: Böhlau Verlag, 1984.

Bezugol'nyi, Aleksei Iu., Nikolai F. Kovalevskii, and Valerii E. Kovalev. *Istoriia voenno-okruzhnoi sistemy v Rossii: 1862–1918.* Moscow: ZAO Izdatel'stvo Tsentropoligraf, 2012.

Blank, Stephen J., ed. *The Russian Military in Contemporary Perspective.* Washington, DC: Strategic Studies Institute, US Army War College, 2019.

Bluth, Christoph. *The Collapse of Soviet Military Power.* Aldershot, UK: Dartmouth Pub., 1995.

Bobryshev, V. S., P. A. Labutin, V. A. Zubkov, N. S. Apenyshev, V. Ia. Khor'kov, A. A. Petrov, A. B. Mikhailovskii, and V. N. Buslovskii. *Peterburgskii, Petrogradskii, Leningradskii voennyi okrug 1864–1999.* St. Petersburg: Poligon, 1999.

Borovik, Artyom. *The Hidden War: A Russian Journalist's Account of the Soviet War in Afghanistan.* New York: Atlantic Monthly Press, 1990.

Braithwaite, Rodric. *Afgantsy: The Russians in Afghanistan 1979–89.* Oxford: Oxford University Press, 2011.

Bubnov, A. S., S. S. Kamenev, M. N. Tukhachevskii, and R. P. Eideman, eds. *The Russian Civil War 1918–1921: An Operational-Strategic Sketch of the Red Army's Combat Operations*. Translated by Richard W. Harrison. Philadelphia: Casemate Academic, 2020.

Bushnell, John. *Mutiny amid Repression: Russian Soldiers in the Revolution of 1905–1906*. Bloomington: Indiana University Press, 1985.

Bushueva, Tatiana. *Krasnaia armiia est' nechto besprimernoe v mirovoi istorii: Ocherki istorii sovetskoi voennoi politiki. 1924 g.–22 iiunia 1941 g. (po rassekrechennym materialam rossiiskikh arkhivov)*. Moscow: Patriot, 2011.

Colton, Timothy J., and Thane Gustafson, eds. *Soldiers and the Soviet State: Civil-Military Relations from Brezhnev to Gorbachev*. Princeton, NJ: Princeton University Press, 1990.

Connaughton, Richard. *Rising Sun and Tumbling Bear: Russia's War with Japan*. London: Cassel, 2003.

Curtiss, John S. *The Russian Army under Nicholas I, 1825–1855*. Durham, NC: Duke University Press, 1965.

Daly, Jonathan, and Leonid Trofimov, eds. *Russia in War and Revolution, 1914–1922: A Documentary History*. Indianapolis: Hackett, 2009.

Eklof, Ben, John Bushnell, and Larissa Zakharova, eds. *Russia's Great Reforms, 1855–1881*. Bloomington: Indiana University Press, 1994.

Erickson, John. *The Soviet High Command: A Military-Political History, 1918–1941*. 3rd ed. London: Frank Cass, 2001.

Figes, Orlando. *The Crimean War: A History*. New York: Metropolitan, 2010.

Frunze, Mikhail V. *Izbrannye Proizvedeniia*. Moscow: Voenizdat, 1984.

Fuller, William C. *Civil-Military Conflict in Imperial Russia, 1881–1914*. Princeton, NJ: Princeton University Press, 1985.

———. *Strategy and Power in Russia, 1600–1914*. New York: Free Press, 1992.

Garthoff, Raymond L. *Deterrence and the Revolution in Soviet Military Doctrine*. Washington, DC: Brookings Institution, 1990.

Gatrell, Peter. *Russia's First World War: A Social and Economic History*. Harlow, UK: Pearson-Longman, 2005.

Golovin, Nikolai N. *The Russian Army in World War I*. 1931; reprint, Hamden, CT: Archon Books, 1969.

Gouré, Leon, Foy D. Kholer, and Mose L. Harvey. *The Role of Nuclear Forces in Current Soviet Strategy*. Washington, DC: Center for Advanced International Studies, University of Miami, 1974.

Grau, Lester W., ed. *The Bear Went over the Mountain: Soviet Combat Tactics in Afghanistan*. Washington, DC: National Defense University Press, n.d.

Green, William C., and Theodore Karasik, eds. *Gorbachev and His Generals: The Reform of Soviet Military Doctrine*. Boulder, CO: Westview Press, 1990.

Greene, Francis V. *Report on the Russian Army and Its Campaigns in Turkey in 1877–1878*. Nashville, TN: Battery Press, 1996.

Gushchin, Andrei V. *Russkaia armiia v voine 1904–1905 gg.: Istoriko-antropologicheskoe issledovanie vliianiia vzaimoostnoshenii voennosluzhashchikh na khod boevykh deistvii*. St. Petersburg: Renome, 2014.

Habeck, Mary R. *Storm of Steel: The Development of Armor Doctrine in Germany and the Soviet Union, 1919–1939*. Ithaca, NY: Cornell University Press, 2003.

Hamilton, R. F., and H. H. Herwig, eds. *War Planning 1914*. Cambridge: Cambridge University Press, 2010.

Harrison, Richard W. *The Russian Way of War: Operational Art, 1904–1940*. Lawrence: University Press of Kansas, 2001.

Hartley, Janet M. *Russia, 1762–1825: Military Power, the State, and the People*. Westport, CT: Praeger, 2008.

Hill, Alexander. *The Red Army and the Second World War*. Cambridge: Cambridge University Press, 2017.

Holden, Gerard. *The Warsaw Pact: Soviet Security and Bloc Politics*. Oxford: Blackwell, 1989.

Irincheev, Bair. *War of the White Death: Finland against the Soviet Union 1939–40*. Barnsley, UK: Pen & Sword, 2011.

Jacob, Frank. *The Russo-Japanese War and Its Shaping of the Twentieth Century*. New York: Routledge, 2013.

Kagan, Frederick W. *The Military Reforms of Nicholas I: The Origins of the Modern Russian Army*. New York: St. Martin's Press, 1999.

Kagan, Frederick W., and Robin D. S. Higham, eds. *The Military History of Tsarist Russia*. New York: Palgrave, 2002.

Keep, John L. H. *Soldiers of the Tsar: Army and Society in Russia 1462–1874*. Oxford: Clarendon Press, 1985.

Kersonovskii, Anton A. *Istoriia russkoi armii*. Vol. 2, *Ot vziatiia parizha do pokoreniia srednei azii 1814–1881 gg*. Moscow: Golos, 1993.

Khrushchev, Sergei N. *Nikita Khrushchev and the Creation of a Superpower*. University Park: Pennsylvania State University Press, 2000.

Knezys, Stasys, and Romanas Sedlickas. *The War in Chechnya*. College Station: Texas A&M University Press, 1999.

Kudriashov, Sergei. *Krasnaia Armiia v 1920-e gody*. Moscow: Arkhiv Prezidental Rossiiskoi Federatsii, 2007.

Kul'kov, Evgenii N., Oleg A. Rzheshevskii, and Harold Shukman, eds. *Stalin and the Soviet-Finnish War 1939–1940*. Translated by Tatiana Sokokina. London: Frank Cass, 2002.

Lee, William T., and Richard F. Starr. *Soviet Military Policy since World War II*. Stanford, CA: Hoover Institution Press, 1986.

Liakhovskii, Aleksandr. *Tragediia i doblest' Afgana*. Moscow: GPI Iskona, 1995/Eksmo, 2009.

Lieven, Anatol. *Chechnya: Tombstone of Russian Power*. New Haven, CT: Yale University Press, 1998.

Lynn-Jones, Sean M., Steven E. Miller, and Stephen Van Evera, eds. *Soviet Military Policy*. Cambridge, MA: MIT Press, 1989.

Mawdsley, Evan. *Thunder in the East: The Nazi-Soviet War 1941–1945*. London: Bloomsbury, 2011.

Menning, Bruce W. *Bayonets before Bullets: The Imperial Russian Army, 1861–1914*. Bloomington: Indiana University Press, 1992.

Merridale, Catherine. *Ivan's War: Life and Death in the Red Army 1939–1945*. New York: Metropolitan, 2006.

Miller, Forrestt A. *Dmitrii Miliutin and the Reform Era in Russia*. Nashville, TN: Vanderbilt University Press, 1968.

Mul'tatuli, Petr V., and Konstantin A. Zalesski. *Russko-iaponskaia voina 1904–1905 gg.* Moscow: RISI, 2015.

Odom, William E. *The Collapse of the Soviet Military.* New Haven, CT: Yale University Press, 1998.

Otte, T. G., and Constantine Pageda, eds. *Personalities, War, and Diplomacy.* Portland, OR: Frank Cass, 1997.

Persson, Gudrun. *Learning from Foreign Wars: Russian Military Thinking 1859–1873.* Workingham, UK: Helion, 2010.

Pynnöniemi, Katri, ed. *Nexus of Patriotism and Militarism in Russia: A Quest for Internal Cohesion.* Helsinki: Helsinki University Press, 2021.

Rediger, Aleksandr. *Istoriia moei zhizni: Vospominaniia voennogo ministera,* vol. 2. Moscow: Kanon-press-ts, 1999.

Reese, Roger R. *The Imperial Russian Army in Peace, War, and Revolution, 1856–1917.* Lawrence: University Press of Kansas, 2019.

———. *Red Commanders: A Social History of the Soviet Army Officer Corps, 1918–1991.* Lawrence: University Press of Kansas, 2005.

———. *The Soviet Military Experience.* London: Routledge, 2000.

———. *Stalin's Reluctant Soldiers: A Social History of the Red Army, 1925–1941.* Lawrence: University Press of Kansas, 1996.

Rich, David A. *The Tsar's Colonels: Professionalism, Strategy, and Subversion in Late Imperial Russia.* Cambridge, MA: Harvard University Press, 1998.

Roberts, Ian W. *Nicholas I and the Russian Intervention in Hungary.* New York: St. Martin's Press, 1991.

Robinson, Paul. *Grand Duke Nikolai Nikolaevich: Supreme Commander of the Russian Army.* DeKalb: Northern Illinois University Press, 2014.

Rybachenok, I. S. *Rossiia: Mezhdunarodnoe polozhenie i voennyi potentsial v seredine XIX-nachale XX Veka; Ocherki.* Moscow: RAN: Institut istorii, 2003.

Rzheshevskii, Oleg A. *Zimniaia voina 1939–1940: Kniga pervaia; Politicheskaia istoriia.* Moscow: Nauka, 1998.

Samuelson, Lennart. *Plans for Stalin's War Machine: Tukhachevskii and Military-Economic Planning, 1925–1941.* New York: St. Martin's Press, 2000.

Sanborn, Josh. *Drafting the Russian Nation: Military Conscription, Total War, and Mass Politics 1905–1925.* DeKalb: Northern Illinois University Press, 2003.

Sarin, Oleg, and Lev Dvoretsky. *The Afghan Syndrome: The Soviet Union's Vietnam.* Novato, CA: Presidio, 1993.

Schimmelpenninck van der Oye, David. *Toward the Rising Sun: Russian Ideologies of Empire and the Path to War with Japan.* DeKalb: Northern Illinois University Press, 2001.

Schimmelpenninck van der Oye, David, and Bruce W. Menning, eds. *Reforming the Tsar's Army: Military Innovation in Imperial Russia from Peter the Great to the Revolution.* New York: Cambridge University Press, 2004.

Sedgwick, F. R. *The Russo-Japanese War on Land: A Brief Account of the Strategy and Grand Tactics of the War,* 2nd ed. London: Forster Groom, 1908.

Shapkina, N. V., ed. Compiled by A. V. Sapranova. *Ot "Krovavogo Voskresen'ia" k tret'eiiun'skoi monarkhii: Materialy nauchno-prakticheskoi knferentsii.* Moscow: AIRO-XXI, 2015.

Shishov, A. V. *Russkie General-Fel'dmarshaly Dibich-Zabalkanskii, Paskevich-Erivanskii.* Moscow: Tsentrpoligraf, 2001.

Simon, Jeffrey. *Warsaw Pact Forces: Problems of Command and Control.* Boulder, CO: Westview Press, 1985.

Smele, Jonathan, and Anthony Heywood, eds. *The Russian Revolution of 1905: Centenary Perspectives.* London: Routledge, 2005.

Stoecker, Sally. *Forging Stalin's Army: Marshal Tukhachevsky and the Politics of Military Innovation.* Boulder, CO: Westview Press, 1998.

Stone, David R. *Hammer and Rifle: The Militarization of the Soviet Union, 1926–1933.* Lawrence: University Press of Kansas, 2000.

———. *The Russian Army in the Great War: The Eastern Front, 1914–1917.* Lawrence: University Press of Kansas, 2015.

———, ed. *The Soviet Union at War, 1941–1945.* Barnsley, UK: Pen & Sword, 2010.

Trotsky, Leon. *How the Revolution Armed: The Military Writings and Speeches of Leon Trotsky.* Vols. 1 and 2. London: New Park, 1979.

Volkov, Sergei V. *Russkii ofitserskii korpus.* Moscow: Voenizdat, 1993.

von Hagen, Mark. *Soldiers in the Proletarian Dictatorship.* Ithaca, NY: Cornell University Press, 1990.

Whitewood, Peter. *The Red Army and the Great Terror: Stalin's Purge of the Soviet Military.* Lawrence: University Press of Kansas, 2015.

Wirtschafter, Elise Kimerling. *From Serf to Russian Soldier.* Princeton, NJ: Princeton University Press, 1990.

Yermolov, Alexey P. *The Czar's General: The Memoirs of a Russian General in the Napoleonic Wars.* Translated and edited by Alexander Mikaberidze. Welwyn Garden City, UK: Ravenhall, 2005.

Zaionchkovskii, Petr A. *Voennye reformy 1860–70 godov v Rossii.* Moscow: Moscow University, 1952.

Zamoyski, Adam. *Moscow 1812: Napoleon's Fatal March.* New York: Harper Collins, 2004.

Zisk, Kimberly M. *Engaging the Enemy: Organization Theory and Soviet Military Innovation, 1955–1991.* Princeton, NJ: Princeton University Press, 1993.

Articles and Book Chapters

Arslanov, R. F., and V. N. Sheptura. "Provedenie mobilizatsii i mobilizatsionnaia rabota v russkoi armii: Vtoriia polovina XIX veka." *Voenno-istoricheskii zhurnal,* no. 1 (2007): 3–10.

Bitis, Alexander. "Reserves under Serfdom? Nicholas I's Attempts to Solve the Russian Army's Manpower Crisis of 1831–32." *Jahrbucher für Geschichte Osteuropas* 51, no. 2 (2003): 185–96.

Bitis, Alexander, and Janet Hartley. "The Russian Military Colonies in 1826." *Slavonic and East European Review* 78, no. 2 (April 2000): 321–30.

Brooks, E. Willis. "Reform in the Russian Army, 1856–1861." *Slavic Review* 43, no. 1 (1984): 63–82.

Epstein, R. M. "Patterns of Change and Continuity in Nineteenth-Century Warfare." *Journal of Military History* 56 (1992): 375–88.

Gokov, O. A. "Ofitsery rossii'skogo genshtaba v Russko-Turetskoi voine 1877–1878 gg." *Voprosy istorii,* no. 7 (July 2006): 142–49.

Grau, Lester W. "Russian Deep Operational Maneuver: From the OMG to the Modern Maneuver Brigade." *Infantry,* April–June 2017, 24–27.

Harrison, Richard W. "Soviet Planning for War, 1936–1941: The 'Preventive Attack' Thesis in Historical Context." *Journal of Military History* 83, no. 3 (July 2019): 769–94.

Hodgson, Quentin. "Is the Russian Bear Learning? An Operational and Tactical Analysis of the Second Chechen War, 1999–2002." *Journal of Strategic Studies* 26, no. 2 (June 2003): 64–90.

Hornsby, Robert. "Soviet Youth on the March: The All-Union Tours of Military Glory, 1965–87." *Journal of Contemporary History* 52, no. 2 (April 2017): 418–45.

Hughes, Geraint. "The Soviet-Afghan War 1978–1989: An Overview." *Defence Studies* 8, no. 3 (Nov. 2008): 326–50.

Khristoforov, V., and Iu. Guseva. "Voennaia strategiia Sovetskogo Soiuza v Afganistane: Proschety planirovaniia i obshchestvennoe nepriiatie." *Quaestio Rossica* 8, no. 2 (2020): 382–98.

Larrabee, F. Stephen. "Gorbachev and the Soviet Military." *Foreign Affairs* 66, no. 5 (1988): 1002–26.

Leggiere, Michael V. "From Berlin to Leipzig: Napoleon's Gamble in North Germany, 1813." *Journal of Military History* 67, no. 1 (Jan. 2003): 39–84.

Mahoney, Shane E. "Defensive Doctrine: The Crisis in Soviet Military Thought." *Slavic Review* 49, no. 3 (Autumn 1990): 398–408.

Maklak, Alena. "*Dedovshchina* on Trial: Some Evidence Concerning the Last Soviet Generation of 'Sons' and 'Grandfathers.'" *Nationalities Papers* 43, no. 5 (2015): 682–99.

Mawdsley, Evan. "Crossing the Rubicon: Soviet Plans for Offensive War in 1940–1941." *International History Review* 25, no. 4 (Dec. 2003): 818–65.

MccGwire, Michael. "Soviet Military Objectives." *World Policy Journal* 3, no. 4 (Fall 1986): 667–95.

Menning, Bruce W. "Pieces of the Puzzle: The Role of Iu. N. Danilov and M. V. Alekseev in Russian War Planning before 1914." *International Historical Review* 25, no. 4 (Dec. 2003): 775–98.

Odom, William E. "Soviet Military Doctrine." *Foreign Affairs* 67, no. 2 (Winter 1988): 114–34.

Reese, Roger R. "Lessons of the Winter War: A Study in the Military Effectiveness of the Red Army, 1939–1940." *Journal of Military History* 72, no. 3 (2008): 825–52.

Shatsillo, Kornelii F. "Poslednie voennye programmy Rossiiskoi imperii." *Voprosy istorii*, nos. 7–8 (1991): 224–33.

Simes, Dimitri K. "The Military and Militarism in Soviet Society." *International Security* 6, no. 3 (Winter 1981–82): 123–43.

Smolin, N. N., ed. "Veshchi omundirovaniia i snariazheniia ves'ma durnogo kachestva': Iz istorii snabzheniia Gosudarstvennogo podvizhnogo opolcheniia. 1855–56 gg." *Istoricheskii arkhiv*, no. 3 (2006): 173–88.

Statiev, Alexander. "The Thorns of the Wild Rose: Russian Ordeals at the Shipka Pass during the Russo-Turkish War of 1877–1878." *Journal of Slavic Military Studies* 32, no. 3 (July–Sept. 2019): 370–86.

Stone, David R. "Misreading Svechin: Attrition, Annihilation, and Historicism." *Journal of Military History* 76, no. 3 (July 2012): 673–94.

Tunstall, Graydon A. "Austria-Hungary and the Brusilov Offensive of 1916." *Historian* 70, no. 1 (2008): 30–53.

Van Dyke, Carl. "The Timoshenko Reforms: March–July 1940." *Journal of Slavic Military Studies* 9, no. 1 (March 1996): 69–96.

Wirtschafter, Elise Kimerling. "The Lower Ranks in the Peacetime Regimental Economy of the Russian Army, 1796–1855." *Slavonic and East European Review* 64, no. 1 (Jan. 1986): 40–65.

INDEX

Printed in the USA
CPSIA information can be obtained
at www.ICGtesting.com
LVHW071211210923
758884LV00004B/38